THE COWBOYS

THE COWBOYS

By the Editors of

TIME-LIFE BOOKS

with text by

William H. Forbis

TIME-LIFE BOOKS / ALEXANDRIA, VIRGINIA

Time-Life Books Inc.
is a wholly owned subsidiary of

TIME INCORPORATED

Founder: Henry R. Luce 1898-1967

Editor-in-Chief: Henry Anatole Grunwald
Chairman of the Board: Andrew Heiskell
President: James R. Shepley
Editorial Director: Ralph Graves
Vice Chairman: Arthur Temple

TIME-LIFE BOOKS INC.

Managing Editor: Jerry Korn
Executive Editor: David Maness
Assistant Managing Editors: Dale M. Brown
(planning), George Constable, George G. Daniels
(acting), Martin Mann, John Paul Porter
Art Director: Tom Suzuki
Chief of Research: David L. Harrison
Director of Photography: Robert G. Mason
Senior Text Editor: Diana Hirsh
Assistant Art Director: Arnold C. Holeywell
Assistant Chief of Research: Carolyn L. Sackett
Assistant Director of Photography: Dolores A. Littles

Chairman: Joan D. Manley
President: John D. McSweeney
Executive Vice Presidents: Carl G. Jaeger,
John Steven Maxwell, David J. Walsh
Vice Presidents: Nicholas Benton (public relations),
Nicholas J. C. Ingleton (Asia), James L. Mercer
(Europe/South Pacific), Herbert Sorkin
(production), Paul R. Stewart (marketing),
Peter G. Barnes, John L. Canova
Personnel Director: Beatrice T. Dobie
Consumer Affairs Director: Carol Flaumenhaft
Comptroller: George Artandi

THE OLD WEST

EDITORIAL STAFF FOR "THE COWBOYS"
Editor: Ezra Bowen
Picture Editor: Carole Kismaric
Text Editors: William Frankel, Anne Horan
Designers: Herbert H. Quarmby, Albert Sherman
Staff Writers: Erik Amfitheatrof, Sam Halper,
Bryce Walker, Peter Wood
Researchers: Joan Mebane, Malabar Brodeur,
Michael Drons, Frances Gardner, Nancy Jacobsen,
Mary Leverty, Mary Kay Moran, Kathryn Ritchell,
Kathy Slate, Jane Sugden

EDITORIAL PRODUCTION
Production Editor: Douglas B. Graham
Operations Manager: Gennaro C. Esposito,
Gordon E. Buck (assistant)
Assistant Production Editor: Feliciano Madrid
Quality Control: Robert L. Young (director),
James J. Cox (assistant), Daniel J. McSweeney,
Michael G. Wight (associates)
Art Coordinator: Anne B. Landry
Copy Staff: Susan B. Galloway (chief),
Roberta Frost, Celia Beattie
Picture Department: Barbara S. Simon

THE AUTHOR: William H. Forbis was born in cowboy country and has returned there. A native of Missoula, Montana, he graduated from the University of Montana with a degree in journalism and left for Central America, where he was to spend more than a decade as a reporter, editor and correspondent. He moved to New York in 1951 to become a writer for TIME and then a senior editor in charge of art, theater, cinema and education. Since his retirement in 1969, he has been dividing his time between freelance writing and teaching at the University of Montana. Before undertaking *The Cowboys,* he completed and edited the late John Gunther's *Inside Australia,* published in 1972.

THE COVER: The spirit and dash—even the titles—of Frederic Remington's cover painting, *The Cowboy,* and his bronze frontispiece, *The Outlaw,* reflect the heroic American conception of the Old West. Remington sold *The Cowboy* to a friend for $2,500 and then, in a grand gesture, lit his cigar with the check.

CORRESPONDENTS: Elisabeth Kraemer (Bonn); Margot Hapgood, Dorothy Bacon, Lesley Coleman (London); Susan Jonas, Lucy T. Voulgaris (New York); Maria Vincenza Aloisi, Josephine du Brusle (Paris); Ann Natanson (Rome). Valuable assistance was also provided by: Blanche Hardin (Denver); Carolyn T. Chubet, Miriam Hsia, Christina Lieberman (New York); Mimi Murphy (Rome); Lynne Waugh (Santa Fe); Alfred Polczinski (Wichita).

Other Publications:

THE EPIC OF FLIGHT
THE GOOD COOK
THE SEAFARERS
THE ENCYCLOPEDIA OF COLLECTIBLES
WORLD WAR II
THE GREAT CITIES
HOME REPAIR AND IMPROVEMENT
THE WORLD'S WILD PLACES
THE TIME-LIFE LIBRARY OF BOATING
HUMAN BEHAVIOR
THE ART OF SEWING
THE EMERGENCE OF MAN
THE AMERICAN WILDERNESS
THE TIME-LIFE ENCYCLOPEDIA OF GARDENING
LIFE LIBRARY OF PHOTOGRAPHY
THIS FABULOUS CENTURY
FOODS OF THE WORLD
TIME-LIFE LIBRARY OF AMERICA
TIME-LIFE LIBRARY OF ART
GREAT AGES OF MAN
LIFE SCIENCE LIBRARY
THE LIFE HISTORY OF THE UNITED STATES
TIME READING PROGRAM
LIFE NATURE LIBRARY
LIFE WORLD LIBRARY
FAMILY LIBRARY:
    HOW THINGS WORK IN YOUR HOME
    THE TIME-LIFE BOOK OF THE FAMILY CAR
    THE TIME-LIFE FAMILY LEGAL GUIDE
    THE TIME-LIFE BOOK OF FAMILY FINANCE

For information about any Time-Life book, please write:
Reader Information
Time-Life Books
541 North Fairbanks Court
Chicago, Illinois 60611

CONTENTS

1 | A sweaty little man, tall in the saddle

This is a painting of the Old West as it never really was. Well, hardly ever. The American cowboy was actually a dirty, overworked laborer who fried his brains under a prairie sun, or rode endless miles in rain and wind to mend fences or look for lost calves. Yet the cowboy had a heroic image of himself as a hard-riding, fast-shooting hombre, and that is how he appears in books and paintings of the Old West.

The image did grow from a seed of reality. Some cowboys actually shot it out with Indians, or broke wild horses and lassoed bears, as they are doing in these paintings by artists Frederic Remington (cover and below) and Charles Russell (following pages). Both painters rode the trails with the cowboy. They recorded every detail of his life, yet they shared his idealized vision. In making him seem larger than life Remington and Russell caught the proportions of a greater reality: the sense, shared by the cowboy and in time the entire nation, that he was indeed the hero of his country's boldest legend.

Helping to trap wild horses, a cowboy who has roped a mustang rises onto his left stirrup, putting all his weight there to keep his saddle from twisting to the right and overturning his horse. This is a typical Russell work — correct in each detail but stressing the drama in a working cowboy's life.

Near the Yellowstone River, in 1881, a trail boss hears a Crow warrior's demand for a toll of $1 a head—indicated by the uplifted finger—before allowing the cattle to cross tribal land. The painting is based on a real event: when the trail boss refused to pay, the braves stampeded the herd, then fled while the cowboys regained control of the cattle.

Charged by a grizzly bear near Timber Creek, Montana, while out herding range horses, a group of cowboys snare the enraged animal with lariats. This actually happened to some cowhands of artist Russell's acquaintance; once the bear was securely trussed up they stoned it to death.

Five whooping, shooting trail hands gallop into a saloon for a celebration before the start of a cattle drive. But such antics were rare, and on some occasions the contrite cowboys returned to reimburse the saloonkeeper for damages.

The real face of the American cowboy

The high time of the American cowboy lasted a bare generation, from the end of the Civil War until the mid-1880s, when bad weather, poor range management and disastrous cattle-market prices forced an end to the old freewheeling ways. In that brief span the number of cowboys who rode the cattle trails across the Great Plains totaled no more than 40,000. As surviving photographs like the one at left suggest, most cowhands were surprisingly young (their average age was only 24), and despite their steely gaze and the guns they may have put on especially for the camera, they seemed to have a lot of the bumpkin in them.

Yet neither flash impressions nor bare statistics can take the true measure of the cowboys or dim the elemental stage presence and the riveting appeal they generated in their own time and forever afterward. They were men of a particular time and place, living by a code compounded of hardfisted frontier desperation and Victorian-era social values, performing body-punishing and hazardous jobs, and pitting themselves against a land of sweeping grandeur that offered prodigious drafts of misery. For each man these harsh realities of range life manifested themselves in different ways, as the following autobiographical excerpts reveal. Yet they also emphasize the enduring quality and the acceptance of his lot that characterized virtually every cowboy.

♦ Trail driver George Duffield drove a herd of longhorns from Texas up to Iowa in 1866 and kept a diary of the ordeal. Agonized phrases leap from the pages.

"Upset our wagon in River & lost Many of our cooking utencils . . . was on my Horse the whole night & it raining hard. . . . Lost my Knife. . . . There was one of our party Drowned to day (Mr. Carr) & Several narrow escapes & I among [them] . . . . Many Men in trouble. Horses *all* give out & Men refused to do anything. . . . Awful night . . . not having had a bite to eat for 60 hours . . . *Tired.* . . . Indians very troublesome. . . . Oh! what a night—Thunder Lightning & rain—we followed our Beeves *all* night as they wandered about. . . . We Hauled cattle out of the Mud with oxen half the day. . . . Dark days are these to me. Nothing but Bread & Coffee. Hands all Growling & Swearing—every thing wet & cold . . . Sick & discouraged. Have *not* got the *Blues* but am in *Hel of a fix* . . . . My back is Blistered badly. . . . I had a sick headache bad . . . *all* our letters have been sent to the dead letter office. . . . Flies was worse than I ever saw them . . . weather very *Hot* . . . Indians saucy . . . one man down with Boils & one with Ague. . . . Found a Human skeleton on the Prairie to day."

♦ John Baumann, an Englishman magnetized by the American West, came to Texas to turn himself into a free-riding frontiersman and perhaps to earn a fortune in the process. He wangled a job as a cowboy, and for his first assignment he helped round up a herd of horses that had been eating locoweed. The effect of this plant on the animals was hallucinogenic and lethal. Some had gone into fits, some lay groaning, some foamed at the mouth, some had fallen dead. Said Baumann: "Having shot two horses which were unable to stand up, we rounded up our cripples and made a start for the headquarters ranch 180 miles due south. In addition to being badly locoed and half-starved, the majority suffered a skin disease which eats the hair off and leaves the shivering creature exposed. Many of them had open kidney sores and wither-galls, swollen running nostrils, watering eyes, and wheezy breathing. Three long weeks did this melancholy procession trail across the prairie.

True-life cowboys like these five in Montana were younger and more self-conscious than Remington's and Russell's heroes. But decked out with guns and scowls for a photographer they could look just as rough.

Every now and then a horse stumbled and fell; generally he was too weak to rise, when a couple of boys dismounted, and, passing a rope under his body and round his shoulders, hoisted the poor beast on his legs again. As a rule this was the beginning of the end, if he managed to hold up until the end of the day's march, the frosty night settled him. Every morning in the chill half-light of early dawn, it was our sad duty to lift those who had lain down to rest, and, by rubbing their stiffened trembling limbs, to restore circulation sufficiently to enable them to stand. Others were beyond help, and several times I have given such their quietus with a six-shooter bullet without drawing more than a faint trickle of blood, so poor were they."

♦ J. L. McCaleb was a boy when he rode up the old Chisholm Trail to Abilene with a herd of longhorns from Texas. After helping bed down the cattle at a good grazing ground, he got permission from the trail boss to head for town: "The boss let myself and another boy go to the city. As it had been a long time since we had seen a house or a woman, they were both good to look at. The first place we visited was a saloon and dance hall. I went to the bar and called for a toddy, and as I was drinking it a girl came up and put her little hand under my chin, and looked me square in the face and said, 'Oh, you pretty Texas boy, give me a drink.' I had a five dollar bill, so I told the girl that she could make herself easy; that I was going to break the monte game, buy out the saloon, and keep her to run it for me when I went back to Texas for my other herd of cattle. Well, I went to the dealer, put my five on the first card, and won. I now had ten dollars, so I put the two bills on the tray and won. Had now twenty dollars and went to get a drink—another toddy but my girl was gone. I went back and soon lost all I had won and my original five . . . and I went out, found my partner and left for camp. The next morning, in place of owning the saloon and going back to Texas after my other herds, I felt—oh! what's the use?"

Duffield, Baumann and McCaleb: the first a dog-

ged, enduring professional; the second a disillusioned adventure seeker from half a world away; the third a good-humored youngster who got his comeuppance trying to act out the role of a swashbuckling trail hand. These were only three of the cowboys of the Old West, and they barely hint at the spectrum of humanity that made up the fraternity of the cowhand. About one cowboy in six or seven was Mexican; a similar proportion was black (most of the blacks had been slaves on Texas ranches, where they had been taught the skills of roping and riding). Others were Indian, or had some Indian blood.

A number of the cowboys were mustered-out Union soldiers unwilling to return to the rocky farms of the dying New England dairy industry or to the dullness of Midwestern homesteads. Even more of them were former Rebels looking for new stakes and perhaps some fast action that would help them work out the frustration lingering from the lost cause. A few sailors exchanged the sea for the arid plains. They brought with them a favorite chantey:

O, bury me not in the deep, deep sea,
Where the dark blue waves will roll over me.

And they remodeled it to go:

O, bury me not on the lone prairee
Where the wild coyotes will howl over me.

Europe contributed moneyed patricians, penniless immigrant peasants and a bizarre lot of Englishmen known as remittance men. These latter were the ne'er-do-well offspring of titled families banished to the plains with regular remittances, to stay until they either disappeared or straightened up and returned home. The typical remittance man was usually besotted and anonymous. Occasionally, however, he would inadvertently reveal his background—like the liquor-wracked cowpoke who, hearing someone mention the results of a British university boat race, forgot himself and suddenly blurted out with hazy enthusiasm: "Thank God we won!" Along with boozy Cantabrigians came some sober Har-

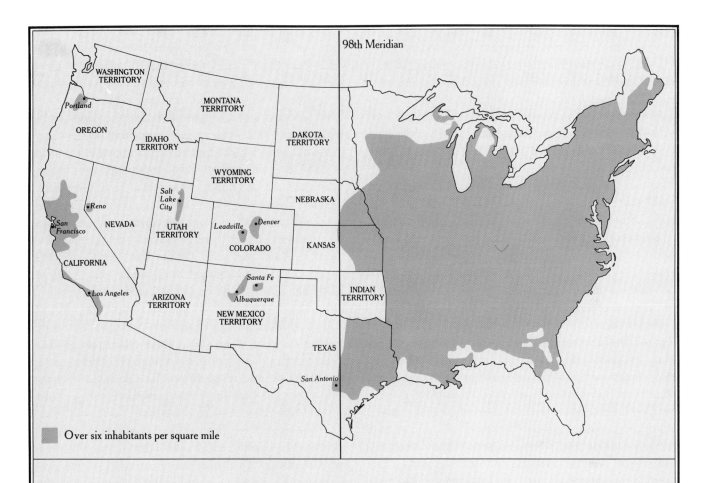

98th Meridian

WASHINGTON TERRITORY
Portland•
OREGON
IDAHO TERRITORY
MONTANA TERRITORY
DAKOTA TERRITORY
WYOMING TERRITORY
NEBRASKA
•Reno
Salt Lake City•
•San Francisco
NEVADA
UTAH TERRITORY
Leadville•
•Denver
COLORADO
KANSAS
CALIFORNIA
•Los Angeles
ARIZONA TERRITORY
NEW MEXICO TERRITORY
Santa Fe•
Albuquerque•
INDIAN TERRITORY
TEXAS
San Antonio•

Over six inhabitants per square mile

The view from the fastidious East

In 1876, the centennial of the Declaration of Independence, the U.S. was still divided into two parts, one settled, one wild. The boundary between them was the 98th meridian, a line where diminishing annual rainfall caused Eastern forests to stop and grasslands to begin. To the east 31 states were settled by 42 million people. To the west of the meridian lay all or parts of seven states and nine territories, populated by a mere two million souls. The few towns of any size were scattered across an enormous territory whose uncivilized land and peoples had long been scorned by even the most farsighted Easterners.

It is to be feared that a great part of [the West] will form a lawless interval between the abodes of civilized men. . . . Here may spring up new and mongrel races, like new formations in geology, the amalgamation of the "debris" and "abrasions" of former races.

Washington Irving, 1836

What do we want with this vast, worthless area? This region of savages and wild beasts, of deserts, shifting sands and whirlwinds of dust, of cactus and prairie dogs? . . . I will never vote one cent from the public treasury [for postal service] to place

the Pacific Coast one inch nearer to Boston than it now is.

Daniel Webster, 1838

We seem to have reached the acme of barrenness and desolation.

Horace Greeley, 1859

Sometimes we have the seasons [in Nevada] in their regular order, and then again we have winter all the summer and summer all winter. . . . It is mighty regular about not raining, though. . . . But as a general thing . . . the climate is good, what there is of it.

Mark Twain, circa 1865

vard men—including one future President of the United States, Teddy Roosevelt *(page 216),* who went to North Dakota to learn to rope and ride. Among the generality of cowboys, however, a college degree was almost unheard of. The more common educational level was reflected in the remark of a Texas-born lad who said, "Well, when I got so I could draw a cow and mark a few brands on the slate, I figured I was getting too smart to stay in school."

Other familiar figures were the drifters who spent their time in the West as rangeland beggars or saddle bums. They regularly took advantage of the Western custom of offering food and tobacco to anyone who happened to show up at a ranch. With typical frontier generosity one rancher tacked the following invitation to his door when he was away: "Help yourself to grub—please feed the chickens."

And there were men on the dodge from the law, bearing such untraceable aliases as Bronco Jim or Wyomin' Pete. It was easy for these characters to stay lost in cattle country because, among cowboys, close inquiry about a man's past was considered discourteous. One cowboy's memoirs recount a childhood incident when a stranger rode into camp. "We ate dinner and then I joined my older brother in asking the stranger what his name was. 'Jones is the name,' he said. As soon as he rode off, our mother laid us boys out for being so ill-mannered as to ask any man his name."

The common denominator for all of these diverse types was the service they paid to the West's sprawling herds of cattle—the work that gave them their name. Actually, the term "cowboy" is of uncertain derivation. In Revolutionary War days it was applied to armed Tories who tinkled cowbells to lure farmer patriots with lost cows into the brush—where the Tories ambushed them. Later the name referred to Texas bandits who stole cattle from Mexicans, sometimes murdering the herders. Only after the Civil War did the term come to signify anyone who tended cattle in the West.

The methods of working cattle could entail a multitude of activities, styles and techniques, depending on when and where in the Old West a man happened to live. In the 1860s the duties of a Texas cowboy—perhaps dressed only in the dilapidated remnants of a Confederate uniform, army-issue marching boots and a floppy woolen hat whose brim was pinned up by thorns

—might be to round up and drive half-wild longhorns 1,000 miles to market across an unfenced and basically unowned range. Thirty years later, in Montana, there was a second-generation cowboy—wearing the now standardized outfit of Levi's, high-heeled boots with hand stitching and a beautifully crafted Stetson—who would spend most of his days mowing hay or helping to breed a rancher's prized shorthorns. Sometimes a cowboy's work even took him away from cattle for a while. In winter he might collect firewood or go bounty hunting for the prairie wolves that preyed on weaker cattle. In fact, many cowboys did not work at all during the winter months, since the ranches laid off more than half their help when the warm-weather roundups and cattle drives were not underway. During the off-season a man might batch up, as the cowboys put it, with friends in town and do such odd jobs as house painting. Yet as long as he called himself a cowboy—which the average man did for only seven years before settling for good in town or on his own ranch—his life centered on those unlovable, thickheaded, panic-prone creatures he referred to as cows, a name that encompassed everything from day-old heifers to 10-year-old bulls.

The approximate midpoint and in many ways the zenith of the cowboy era was 1876. Yet in that year most of America's 44 million citizens were still only dimly aware of either the cowboy or the burgeoning cattle business that supported him. In 1876 a great exposition in Philadelphia celebrated the hundredth anniversary of the signing of the Declaration of Independence. This ostensible showcase for the nation's activities found little of value in the West, an attitude that had long been shared by prominent personages of the day *(box, page 19).* The livestock section of the exposition had been crammed with purebred Aberdeens and Herefords, but there were no longhorns—and hardly anything else from west of the Mississippi. By far the heaviest emphasis of the show was on manufacturing, the great activity of the industrial East.

The fact was that at this time the United States was still two countries. From the Atlantic Coast to just west beyond the Mississippi lay a settled, powerful, productive nation. In this America, steel was forged by the fiery new Bessemer process in Pittsburgh, thread was spun by the mile in New England mills and a tracework of 50,000 miles of railroad track—more than in any other nation—linked every port and factory town and farming center. It was a land of dense cities clogged with carriages and horse trolleys; of gaslit homes with linoleum floors; of soot-blackened ghettos where the immigrants from Europe arrived at a rate of half a million a year; of nine-course dinners at Delmonico's and whiskey at 10 cents a pint at the corner saloon; of dare-anything financial manipulators like Jay Gould and Jim Fisk, and a onetime ferryboat captain named Cornelius Vanderbilt, now 82 and dying of old age, who had hustled together the world's largest fortune—$103 million.

A side effect of this booming growth was a bad case of growing pains. In 1876 the nation was still in the throes of a terrible depression that had caused the collapse of the banking system three years earlier. Florida, Louisiana and South Carolina, scarred by the Civil War, were still under martial law. The scandal-racked administration of Ulysses S. Grant was about to leave office, and a colorless Ohioan named Rutherford Hayes would take Grant's place in the White House, bringing along a strait-laced wife known as Lemonade Lucy because she forbade the use of alcohol.

Measured against the tumultuous energies of civilized America, the Wild West indeed seemed like a second country, a howling wasteland. Between California and the first tier of states west of the Mississippi, an expanse of desolate plains stretched across a third of the continent's width, broken by harsh mountain ranges and containing only half a dozen towns with populations over 5,000. Across this void in 1876 wandered a single railroad: the Union Pacific, which had joined the Central Pacific in 1869 to link California to the East and ran sometimes only a single, rattling train a day over a jerry-built railbed. Some old geography textbooks still in circulation referred to the area as "the Great American Desert"—a description that held more than a grain of truth. From Canada to the Rio Grande, from the 98th meridian bisecting Kansas to the slopes of the Sierra, annual rainfall in the lowlands averaged less than 20 inches, and evaporation and wind velocity were apparently too high for farming. East of the Rockies, the only trees that grew were cottonwoods and hackberries in the creek bottoms, and some cedar and pine in the canyons. These plains were mostly made up of clay, sand and pebbles washed off the eastern face of the Rockies by rivers like the Platte and the Arkansas, and

eroded into diverse contours—most of them stupefyingly flat, or carved into grotesque clefts and pinnacles.

For a full half century westering Americans had probed in vain for a way to exploit the Great American Desert, but the entire area seemed wretchedly unpromising. Francis Parkman, a historian from Boston who crossed the plains in 1846, wrote gloomily: "No living thing was moving throughout that vast landscape, except the lizards that darted over the sand and through the rank grass and prickly pears at our feet. . . . Before and behind us, the level monotony of the plain was unbroken as far as the eye could reach. Sometimes it glared in the sun, an expanse of hot, bare sand; sometimes it was veiled by coarse grass. Skulls and whitening bones of buffalo were scattered everywhere."

But Parkman and others missed the significance of one vital ingredient—grass. The semiarid plains were covered by grasses, and these were, in fact, remarkably nutritious. The two main varieties were grama and buffalo grass, the latter growing even in the more parched areas where less than 15 inches of rain might fall in a year. Both of these grasses could stand long drought; broiled by the sun, they cured on the ground to a haylike quality that remained nourishing all winter. Once this rangeland had supported perhaps 75 million buffalo. But in the years following the Civil War the buffalo were slaughtered for their hides—and now the grass lay there unused, awaiting any grazing creature that could withstand the rigors of the climate.

Texas supplied the creature—the hardy longhorn, descended from cattle brought by the Spaniards. And that was the real news of the West in 1876. It was, in fact, a major piece of news for all America, the kind of thing that should have been represented front and center at the Centennial Exhibition. From April to October of that year 321,998 longhorns moved north on cattle trails, to be shipped from Kansas railheads to the beef-hungry East or to provide seed herds for new ranches springing up across the northern plains. Still more cattle were fattening and multiplying back in Texas. In the two decades between 1867 and 1887 a total of 5.5 million head of cattle were trailed north, a momentum of animals, men and money that in turn drew merchants and settlers to a region that had long been regarded as worthless. The chief agents of this colonization were the mounted cattle tenders of the West, the cowboys.

This trail boss wears, or carries on his saddle, everything he needs to live and work in the open. While tending cattle, however, he would not normally carry the rifle since it could easily snag his reins or lariat.

The uniform of the range

Fully outfitted for work on the range, a cowboy was covered from head to foot in a protective costume that identified him as distinctly as a knight's armor identified its owner. But every item of dress had a useful purpose, from the broad-brimmed hat that kept sun and rain off his head to the spurs fastened to the backs of his boots. Even the cowboy's ornamental-looking bandanna had various functions—as a mask to keep out trail dust, as insulation against the desert sun when wadded up and stuck in a hat crown, even as a tourniquet in case of rattlesnake bite.

Beneath this glamorous but utilitarian garb, the cowhand was dressed like any other laborer. He normally wore long johns—unless it was too hot. His shirt was typically collarless and made of cotton or flannel. His woolen pants were sometimes fortified with buckskin

sewn over the seat and down the inner thighs to keep them from fraying where they rubbed against the saddle. He rarely used suspenders, since they chafed him, and just as rarely wore a belt unless, as in later days, he was a rodeo rider hankering to show off a fancy belt buckle won in the arena. As a practical measure his pants had to stay up by themselves and thus were bought to fit tight around the waist. Because it was inconvenient to carry anything in pants pockets while riding, the cowboy usually had on a vest with deep pockets where he kept his Bull Durham tobacco, and perhaps a tally book for keeping count of the cattle.

Attire varied according to region and a man's own taste. In the Southwest many ranch hands wore heavy canvaslike jackets to protect themselves from thorns; Northern cowboys had knee-

length, fur-lined overcoats. Some men wore buckskin gauntlets to protect their hands from rope burns or from blisters caused by the reins. Others, accepting these hazards, scorned gloves of any kind, claiming they robbed a man of a good feel on the rope.

There was one item, however, that everyone wore. That was the hat. Along with saddle and boots, the hat was the cowboy's proudest, most personal possession. Besides warding off everything from hailstones to low-lying branches, it could be used to fan a fire or to carry water. A cowboy so hated to be without his hat that Western etiquette allowed him to wear it even when he sat down to a meal indoors, or while he was hopping around the dance floor with a cattle-town belle in a saloon at trail's end. Sometimes he even wore his hat to bed (*pages 96-97*).

FOUR DISTINCTIVE STYLES IN COWBOY HEADGEAR

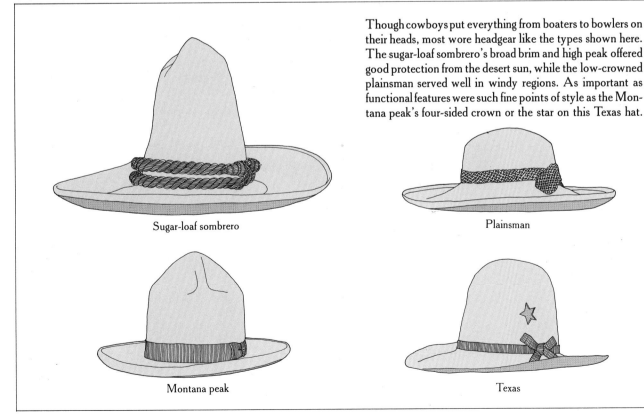

Though cowboys put everything from boaters to bowlers on their heads, most wore headgear like the types shown here. The sugar-loaf sombrero's broad brim and high peak offered good protection from the desert sun, while the low-crowned plainsman served well in windy regions. As important as functional features were such fine points of style as the Montana peak's four-sided crown or the star on this Texas hat.

Sugar-loaf sombrero

Plainsman

Montana peak

Texas

Shotguns

Batwings

Woollies

Before mounting up, a cowpuncher would often pull on a pair of chaps. These were seatless coverings first used by vaqueros who had to hunt cattle in heavy brush. Cowhands found they also gave good protection against rope burns, abrasions from corral poles and even horse bites.

Chaps came in three basic styles, shown here in front *(far left)* and rear views. The earlier chaps were climb-in models called shotguns, because they resembled parallel tubes. Like later chaps, they buckled at the waist. Many riders came to prefer batwing chaps, with wrap-around leggings that fastened at the back and could be snapped on without removing boots and spurs. On the cold northern ranges cowboys pulled on woollies, wintertime chaps covered on the front with wool or sometimes with fur.

THE EVOLUTION OF THE COWBOY BOOT

Early cowhands wore flat-heeled, round-toed boots they brought home from the Civil War. In the 1860s the true cowboy boot appeared, featuring a reinforced arch and higher heel. Later boots took on semi-functional frills, such as a more pointed toe and floppy grips called mule ears to make them easier to pull on. The fanciest boots, made after the mid-1880s, were of soft leather with decorative stitching, which some cowboys claimed gave a snugger fit.

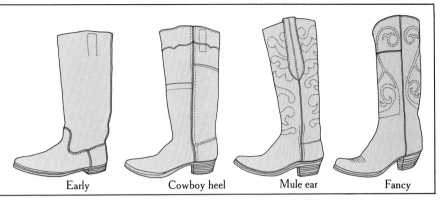

Early   Cowboy heel   Mule ear   Fancy

SPURS FOR RANGE WORK AND DISPLAY

Highly practical, spurs were also a vital part of the cowboy's image, and he rarely took them off. The spur's heel band fit over the back of the boot, while the spur strap fastened across the instep. The heel chain not only kept the spur from riding up but, along with the jinglebobs, produced a sound that was music to any strutting cowboy's ears. Most Americans shunned Mexican spurs, with their spiky rowels, and used models like the OK, with rowels filed down to avoid scouring the pony's flanks. The plainest type was a work spur, with a gentle, star-shaped rowel. However, many cowboys also owned a pair of fancy silver spurs like those shown at lower right.

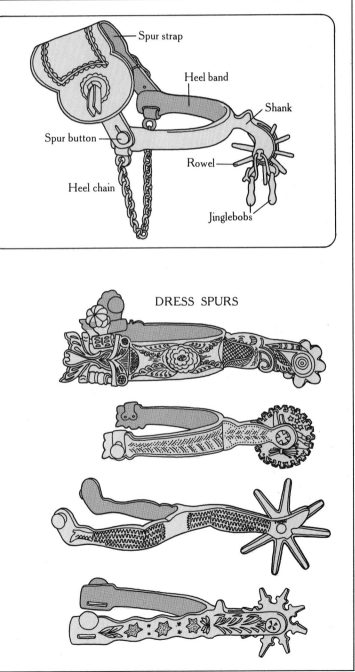

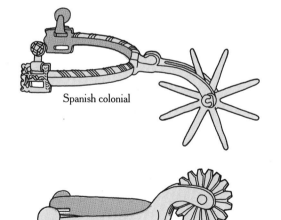

Spanish colonial

OK

Work spur

DRESS SPURS

The basic ingredient of the cowboy's function and his identity was the horse. An early chronicler of the cattle industry speaks mystically of "the strange mastery the mounted man has always had over the horned creatures of the range." There was nothing very strange about it. The horse was simply a serviceable tool that greatly augmented the muscle power and mobility of the rider. The range was no place for a man on foot. Distances were too great, and without horses it would have been impossible to round up, brand and drive millions of longhorns over those plains. Few cowboys actually owned a horse, but they all rode. Their mounts were supplied by the ranch they worked for. If a cowboy did happen to have his own horse, he put it into the ranch's common pool as a gesture of his commitment. And he always treated it as a tool, feeding it when he had to and burning it out after seven years of hard riding. Sometimes, in emergency situations on a long trail drive or a grueling roundup, horses were literally ridden to death.

Although the relationship between man and horse was a practical arrangement, rather than a love affair between a kindly master and a faithful servant, the horse nevertheless became the major element in the self-image of the cowboy. Veteran cowhands, proud of the feelings of height and power that came from being mounted, displayed an aversion to walking any distance greater than from the corral to the bunkhouse. A favorite range story tells of three cowboys who rode their horses into a desert saloon where an Easterner was having a drink at the bar. The stranger was jostled, and he complained about it to the bartender, who happened to be an ex-puncher himself. The bartender said coldly: "What the hell you doing in here afoot anyhow?" Most cowboys were resolute in their judgment that "a man afoot is no man at all." And it was true, as cowpuncher Jo Mora put it, that, dismounted and viewed dispassionately, the cowboy was "just a plain bowlegged human who smelled very horsey at times, slept in his underwear and was subject to boils and dyspepsia."

A second tool, indispensable to both the cowboy's work and his image, was the rope, or lariat. Expertly thrown, a rope could snare a cow's horns or a horse's neck, or the hooves of either, enabling a 140-pound man to capture and subdue a 1,000-pound animal. A rope could be transformed into an instant corral when it was stretched taut by several men. It could be used as a hobble to keep a horse from straying away in the night. Hitched around a saddle horn, it served to drag firewood or pull a mired cow out of a bog. And although violence was far less common in the West than the legends have it, the rope was on certain rare occasions shaped into a hangman's noose to carry out short-order justice, served up quick and hot when someone was caught in an absolutely unforgivable crime such as horse stealing. Cowboys even dreamed up some magical functions for rope; they believed, for example, that if one made of horsehair was placed in a circle around a sleeping man it would protect him from snakes.

Another proud cowboy possession was a gun, although it was not so much in evidence as the horse or rope. A lot of cowhands used their guns as playthings, passing time by firing at casual targets. The most common practical use was for hunting. When a cowboy went out to kill an antelope or a jack rabbit for his supper, he took a rifle or a shotgun. But he did not take it far, because a large firearm was awkward to hand-hold and when carried in a saddle scabbard it rubbed against the horse, producing sores. The cowboy's celebrated Colt revolver, although it was often left back at the bunkhouse or tucked away in his bedroll, had considerably more versatility than the cumbersome rifle. Despite the revolver's woeful inaccuracy, it was convenient to carry and served to kill rattlesnakes, to finish off a horse that had a broken leg or to turn aside a stampede when it was fired directly in front of the leaders.

In the early days the revolver was also used against Indians or Mexicans—but flash-tempered shoot-outs with fellow cowboys rarely occurred. Homer Grigsby, a cowhand who spent many years on the Arizona-New Mexico range, declared that he never saw a gun drawn on another man except by a feverish greenhorn who had heard that courage in the West was proved with a Colt. There were exceptions, of course. Some cowboys had been schooled in the Southern view that a gentleman had not only the right but the obligation to defend his honor with a gun. And whether from the North or from the South, cowboys on a trail's-end spree in a cattle town sometimes succumbed to both liquor and a compulsion to demonstrate their manhood with six-shooters. The cattle trade also embraced a fair number of outright thugs who doubled as cowhands when not

By the 1880s cowboys were parodying the Old West's reputation for lawlessness. At top Montana hands stage a mock lynching. In the other picture four men spoof the quick draw at an impromptu card game.

rustling or working as enforcers for autocratic ranch owners. One so-called puncher named Scharbar was described by a misled admirer as a "square, law-abiding man if I ever saw one. . . . Always backing up law and order and never killed anybody but hard eggs trying to run over somebody." In the course of his violent career Scharbar found 32 such hard eggs and killed every one of them. But he was unusual.

Cowboys were certainly aware of the aura of lethal manliness that guns gave them, and they weighed themselves down with firearms whenever they paid a call on a girl, confident that she would be impressed. But in trying to appear manly, more than one cowboy managed to look just plain silly. A Montana man remembered a cowboy relative who returned from town with a bandage on one hand covering a bullet wound. Presumably he had been wounded in a saloon battle. In fact, the poor puncher had shot himself, though not seriously, when a photographer handed him the gun so he could pose looking fierce for the home folks.

In other ways, too, cowboys were singularly conscious of their appearance, real dandies in their own steel-and-leather fashion. They would spend as much as four months' wages on a hat with a fancy sweatband. Their boots were custom-made, costing sometimes more than $50 per pair—two months' wages. If a cowboy could not get to a bootmaker in person, he would spread an order blank on the bunkhouse floor and trace the shape of his feet. The vamp of the boot had to be skintight so that his feet would look small—a point upon which cowboys were particularly sensitive, not wanting to be confused with any big-footed groundling. But boots were also highly functional in design. The sole was made of thin leather to permit a good feel of the stirrup, and the tops were generally at least 17 inches high to prevent twigs or pebbles from getting inside. Heels were high, narrow and undersloped to hold the stirrup firmly, and the pointed toe helped a rider slip easily into the stirrup—and slip free if he was thrown. (The most common form of death among cowboys was to be dragged by a horse.)

As befits a mounted cavalier, the cowboy carried himself with a sort of vinegary pride, fully convinced that he was the aristocrat among the workingmen of the West. An Englishman visiting a friend on a ranch in Wyoming discovered this quality when he inquired of the foreman, "Is your master at home?" The foreman looked at him levelly and replied, "The son of a bitch hasn't been born yet." A wiser New Yorker traveling across the plains reported: "There is no use trying to be overbearing with them, for they will not stand the least assumption of superiority."

This cowboy pride had its ugly side, too. Like other men of the late 19th Century, the white majority of cowhands were unabashed racists. Blacks were casually referred to as "niggers." Mexicans were "greasers." And the white cowboys sometimes expressed these attitudes in deeds as well as words. On one occasion a black man entered a hotel in Cheyenne, Wyoming, and took a seat in the dining room next to a trail boss. Without a word, the trail boss arose and smashed a chair over the man's head. The trail boss was subsequently arrested and fined heavily for assault under an equal-rights act passed just after the Civil War.

Cowboys also tended to be rough in their humor. In one typical practical joke a trail cook would tie all the sleeping cowboys' spurs to a log and then rouse them with a shout that breakfast was ready. Another joke was to put pie dough in a sleeping man's beard. And the funniest sight in the world to a veteran cowhand was a greenhorn who had suffered a sprained ankle or dislocated shoulder from falling off his horse.

There was also a surprising amount of cruelty to animals. During the early days of cattle tending in Texas, punchers sometimes adopted the brutal practices of the Mexican vaqueros, making a sulky cow move by rubbing sand in its eyes, or by twisting its tail until the bone snapped. Horses were individually more valuable than cattle, but they, too, came in for a good deal of sadism at the hands of cowboys. A young cowhand named Pinnacle Jake recalled how he vented his exasperation against a wild sorrel that refused to be bridled. He climbed on a big horse called Smoky, known "to be a fine roping horse, except that he broke the necks of everything that was roped off him." With deadly intent Pinnacle Jake roped the uncooperative sorrel: "He jumped over the loop and started to run. I took two or three quick turns of the rope around my saddle horn, and old Smoky began to sag back against the rope just as the sorrel hit the end of it. The little bronc sort of went straight up in the air, turned over and come down square on his head. His neck popped like a pistol shot. It seemed like it was all done in twenty seconds."

But the cowboy's harsh way had a more attractive counterpoint—stoicism, a deeply rooted trait among range hands. Complaining was considered unprofessional. It irritated others and evoked no sympathy whatever. The Englishman John Baumann, who found much to deplore in the Old West, was astonished at the ability of his fellow workers to endure pain without making a fuss. He remembered with particular admiration the cowhand who rode off one morning to shoot a wild turkey. A distant gunshot was heard, and a while later the cowboy returned to camp, sat down and began to whittle a stick. After he had finished shaving the stick he bared his leg and revealed a deep bullet wound in the thigh. The horse had stumbled, he told onlookers, and the six-shooter in his hand had gone off accidentally. Having done all the explaining he considered necessary, he wrapped a rag around the stick, pushed it into the wound to scrape out the gunpowder and then rode 30 miles to a surgeon with his leg across the saddle horn.

This kind of ability to endure was fundamental to a cowboy's survival, for few professions have ever offered more occasions for complaint. On a given day a cowboy could find himself in the middle of a prairie fire, quicksand or a stampede. And on any day he could be thrown or kicked by a horse, charged by a steer or half frozen on a winter search for strayed livestock. His reserve of strength was ground down by these—and other—rigors of the job. On a trail drive a puncher might work 18 hours a day seven days a week, and he might have to travel 1,800 miles with no comforts other than a campfire and his bedroll. The constant moaning of the prairie wind rubbed men's nerves raw—and literally drove some ranch wives mad. At times the weather turned so infernally hot that a cowboy had to cool his horse's bit in water to keep the hot metal from blistering the animal's mouth.

Yet such tribulations were part of the game and, if mentioned at all, were discussed in tones of rueful understatement. After one bitter winter that killed off cattle by the thousands gave way to furnacelike heat, a cowhand was observed addressing himself to the sun with the words, "Where the hell was you last January?" A typical comment on a long drought was: "We're closer to the next rain than we ever was before." A piece of advice about the winds of the Great

Plains ran: "Hang a logchain on a post. If the wind raises the chain straight out from the post it's a calm day. But when the end links start snapping off, expect rough weather." This Bunyanesque humor concealed a grim fact of life: exposure to the extremes of the weather in the cattle country frequently brought on pneumonia—after riding accidents, the leading cause of cowboy deaths.

Understatement about hardship merely reflected a more general taciturnity. Silence at meals was the general custom, and big talkers were derisively called leaky mouths. An old anecdote told of the two partners in a lonely cow camp who heard bellowing noises in the night. One of them suggested: "Bull." The other said, "Sounds like an old steer to me." Not another word was spoken, and the two went to bed. The next morning one of the cowboys began packing up his horse. "Leaving?" asked his companion. The other replied, "Yes, too much argument."

About the only time a cowboy let his tongue run free was in swearing. Cowboy talk assayed somewhere around one third profanity and obscenity, which was either directed at horses and cattle or used as the salt and pepper of ordinary speech. "Son of a bitch" in particular seems to have been part of every other sentence. Swearing, it was said, "takes the strain off the liver." However, it was not permitted everywhere; a number of cattle owners forbade profanity on their ranches and fired men who did not keep their language clean.

The prohibition did not weigh too heavily on all cowboys, for a number of them were raised to be good Christians and remained God-fearing men all their lives. Some even became preachers after they left the range. But most cowboys did not want to be thought of as Sunday-schoolish, and they behaved accordingly. A cowpuncher named Teddy Blue Abbott commented of his acquaintances that "ninety per cent of them was infidels." Documentary support for his assessment still survives in period pamphlets bearing such titles as "Help the Heathen Cowboys of the West."

The most reverent feelings of cowboys in this Victorian time were reserved for womankind—that is, for the nice-girl portion of womankind. It was a remote kind of reverence. For marriage was a mode of life that most men had to shun as cowboys, since they were always on the move, nice girls were few, and their pay was too low to support a family in any case. But all the

Fred P.O. Indian T.Y.

Mr A H Pierce
                    Dear Sir
not having herd from you since
we left I thought I would write
you so that you would know
whare to find us I am now
Camped on bitter Creek between
the Washata & Cadanian Rivers
You had better write to us here
as we will remain in this
visinety some time unless we
receive orders from you to move
on we have not had eny rain
yet and this is the first place
that I have been where we could
improve the Cattle and Horses Wylies
men have been having the Measles
Bob Logan has them now but
is getting all right my Cattle have
been running badly but are getting
all right now the grass and water
is fine and Cattle ought to improve
very fast I have 2000 head in my herd,
had to let Wylie have one of my
hands to help him out have had
no Chance to sell my Cattle yet

For reasons known only to themselves, these cowboys proudly laid out their spurs when they gathered in front of the chuck wagon at a Colorado range in the 1880s.

while they rode the trails, consorting with an occasional cattle-town prostitute, they yearned for the company of virtuous women. A lonesome young cowboy would travel miles, by one account, "just to sit on a porch for an hour or two and watch some homesteader's red-faced daughter rock her chair and scratch her elbows —and not a smack or a hug." The Denver *Republican* commented: "Let a cowboy be alone in the presence of a good woman, and there is no finer gentleman produced by nature." At a trial in Randall County, Texas, in 1889, a jury of cowboys displayed their gallantry by not only acquitting a nester accused of claim jumping, but awarding him a section of land on the grounds that the nester had "comely daughters."

Cowboys were proud of their prowess at their jobs and did a good deal of bragging about it. They bragged even more about acquaintances who were better men than themselves—and none better than puncher Ed Lemmon, who by his own estimate saddle-handled more than a million cattle in his lifetime. Lemmon at one point knew every important brand in the West and set the record for the most cows—900—cut out of a herd and branded in a single day. An Arizona rancher once boasted that he had riders who could calmly roll and light a cigarette while busting mustangs—an act, he pointed out to a friend, that made the horse realize the hopelessness of bucking any more. The friend, a Montana man, solemnly replied that his riders broke horses with the same technique, except that what the horse saw when he looked back was the cowboy "quietly shaving, holding a small mirror in one hand and the razor in the other, with the mug, hot water and bay rum in a little basket on his arm."

But such good-humored bravado, while it provided a few light moments, did not alter the fact that the cowboy's life was often bitterly hard. And it is not difficult to find in this harshness the sources of the Western legend. Perhaps the best summary of the grueling, lonely and sometimes violent substance of life on the range was contained in one man's brief year-end written report to an absentee ranch owner back East. "Deer sur," it went, "we have brand 800 caves this roundup we have made sum hay potatoes is a fare crop. That Inglishman yu lef in charge at the other camp got to fresh and we had to kill the son of a bitch. Nothing much has hapened sence yu lef. Yurs truely, Jim."

33

The limitless land that he roamed

No folk hero, real or fanciful, ever acted out his role on a more spectacular stage than the Old West provided for cowboys like those shown here, silhouetted against the Arizona sky. West of the Mississippi, the prairie undulated in ripples of grass for a thousand miles, then rose toward the cool summer pastures of the high Rockies. Beyond the Rockies the land dropped to the red-brown wash of the intermountain basin, then climbed again to the pastures of the Sierra foothills in California.

Few pieces of country had seemed more inviting to a cattleman—"land for nothing!" as one exulted. But though the West may have looked like paradise to the cattle investors and ranch owners, there were days when it could feel like hell to the ordinary cowhands. The contrast in altitude between mountains and lowlands bred killing extremes of hot and cold. A Montana winter night could freeze a steer in its tracks at 50° below, while a summer noon on the Arizona desert might well be more than 110°. The winds could be deadly, rolling over the treeless prairie from Hudson Bay to Texas, dropping the thermometer 50° in one day. Ranch hands called such winds "blue northers" and despised them. These brutal elements helped to carve the shape of the land. And together with the land they shaped the character of the cowpuncher, as hard-scrabble tough as the mesas that he rode and in his resolute way a more fascinating man than the half-fanciful hero of the Western sagas.

Mounted cowboys line up on the dry range of Pima County, Arizona. Even here on the desert fringe four inches of rain per year helped to provide grazing for longhorns.

The broad flood plain of the Sweetwater River stretches away from Devil's Gate Pass in the mountains of Wyoming. Traveled mainly by fur trappers and a few emigrants up to the end of the Civil War, the Sweetwater country, by 1880, was a major grazing ground. That year the Wyoming cattle herds numbered more than half a million head.

Twin Sisters buttes stand watch over the narrow pastures of the Green River Valley. Trail bosses on the long drives often navigated by such stark landmarks, but the blasting, erosive action of wind-borne sand and freezing rain could, within a few years, change the shape of lesser beacons to make them unrecognizable to cowhands lost on the trails.

A sagebrush plateau west of Craig, Colorado, presents the sterile-looking appearance that led early explorers to condemn such terrain as "substantially uninhabitable." Cattlemen grabbed up huge tracts of this bleak land, knowing its thin ration of needle grass and balsamroot scattered through the sage could support one hardy longhorn every 36 acres.

Half-wild range horses gather at a water hole near the crest of the Rockies. The high pastures were closed from November to May by snow and cold, but they became prime grazing ground in summer, when lowland water sources dried up and the prairie grass had been cropped to the roots.

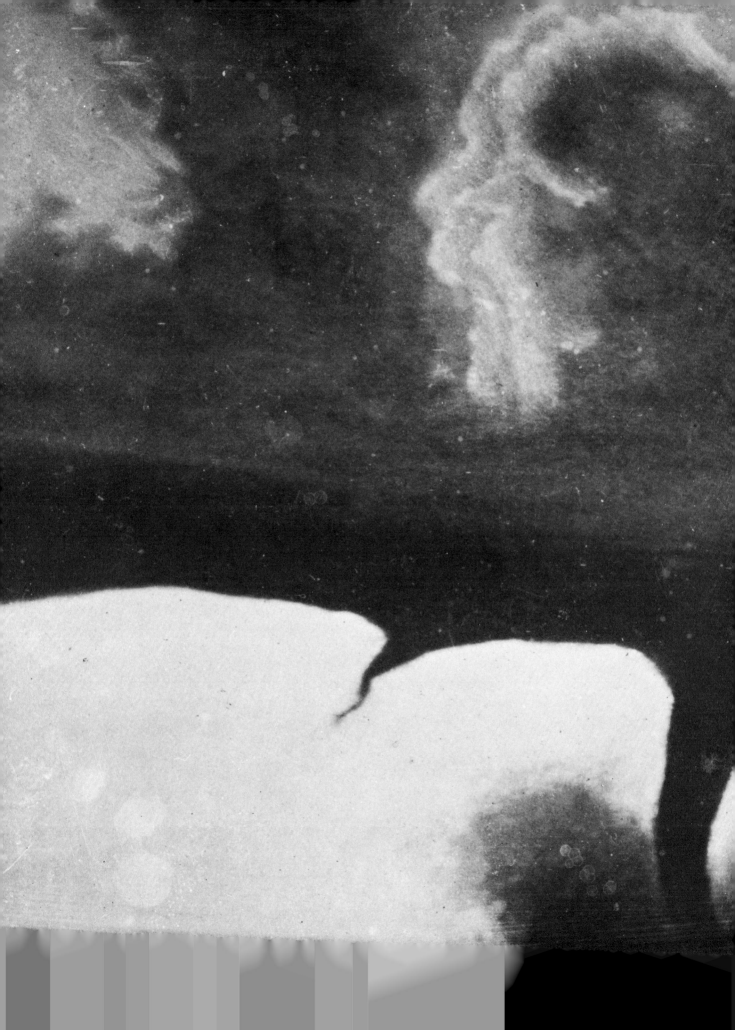

A tornado, hatching a pair of young twisters on either side, tears into the Dakota prairie in this first photograph of a live cyclone, taken in 1884. Storms on the Great Plains were often quick, violent and lethal. One thundersquall in 1882 killed two men, half a dozen horses and 14 head of cattle.

2 | The cattle barons

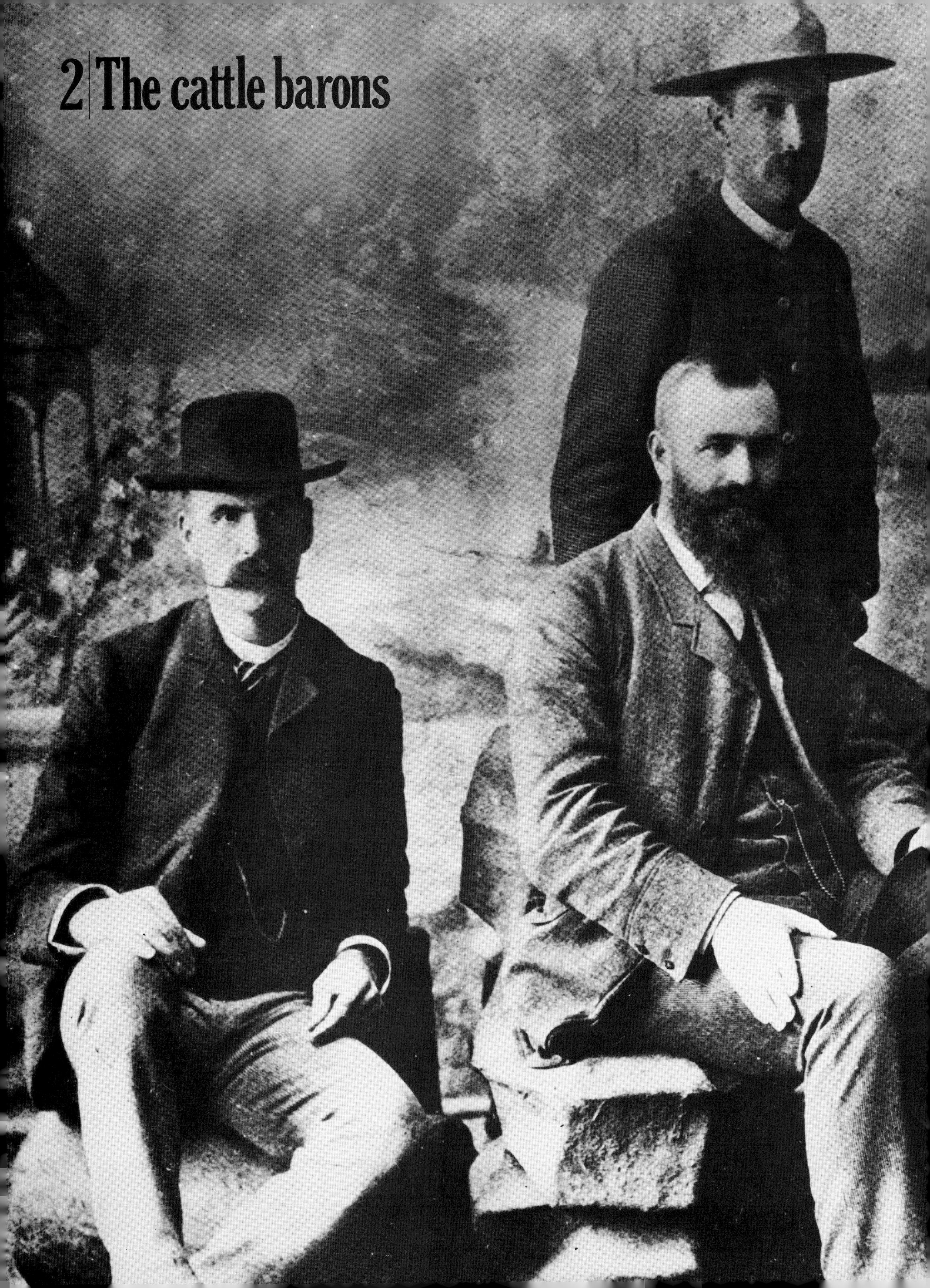

The reason that the American cowboy loped onto the prairie, bigger than life and brandishing his six-shooter, was to work for a bunch of straight-eyed entrepreneurs like those at left. These were the businessmen who built the Western livestock industry, the milieu within which the cowboy flourished. They were known as the cattle barons, a term they detested, and they ruled enormous fiefs that as of 1883 held half of the West's 23 million cows.

The quartet shown here managed the Prairie Cattle Company, Limited, whose 156,000 cows roamed across five million acres. So vast was the Prairie spread—and others like it, such as the Matador, XIT and King Ranch—that an old hand equated the annual roundup to "a farmer in Massachusetts turning out a cow to graze and finding her months later in Delaware." A few barons started as cowpokes; one such was Charles Goodnight (next page). But most of the others never knew how to hold a Colt or a branding iron. For example, Murdo Mackenzie, the hatless, bearded gentleman at left, detested guns and generally avoided the grubby life of the range. However, all the barons were alike in one respect: they kept their eyes fixed on the profit-and-loss statement. And in so doing they managed to establish a business—and a way of life—that the world would see only once, in the Old West they ruled.

Cattle baron Murdo Mackenzie (at center in foreground) sits for a corporate portrait in 1886 with three fellow officers in the powerful Prairie Cattle Company, Limited.

47

The men who turned the longhorn into big business

During the summer of 1876 a group of trail riders pushed a herd of 1,600 cows through the Texas Panhandle, looking for a promised land that Mexican friends had told them of — a great valley where they could settle the cattle amid sweet grass and good water. The men had been out several months now, and for all that time the Panhandle had appeared a harsh and inhospitable place. The surrounding plains seemed stove-lid flat and boundless, a parched surface empty of all but gray soil and dry grass. Then the riders saw a dark slash across the land. Suddenly they found themselves on the brink of a gorge, the wild and mighty Palo Duro Canyon cut cleanly to a depth of 700 feet by the headwaters of the Red River in the center of the Texas Panhandle.

Charles Goodnight, a bowlegged, bearded bull of a man, gazed into the canyon. At this upper western end the chasm was narrow and cliff-sided, lined with cedars and wild china; but eastward it widened to embrace a cattleman's Eden — a vast, sheltered, well-watered pasture, fenced naturally on the north and south by its own towering bluffs. Goodnight made an abrupt decision. As of that day Palo Duro Canyon was his. He would, he told himself, acquire the land by any means necessary — legal, illegal or extralegal. He would drive out any Comanches who camped there; he would oust or kill the buffalo that ranged on the canyon floor and replace them with his cows; when the time came he would get a moneyed investor to provide needed capital. Already

A cowboy who made it up the ladder to baron, Charlie Goodnight stole when he wanted to, lynched when he had to and died having ruled millions of acres of Texas rangelands.

famous as a pioneer trail driver and cattle raiser, he would go on to dominate this vast and precious land.

Goodnight did all of this and more. Within five years he ruled not only the Palo Duro but the outlying plains for farther than a man could see. He presided over a herd that numbered upward of 100,000 head, from which he sold some 30,000 animals in an average season for a gross income of around half a million dollars. His hegemony over the area was as absolute as that of any medieval liege lord: when some armed neighbors appeared and said they intended to wipe out a harmless group of local sheepherders Charlie's curt order to desist was enough to send the abashed gunmen quietly back to their ranches.

The details of Goodnight's personal history were in many ways unique — and as fascinating as those of any Western cattleman, for the wealth he made on the Palo Duro was not his first fortune but his second. Yet his general *modus operandi* was in the classic pattern of the handful of extraordinary men who became the cattle barons of the West and created the backdrop against which the cowboy lived and worked. As a matter of historical fact, the cowboy was not in the saddle to create a legend or to win the West. He was there because hardheaded businessmen — most of them Texans, at first — decided that they could make money in cattle. And they did. By 1885 beef cattle represented by far the biggest business in all the Old West. And by that time this cabal of no more than perhaps three dozen rangeland rajahs controlled more than 20 million acres of United States soil, private and public, and owned at least one third of the beeves that grazed the Western prairie.

In background these businessmen varied widely. A would-be baron often started as a cowhand himself

49

—perhaps one of the men who had drifted into the brushlands after fighting in the Texas Revolution of 1836. Or he might be a refugee from a burned-out farm in the Old South, one of the GTTs, whose nickname derived from the "Gone to Texas" signs they left behind. Or he might be an Easterner seeking a new life and fortune on the frontier. In any case he was likely to be an adventurous man, accustomed to hard work and violence, and ready for both.

Commonly, the baron-to-be started operations on a shoestring, usually hiring a few cowhands to round up wild cattle on the open range, sometimes seizing and branding strays or alleged strays, or even already branded cattle whose existing markings were alterable with a skillfully placed iron. Then he and his men drove them to market. If he hit it lucky for a couple of years—which meant the weather stayed good and commodity prices high and a thousand other factors remained favorable —he then expanded his operation. He might reach out for control of vast tracts of grazing land, first nailing down—either by claim or by plain six-gun fiat—the crucial water holes or streams upon which all cattle raising depended. He then set himself to master the special skills, ever more sophisticated, of ranch management and marketing. Eventually, to consolidate his holdings and further expand his business, he went after fresh capital any way he could get it, frequently by wooing free-wheeling foreign investors. For while America was rich in land and cattle, it was still relatively poor in money.

Charles Goodnight, who drove his way through every one of these stages of growth, stands as a prototype of the successful cattle baron. He was born in 1836 on a farm in southern Illinois and got his only schooling there. In 1845 Goodnight's family set him bareback onto a white-faced mare, climbed into a wagon themselves and journeyed for some 800 miles to the Brazos River deep in the plains of Texas. In those days, just after Texas was admitted to the Union, this was Far West, frontier country. Young Charlie encountered more than enough buffalo and Indians to thrill an Illinois boy. But the longhorn cows, roaming everywhere, were the creatures that tantalized him.

These cattle were authentic wild animals, living in the thickets like game—and in fact often shot as game. Nearly as wild and even more numerous were the cattle in the country south of San Antonio, abandoned by

their Mexican owners after the Texas war and the subsequent border fighting. Taken together, the cattle running loose in Texas numbered close to 300,000 in 1845. "We have only to go out a few miles into a swamp between the Big and Little Brazos to find as many cattle as one could wish," wrote one visitor to the region where Goodnight's family settled.

By the time Charles Goodnight arrived in the Brazos some Texas men already were building careers on these cattle. For most of their history Americans had shown a preference for pork; now, for some reason, they were evidencing a new taste for beef. To meet this new demand, entrepreneurs in Texas had begun to round up cattle and drive them toward the rich markets of the East. Herds went to New Orleans and to Missouri in 1842, and in 1846 a drover named Edward Piper pushed a thousand head all the way to Ohio. For part of the trek Piper used the first of the long trails —the Shawnee Trail, from the Brazos country to a railhead at St. Louis. Starting on this same trail, drover Tom Candy Ponting took Texas cattle by foot and rail all the way to cattle pens at the corner of 44th Street and Fourth Avenue in Manhattan. New Yorkers, even in this early day, were more interested in the quality of the beef than in the first sight of a longhorn cow. Commented the *New York Tribune* of July 4, 1854: "The meat is fine-grained and close, somewhat like venison. It is apt to be a little tough."

Growing up in the Brazos country, young Charlie was a cowboy before he ever thought of being a cattle dealer. On the family farm he became familiar with the distinctive ways of cattle—in the Western phrase he "learned cow." He also became a clever hand at busting mustangs, whacking bulls, splitting rails and racing horses. All this time he watched the herds go north. Then, in 1856, Goodnight made his own first modest venture into the cattle business. He and a stepbrother took on the care of 430 cows bearing the brand of the neighboring C V Ranch. As pay, the boys were allowed to keep every fourth calf that was born; in four years they owned 180 head.

During those years Goodnight also picked up some of the subtleties of scouting lore and of survival on the frontier—all matters of the utmost importance to the cattle drive. He learned to locate water by watching swallows; if they carried mud for nest building in their mouths, a water hole lay in the direction from which they came. He learned to stop thirst by sucking a bullet, to stay hunger by chewing tobacco, to make rich soup by boiling prairie dogs with flour. He discovered in himself a sure sense of direction and found how to judge the freshness of a hoofprint by counting the insect tracks across it.

He learned, too, to recognize the precious grasses of the plains, grasses that in three years could transform a four-dollar yearling into a twenty-dollar steer or heifer. He discovered that a single cow needed 10 acres of this grass to graze in a year if the underlying soil was good—and half again as much if the land was dry and scrubby. But no matter how lush or poor the grass, the critical factor was water. Each cow might drink up to 30 gallons a day. Furthermore, to a cattleman, control of the water meant control of an entire region. A rancher who held a river or water hole might claim the surrounding range for at least 10 miles (as far as a cow could walk to water) plus elbow room, maybe 15 to 25 miles in all. Thus, once he had clinched a firm claim to the water, all the pasture was automatically his; no other cowman would move into even the lushest grass if a predecessor had taken over the vital water supply for his own stock.

It was a good time to be learning facts like these. By 1860 Texas herds had grown to some 3.5 million head, and the new Western cattle business was beginning to burgeon. But then came a hiatus that was to last for five years: while their cattle, untended and undriven, continued to multiply on the open range, ranchers and cowboys went off to fight in the Civil War.

As his service to the Confederacy, Charles Goodnight joined the Texas Rangers, whose main job was fending off Comanches and Kiowas on the Western frontier. He served as scout and guide, sometimes moving west into the virtually unexplored Staked Plains. Mustered out early in 1864, Goodnight set off with his stepbrother to gather their portion of the C V herd, which had grown, they estimated, to 5,000 head, part of the astonishing increase that crammed Texas by war's end with five million longhorns. It was these longhorn cattle and their progeny, either driven or shipped across the West into 16 new states and territories, that provided virtually all the barons with the basic brood stock for their herds—and in fact was the base from

which the entire Western cattle business developed.

Right after the war, however, most of the longhorns were wandering, lost in the vastness of the Texas brush country. Goodnight later recalled, "Certain scattered men over the country could not resist the temptation and went to branding those cattle for themselves." He estimated that in Texas there were two or three mavericks—unbranded calves—for every branded one. The word maverick itself carried a warning. It came from Sam Maverick, a cattleman on the San Antonio River who neglected his branding and discovered, after only a year of ranching on this rich, well-watered ground, that he had been forced out of business by avaricious neighbors and outright rustlers who had made off with his unmarked stock.

But Goodnight was too tough and smart to suffer any such fate. First, he and his stepbrother bought the whole C V herd on credit. Then by buying still more cattle (and also, in truth, by stealing a bit from the open range) Charlie and the stepbrother put together a herd of 8,000 head by the spring of 1865.

All around them equally hard, resolute—and often eccentric—men were building herds and driving them to market. One pre-Civil War neighbor, George Webb Slaughter, had a flourishing ranch near the Goodnight outfit on the Brazos River, where he occasionally shot Indians with the same rifle that he rested every Sunday against the pulpit of the Baptist church in which he served as an ordained preacher. As early as 1860 Slaughter owned 1,500 head of longhorns.

Another Texan, an up-from-broncobuster rancher named Abel (Shanghai) Pierce, represented a more flamboyant side of the business. At one point in his early career he hired three brothers to round up mavericks for him; when they began doing some mavericking on their own he took it badly and had them strung up. The flavor of Pierce's personality comes across in the response he once made when a neighbor boasted about his cow. "If I had a cow that would give five gallons of milk, I tell you, I'd never touch a teat," bellowed Shanghai. "I'd make her stick out her tongue, and I'd dip out the milk with a long-handled gourd!"

Dudley Snyder was just the reverse: a sober and self-righteous man, certain to deliver what he contracted to deliver. On his first drive, in 1862, taking cattle to the Confederate Army, he swam the animals across the

Mississippi, an astonishing feat. Snyder's mercantile philosophy as it evolved after the war was that a man never makes money selling a horse—the money is made in buying it. Buying shrewdly, he eventually acquired ranches in Colorado and Wyoming as well as Texas.

If Dudley Snyder was conservative in his plans, the same could not be said of Charles Goodnight. In the spring of 1866, while most drovers made plans to take their cattle to the railheads in Kansas for shipment to the East, Goodnight decided to open a route to Colorado, hoping for a lucrative new market for his cattle in the mines and military posts there. While buying provisions in a town near his home, Goodnight encountered Oliver Loving, a 54-year-old cattleman renowned for his knowledge of both livestock and the frontier. A real pioneer in the cattle business, Loving had been in Tex-

as since 1845. In 1855 he had driven a herd to Illinois, and a few years later he became the first man ever to trail cattle to Colorado. Now he listened carefully as Goodnight outlined a plan to establish the regular new cattle trail. To avoid traversing Comanche country that lay across the northern Texas border, Charlie proposed to start for Colorado by heading in a roundabout direction, southwest rather than northwest, along an old trail from the Brazos to the Pecos River in western Texas; he would then strike northward through New Mexico. Loving frowned over the dangers and difficulties of Goodnight's proposed route. But he could envision the soundness of the basic plan, for abruptly he said: "If you will let me go, I will go with you."

In June 1866 the two men gathered 2,000 trail-ready cattle and 18 riders at a point on the trace of the

The original American cowboy, a California vaquero of the 1830s, throws a bull with the style of a latter-day rodeo showman.

Southern Overland Mail. This road brought them, 250 miles later, to the head of the Concho River. There Goodnight and Loving watered the herd until the thirstiest old cow could drink no more. Over the next 80 miles the herd encountered not a single stream, in fact nothing wetter than the sun-baked mud of former water holes. With frightening frequency, an exhausted cow would drop out of the drove to die. At 2 a.m. on the third night the cattle smelled water ahead and Goodnight let the strongest run the final miles to the Pecos.

"When they reached the river those behind pushed the ones in the lead right on across before they had time to stop and drink," he later recollected. In the rush to water, others were trampled, drowned and bogged in quicksand. More than a hundred were lost—to add to the 300 whose carcasses littered the trail behind.

But despite its livestock losses the drive made money—and lots of it. The entire herd was sold in two bunches. At Fort Sumner, a reservation of Navahos and Apaches in northern New Mexico, the government paid eight cents a pound for all the steers. Loving took the cows and calves on to the vicinity of Denver and sold them to a cattleman named John Wesley Iliff. Goodnight packed a mule with $12,000 in gold and headed back down the trail toward Texas.

The partnership did not last much longer. A year after that first drive Oliver Loving was trapped at the Pecos River by a party of some 500 Comanche braves, and was shot in the arm and side. He eluded his pursuers and traveled overland for seven days without food, then was taken by a group of Mexicans to Fort Sumner. There Loving died of an infection—needlessly,

The cowboy's elegant Spanish ancestry

A good half century before the Western beef-cattle industry blossomed in Texas, a singular breed of professional horsemen calling themselves vaqueros had already set the style, evolved the equipment and techniques *(left)*, and even developed much of the vocabulary that would become the stamp of the American cowboy. The range of the vaquero was Spanish California. There, roughly from the time George Washington crossed the Delaware until the United States annexed Upper California in 1848, a unique pastoral society evolved, founded on Christ but ultimately flourishing on the cow.

When Franciscan missionaries first arrived in California around 1769 they brought with them a few modest herds of domestic cattle for dairy and brood stock. In the warm, grassy valleys of California the cows thrived and became an unexpected source of profit to the fathers. At San Diego and other California ports they had begun trading with Yankee ships like the *Pilgrim*, which Richard Henry Dana made famous in

his book *Two Years before the Mast.*

On a more modest scale the same thing was happening at missions along the lower Rio Grande. There was, however, a major difference between this embryonic, California-centered cattle industry and the one that later grew on the prairies of the U.S. To the padres, beef was actually a by-product. Profits came from hides and tallow, the raw materials used by New England factories to manufacture leather goods, candles and soap. And from the first, profits were very good.

In consequence, the mission fathers were soon saving as many pesos as souls, and local Indians found themselves learning as much about cattle as about the Trinity. For as the business and the herds increased, the priests, many of them sons of Spanish nobility trained from birth as superb horsemen, needed help handling the cows. The only laborers available were their Indian converts, who were known as neophytes—a religious euphemism meaning trained slaves. Those selected by the

padres became skilled horsemen themselves, as they had to be to handle big herds of cattle on an open range.

The need to teach the Indians to ride created something of a dilemma, for an ancient Spanish colonial law, dating back to the time of the conquistadors, forbade the Indians the use of horses, which were then considered primarily tools of war. But the padres, laws unto themselves on the early frontier, decided to ignore the old edict in the interests of expediency. They also set about teaching the Indians how to snare a steer on the run by throwing a loop of braided rawhide rope, known for centuries in Spain as *la reata* and later Americanized to "lariat."

The Indian horsemen used a horn-equipped modification of the old Spanish war saddle *(page 105)*. Once a steer had been caught, they learned to bring the animal to a stop by taking quick turns of the lariat around the horn. This they called *dar la vuelta* (to make the turn), which came to be the American Cowboys' "dally." To

according to a companion, because the doctor at the fort "had never amputated any limbs and did not want to undertake such work."

Goodnight survived and prospered. During the next few years he drove herd after herd up the Goodnight-Loving Trail from Texas to Colorado. It was good business, but wearing and dangerous. By 1870 he was ready to move up from the role of drover to that of bona fide rancher, and he was willing to leave Texas to do it. On his cattle drives he had come to admire a patch of land near Pueblo, Colorado. Now he bought strategic plots of it along 25 miles of the Arkansas River. He married, built a home, planted apple trees, dug ditches. For stock he trailed cattle up from Texas.

His new headquarters was in a sector of the West that cattlemen called the northern range, a vast tract of cow country that extended from northern Colorado up through Wyoming, Montana and the Dakotas. Here, Goodnight began to learn the cattle business in a new way. He was now a neighbor of John Wesley Iliff, the man who had bought part of Goodnight's first herd back in 1866. Under the management of men like Iliff the business was beginning to grow up. Iliff himself was well on his way to full cattle-baron status. Eventually, he would plant so many ranches along the South Platte River in Colorado that he could, if he wished, sleep at a different headquarters every night for a week. Iliff had got his own start by buying weak, thin work oxen, which he fattened on range grass and sold as beef in Denver. Later he picked up cattle in big bunches (including that herd from Goodnight and Loving) and sold them to miners, Indian agencies and the Union Pacific

protect their legs while riding through chaparral thickets, the mission hands wore heavy leather trousers called *chaparreras* — subsequently abbreviated to "chaps." As for themselves, the cowhands came to be called vaqueros (an extension of the Spanish *vaca,* meaning cow), and their American heirs changed it to "buckaroo."

Mexico broke away from Spain in 1821, and 12 years later the new republic took the mission range away from the Spanish padres. The holdings were then snatched up by private rancheros, the first real cattle barons of the West. The vaquero threw off his peonage and then went to work for the ranchero, becoming in the process a proud and independent range hand, who boasted the princely salary of up to $14 a month. His clothing became tight fitting and decorative, while his saddle and bridle flashed with silver trimming. And, of course, his horsemanship was superb. At the annual *rodeo* (roundup) he drove his pony through milling seas of cows, cutting out his ranchero's stock from that of neighboring herds and then branding it. Sometimes he would ride up behind a running steer, and rather than rope it he would grab its tail and flip the beast hind over horn, stunning it.

After the roundup, at the mass cattle slaughters known as *matanzas,* he would ride down upon one steer after another, killing each beast with a single flashing thrust of the long knife carried in a boot scabbard. During lulls in the matanza or the rodeo he amused himself with competitions against other vaqueros: one favorite stunt was to lean out of the saddle at a full gallop and pluck from the ground a rooster buried up to the head.

A French sea captain who visited California, after noting all this in his diary, added that the California horsemen "are so little accustomed to make use of their legs in walking they carry the entire weight of their body from one side to the other, as if they were lame." Thus the vaquero had developed, along with everything else, the characteristic bowlegged cowboy walk.

His day, however, was short. In 1846, when Mexico and the United States went to war, Mexican troops retreated below the Rio Grande, leaving the ranchos at the mercy of marauders, both Indian and white. Cattle were slaughtered and driven off by the thousands. Drought killed many more, and those that survived were herded north to feed hungry miners in the newly opened gold fields around San Francisco. Ranges that once swarmed with cows were emptied even of breeding stock. By the time the herds began to recover decades later, the emphasis of the cattle business had changed from hides and tallow to beef. And the center of the industry had moved to Texas, nearer the railheads leading to Eastern markets. The men who worked beef cattle spoke English and called themselves cowboys. But whenever they swung a lariat, held a rodeo, or pulled on their chaps and wore wide-brimmed hats they were paying mute tribute to the vaquero who had started it all.

Railroad. Iliff never wore a gun, but by sheer force of personality and a commanding manner he made his word law for miles around.

On the Northern ranches the method of operating became quite different from that on the Texas spreads. The long drives to distant railroads were less important here in the North; the main job of these other ranchers was to fatten cattle for market and to nurse them through the bitterest of blizzard-bound winters. Accordingly, a Goodnight or an Iliff hired cowboys who were not casual or temporary hands, but canny and farsighted permanent employees—men who carefully separated and sorted out breeding cattle, who gentled a herd for maximum growth, who cut and stored hay for use as winter feed. And the barons themselves came to operate on a different scale, dealing in tens of thousands of cattle and managing hundreds of thousands of acres.

The problems were different from those of Texas, too. At South Dakota's VVV Ranch, for example, the problem one season was, paradoxically, good weather. The pasture was so rich and high that the steers did not even have to stretch their necks to nip the fat seed buds dangling like ears of wheat from the thriving prairie grass. A morning finally came when manager John Clay faced a decision: Should he let his cattle continue to fatten on this abundant feed, and thus gain pounds that could mean dollars, or should he ship the animals right away to sell on a market that was then riding high? He decided to wait two weeks, and during that time the Chicago market took a nose dive. "That morning cost the company $10,000," he wrote later. But guessing when to sell was only one of the intricacies of

Vaqueros drive livestock past San Gabriel, one of 21 Spanish missions that prospered by selling hides and tallow to Yankee traders.

the business. Raising beef was a complex process, and cattle might change hands as many as half a dozen times between birth and slaughterhouse. Some ranchers bought yearling steers and sold them later, after fattening, as lucrative four-year-old beeves. Other ranchers focused on the specialized jobs of breeding and calf production. Still others might tailor their cattle for sale as feeders to Midwesterners, who would pack on more pounds by giving the animals corn.

A revealing account of shrewdness, risk and luck in a cattle deal is that of a rancher named James Haft, who in 1881 bought three quarters of a small spread on Box Elder Creek in South Dakota. To stock it he picked up a thousand head of cattle in Washington Territory, and to help finance the herd he took in a silent partner, a Kansas farmer, each man committing himself to invest up to $8,000. As Haft's trail boss prepared to drive the cattle from Washington to Dakota, the outlay stood at $15,947.20.

For six months the trail boss and a crew of 20 men drove the cattle eastward. The boss's letters were a litany of troubles with his crew ("Jim Stewart left long ago he is a little Son of a bich") and appeals for money, but the cattle throve. Meanwhile, back in Dakota, Haft built a 14-by-16-foot ranch house, brought in 100 tons of hay and on October 30 received the cattle, minus 100 dead on the trail. He hired three men to help him tend the cattle through the winter. The temperature fell as low as 37° below; Haft froze his fingers, ears and nose. But in August the tally after the branding showed 1,508 head in the herd, including the spring calves. In 1883 Haft took 271 steers to Chicago and sold them for $10,656 — a fine return on the original investment, considering that Haft and his partner still held more than 1,200 head of cattle.

Throughout the deal, Haft frequently used bank credit to pay bills, though he resented forking over 2 per cent a month in interest. Earlier, in the days of the first cattle drives, credit was mostly a matter of word of mouth. Texas herd owners gave the men who took the cattle north a simple bill of sale. The bill sufficed for the drover to sell the herd to a shipper, and finally the money filtered back from slaughterhouse to shipper to drover to cattle raiser, all at prices agreed upon by handshake. Then the cattlemen began to give one another promissory notes, whereupon banks began to buy the notes at discounts, which led them to start making direct loans on cattle. Ultimately credit, and how to get it, became as much of a concern for the cowman as whether the range greened up well.

Charles Goodnight was one of the richest cattlemen in Colorado by 1873, but he was still a heavy user of credit and resentful of the high interest he had to pay — often as much as the 2 per cent a month that James Haft had to bear. To beat the bankers, Goodnight decided to become one himself, joining in the organization of the Stock Growers Bank of Pueblo. This unhappy enterprise got going in the same month as the great crash of 1873, which, Goodnight said, "wiped me off the face of the earth." (Another rancher, in the same plight as Goodnight, remarked to friends: "I'm all right, I'll come back. I came here fifty years ago with only sixty-five cents and asthma, and I still got the asthma.") Trying to recover his losses, Goodnight overstocked his range — and as a result lost most of his remaining livestock and money.

Slowly Goodnight formed a resolution to find yet another new range and maybe a new stake. His mind's eye turned southeast, back to the Texas Panhandle, a realm so apparently uninviting that the first rush of westward settlement had swept around it like water around an island. It was there that, in 1876, he discovered the Palo Duro Canyon — the event that started him on the giant step from ruined rancher to prosperous baron. To the canyon he brought the remains of the herd from his old Colorado range and led them down an Indian trail along the canyon wall. In the ensuing months he built corrals and a small house beside a creek.

Early the following year Goodnight invited to the Palo Duro a well-to-do young couple, John and Cornelia Adair, whom he had met in Denver and who had a sporting impulse to learn about ranching life in the West. As host, Charlie, who had an ulterior motive, did it up brown. He went all the way to Denver to pick up the Adairs — plus a few more head of cattle — and their arrival at Palo Duro was carried out in high style. Up ahead galloped John Adair, a debonair Irishman who had inherited a fortune. Next, graceful on sidesaddle, came his wife Cornelia, the daughter of a New York banking tycoon and the sister of a senator. At the reins of a wagon behind them was Charles Goodnight's plain-spoken wife, Mary Ann. Goodnight brought up

the rear driving a herd of 100 shorthorn bulls.

Settled at the ranch, the high-spirited Adairs reveled in the grandeur of the West, the bracing air, the buffalo hunting—but they also talked business. For Charlie's underlying purpose in asking the Adairs to Palo Duro was to induce them to invest enough money in the ranch to finance an enormous expansion. It worked. The upshot of the visit was the first of a long series of big deals that brought foreign money to the American cattle industry.

Using Adair's investment of nearly half a million dollars (and taking his initials, J A, as a brand), Charles Goodnight launched the kind of land-grabbing exercise that was standard among the barons. In effect, Goodnight bought a little to get a lot. He actually purchased only 24,000 acres of public lands at 75 cents an acre —but the land was so crazy-quilted on waterfronts, hay fields and ranch-house sites that he got control of the whole of the Palo Duro Canyon. On this land he put an entire community of nearly 50 more houses. Headquarters was a small village, with a stone residence for the rare visits of the Adairs, a two-story house of logs and broad planks for the Goodnights, a large mess house, a dairy, a blacksmith shop for mending wagons and shoeing horses, and a tin shop that made plates and cups. Using $150,000 worth of blooded bulls—2,000 of them—Goodnight built up the herds until they numbered 100,000. By 1882, with the help of Charlie's

good cattlemanship (and land grabbing), John Adair had made a clear profit of $512,000.

In much the same way that Charlie Goodnight had grabbed the Palo Duro other budding American barons were grabbing land every way they could. One favorite method was indicated in an advertisement that appeared in the *Glendive* (Montana) *Times* of April 12, 1884: "I, the undersigned, do hereby notify the public that I claim the valley branching off the Glendive Creek, four miles east of the Allard and extending to its source on the south side of the Northern Pacific Railroad as a stock range. Chas. S. Johnson." Western papers in the '70s and '80s carried whole columns of such ads. They read like legal notices. Actually, they had no legal standing whatever, but they worked.

Centering a spread around a river or water hole, as Goodnight had done, the typical baron would claim land that backed up to some sort of natural boundary separating him from his neighbor—maybe a mountain range, often the highest point between the watershed of his stream and the one beyond. In a token effort to legalize his occupancy of the land, he might even file a homestead claim for the 160 acres around his water. Then he simply took possession of all the rest. Even Theodore Roosevelt, as a new arrival from the law-abiding East, neglected to take legal ownership of his lands in the Dakotas; both his Maltese Cross and Elkhorn Ranch buildings were built on the public domain.

57

JOHN WESLEY ILIFF

JOHN B. KENDRICK

ABEL (SHANGHAI) PIERCE

C. C. SLAUGHTER

GEORGE LITTLEFIELD

DUDLEY H. SNYDER

Peers of the Western realm

JOHN WESLEY ILIFF, son of an Ohio livestock breeder, turned down his father's offer of a $7,500 interest in the family farm, took $500 cash instead and headed west to build a cattle fortune. Devout, teetotaling, stern, he dedicated a large part of his estate to the founding of the Iliff School of Theology in Denver.

JOHN B. KENDRICK left school in Texas at the age of 15, trailed rancher Charles Wulfjen's cattle north to Cheyenne, Wyoming, married the boss's daughter, Eula, and built three of the biggest spreads on the northern range. He then vaulted into a successful political career — as Governor and later Senator from Wyoming.

ABEL (SHANGHAI) PIERCE, "as uncouth as the cattle he drove," according to a neighbor, became a baron on sheer gall, augmented by anything he could grab. At one point early in his career he was running more than 50,000 cattle while owning only 11 acres of land; eventually he took control of more than a million acres.

CHRISTOPHER COLUMBUS SLAUGHTER learned the cattle business from his baronesque father, George. A notorious nickel nurser, C. C. grew to be the largest individual landholder in all of Texas, and after amassing a truly baronial fortune admitted, almost grudgingly, that "from all appearances we are all ok financially."

GEORGE LITTLEFIELD, a Southern aristocrat, came out of the Civil War a pauper on crutches and hit it big as a cattleman. But he was apparently prouder of his roles as a banker and as a regent of the University of Texas. "The only practical knowledge I have gained in ranching," he remarked once, "is that a cow will have a calf."

DUDLEY H. SNYDER, surely the most proper of all the barons, was famous for the strict blue laws that he laid down to his cowpunchers: "First, you can't drink whiskey and work for us. Second, you can't play cards and gamble and work for us. Third, you can't curse or swear in our camps or in our presence and work for us."

58

PIERRE WIBAUX

ALEXANDER H. SWAN

GRANVILLE STUART

MORETON FREWEN

CONRAD KOHRS

THE MARQUIS DE MORÈS

PIERRE WIBAUX brought his money from France to the northern range, reckoned his profit in francs and outsmarted every cattleman in his neighborhood. He had the self-esteem of a proper baron, too: patrons of his bank were greeted by a bronze statue of the owner and by a photograph of Wibaux mounted on his horse Tic-Tac.

ALEXANDER H. SWAN — cattleman, businessman and promoter extraordinary — rose high, then fell with a crash. Creator of the Swan Land and Cattle Company Ltd., which in its palmy days mounted Wyoming's first rodeo (complete with a barbecue and a Wild West show), he ran his fief into ruin and ended up in an asylum.

GRANVILLE STUART got his start by making the first gold strike in Montana and went on to become a hardfisted patriarch of the cattlemen on the northern range. He came to have no patience with any prairie enterprise but beef raising and sent his men to poison sheepmen's dogs and to run homesteaders off the range.

MORETON FREWEN was called a "sublime failure" — and he did fail constantly, in India, Australia, Canada and the United States. During his fling as a cattle baron in the Old West he was said to have bought a herd of cattle twice, when the shrewd seller drove the steers around a hill and brought them back as a second herd.

CONRAD KOHRS built his cattle business on solid experience as a butcher. He replaced stringy longhorns with the first Herefords in Montana and persuaded his neighbors to import other breeds of shorthorns. But not all his experiments worked. Kohrs once said, "I guess I've been broke oftener than any man in Montana."

THE MARQUIS DE MORÈS, a fine figure of a man with black curly hair, and mustaches waxed to pinpoints, was the dandy and social leader of the Dakota Badlands — but as a cattle baron he was a disaster. When he finally returned to his native France in 1889 he left a record of business failure even more spectacular than Frewen's.

AWBONNIE STUART

EULA KENDRICK

ELIZABETH ILIFF

NELLIE WIBAUX

AUGUSTA KOHRS

MARY ANN GOODNIGHT

Six baronesses of the prairie

AWBONNIE STUART and her husband Granville made an unlikely but perfect marriage in a period when Indian-white hostility was at its peak. A full-blooded Shoshone, Awbonnie settled easily into her mixed marriage. She bore Granville nine children and later adopted and raised two children of his dead brother James.

EULA KENDRICK lived and dressed stylishly even on the frontier. A friend said her "trim, erect figure sets off to perfection frocks which are always the last word in smartness and elegance." She also kept her husband's books and happily shared his retirement at the Sheridan, Wyoming, home they called Trail's End.

ELIZABETH ILIFF was a young Singer sewing-machine saleswoman when John Iliff met her trudging up a country road. She was a perfect baroness, handling whatever crises arose. When he died at 48, her cool first thought was to telegraph his ranch foreman to double the guard on the herds before rustlers could move in.

NELLIE WIBAUX had a flair to match that of husband Pierre. Though their first home was a log cabin with a sod roof, at Christmas they prepared turkey, plum pudding and mince pie—she working over the stove in a gown, he with a glass of champagne in hand and a flour sack over his shirt and swallow-tailed coat.

AUGUSTA KOHRS ran the domestic half of husband Conrad's domain in decisive Teutonic style. She started by firing the cook and taking over his duties. Later, with the staff trained to her satisfaction, she made tours to Europe and an annual visit to New York's Metropolitan Opera, which she last attended in 1942 at 93.

MARY ANN GOODNIGHT was as tough and patient as her husband. She waited to marry until age 31, when Charlie had established his Colorado spread. Later she helped him get through his financial crash; eventually she presided over their Palo Duro spread, where she was the only white woman for hundreds of miles.

60

With all parties in on the grab, the cattlemen decided they needed some house rules for splitting the swag and keeping the peace. A body of informal regulations grew up, variously called cow custom, range privilege, possessory rights, accustomed range, range rights. All of these terms were euphemisms for stealing but they tended to lend a sort of formality to the usurpation. Possessory rights, for instance, meant that government land sold by a rancher carried with it the right of occupancy.

Fortunes came to depend on these extralegal institutions. For example, when the Coad brothers in western Nebraska sold ranch property for $912,853 the legal inventory of the property made it perfectly plain that the Coads were selling actual title to only 527 acres of land. The vast bulk of the land conveyed in the legal inventory consisted of possessory rights to most of one county plus "a main pasture of 143,000 acres" to which the Coad brothers, the legal inventory carefully added, "have no title except a possessory title or right thereto."

Competition in the big grab fostered other kinds of hardhanded ingenuity. To nail down their property claims the barons threw barbed wire around the public land on which their cattle grazed. And how they fenced! In Colorado alone, the fast-growing Arkansas Valley Cattle Company took part in the encircling of more than one million acres of public land with private barbed wire. Whole towns were fenced in and made inaccessible; postal men plaintively wrote Washington that they had to go out of their way to effect deliveries. "I must drive through such gates as they choose to put up," wrote the mail carrier in the Loup River Valley, Custer County, Nebraska. "Some morning," rasped the *Wyoming Sentinel,* "we will wake up to find that a corporation has run a wire fence about the boundary lines of Wyoming, and all within the same have been notified to move."

Complaints poured into Washington. Four farmers from Stratton, Nebraska, wrote that 12 ranchers had strung 22 miles of fence around government land. "They claim that if anyone interferes with their fence they must be bulletproof." From B. A. Arnold of Walsenburg, Colorado: "Will the government protect us if we poor unite and cut down their fences and let our stock have some of Uncle Sam's feed as well as them?"

The government would. Belatedly, the Interior Secretary invited bona fide settlers to cut illegal fences. This brought warnings from cattlemen, such as this posted on a Nebraska fence and forwarded to the Secretary: "The man who opens the fence had better look out for his scalp." The House Public Lands Committee bristled: "There is not another nation on the earth that would permit such outrages." President Grover Cleveland agreed. He ordered federal officials to prosecute the illegal fencers; slowly the barbed wire on public lands began to come down.

The cattle barons' response was to order their own cowboys to file temporary homestead claims on public lands. These were then transferred to the ranchers for a small consideration 24 hours after title was secured. One cowboy using fictitious names scrounged 7,200 acres of public domain for cattle in New Mexico Territory. Land agents for the cowmen sought out soldiers' widows as far away as Boston and persuaded them to file for homesteads under special land-bonus privileges that had been voted them by Congress. The widows then conveyed the homestead land to the cowmen and the cowmen conveyed $200 to $400 per widow to supplement their meager pensions.

Local politicians and state legislatures also were diligently exploited, nowhere more successfully than in Wyoming. In the management of rangelands, the Wyoming Legislature actually adopted the rules and regulations of the Wyoming Stock Growers' Association as the law of the territory. WSGA detectives, paid territorial funds to enforce WSGA stock regulations, arrested and even killed men.

Finally, to defend the big steal, some last-ditch cowmen used threats of violence without even the pretext of the law: a grisly dried human ear tacked to the interloper's door or a rope knotted into a noose and tossed onto his steps. In the final analysis, commented Charlie Goodnight, free grass and the six-shooter went together. The manager of the well-directed, British-financed, 500,000-acre Spur Ranch made an entry in the headquarters diary: "Lomax and Davis went down to see about firing out the settlers on the Catfish." Some years later Spur employee Pinckney Higgins shot a small local rancher suspected of rustling on company land, stuffed the man's body into the carcass of a fresh-killed cow and coolly rode into town to invite the sheriff to take a look at "a real freak of nature — a cow giving birth to a man." And in Montana and western Dakota the ultrarespectable cattleman Granville Stuart and his friends secretly organized and financed clandestine groups of law-and-order vigilantes called the Stranglers. Armed with hanging hemp, the Stranglers would come in the night, and dawn would find their victims — often peaceable homesteaders or small stockmen — dangling from cottonwood trees.

Goodnight was no better than the rest. Once when his wife expressed shock at some vigilante hangings ("I understand," she exclaimed, "they hanged them to a telegraph pole!") Charlie replied quietly, "Well, I don't think it hurt the telegraph pole." What she didn't know was that the victims had actually been strung up with Goodnight's full approval.

Underlying all the turbulence was the fact that the cattlemen were playing for huge stakes: for the first time in the history of the world, ranching had become Big Business. By 1880 the northern range and Texas alone pastured no less than 11 million cattle. Once the land for grazing had been sewn up, the exploitation of these giant herds called for constant infusions of money. That, of course, meant drumming up a steady stream of investors. Just as Goodnight had found his Adair, so the other barons proceeded to find their own angels, and often to treat them in much the way they had treated the land — as an inexhaustible opportunity to be grabbed. And as usual the barons did not trouble themselves with fussy ethics.

A promotional brochure whipped up by West Texas cattlemen depicted steamboats serenely plying the Pecos River, which was in reality a swift, shallow stream about 100 feet wide. The Governor of Wyoming Territory, doing his bit, argued that the dryness of the Western atmosphere gave it "the property of a non-conductor of heat and electricity, so that exposed animals better retain their animal heat and keep their vital forces in full reserve."

Probably the most colorful of the boasters was a German immigrant named Walter Baron von Richthofen, a true spiritual descendant of Baron Munchausen, and an uncle of the Red Baron of World War I. A rich and genial former officer of the Prussian Army, Richthofen went to Denver in the middle 1870s and plunged into numerous enterprises (though never, apparently, ranch-

ing). In 1885 he wrote an influential book, *Cattle-Raising on the Plains of North America,* in which he blithely argued that "there is not the slightest element of uncertainty in cattle-raising." Richthofen's basic contention, studded with examples of vast profits, was that in 10 years 100 cows could become a herd of 2,856 cattle, provided that four out of five cows gave birth each year and that the heifers among their offspring started bearing in two years. There was nothing wrong with his figures, except that they largely ignored the realities of cattle raising on the open range — realities that included stillborn calves, killing weather, various ailments and a host of other natural disasters. To obtain equally fantastic estimates of the money to be made in the cattle business, he omitted necessary expenditures, minimized inevitable losses and preposterously overvalued potential profits.

The baron was not alone in his fantasies. In *The Beef Bonanza; or How to Get Rich on the Plains,* one James S. Brisbin presented figures to show that $250,000 borrowed at 10 per cent and invested in cattle would yield $810,000 clear in five years.

Who bought this fantastic bill of goods? Among others, a good number of ostensibly shrewd Easterners. William Rockefeller, brother of John D. and himself an organizer of Standard Oil. James Gordon Bennett, editor of the *New York Herald.* Marshall Field of Chicago. Teddy Roosevelt. Russell B. Harrison, son of President Benjamin Harrison. August Busch, the St. Louis brewer. Nelson Morris, the Chicago packer, who never even bothered to visit his 250,000-acre ranch. Alexander Agassiz, son of the great Swiss-American naturalist Louis Agassiz. William K. Vanderbilt. And many others, mostly from the Eastern seaboard. "With little distortion, it could be said that the membership of the Union League Club of New York, the Harvard Club of Boston and the Union League Club of Chicago controlled the major portion of Eastern capital in the range cattle industry," Professor Gene M. Gressley of the University of Wyoming has said.

Right along with the rich Eastern investors came a horde of money-heavy Scots, Englishmen and other Europeans. They had heard from such sources as a report made by two touring British Members of Parliament that 33 per cent was the normal annual profit in ranching. More specifically, and even more effectively, foreign

Mixed blessings from a range mongrel

It should have been the perfect animal to produce profits on the range—beefier than a longhorn, stronger than an ox, hardy and independent. Its tough, woolly hide could be tanned into fine shoe leather or stretched to make luxuriant fur coats. This marvelous beast grew fat on the scrubbiest grass and lasted out the harshest of winters and most searing dry spells. Half cow and half buffalo, it was called the cattalo, and it promised to be a kind of bovine Santa Claus, giving everything and asking nothing in return.

And the Western range, in the late 1880s, badly needed a Santa Claus. Following a summer of devastating drought, severe blizzards during the winter of '86 left frozen cattle strewn for miles along drift lines. Ranchers were looking for herd replacements of the hardiest possible stock. The question was where to find them.

The answer seemed obvious, once someone had thought of it: create a brand-new animal, starting with the hardiest of all range creatures—the native American buffalo. For numberless centuries the buffalo had withstood blizzards and dry-ups on the high plains. But the beast was virtually untamable, difficult to herd and almost impossible to rope and brand without risking a terrible injury. Genetically, however, the buffalo was a distant cousin to the more tractable cow. So why not mate the two, combining the better nature of the longhorn with the buffalo's ruggedness and heft?

The first man publicly to claim credit for the idea was a onetime hide hunter, Colonel Charles J. (Buffalo) Jones (above). A spare, swashbuck-

Breeder Charles Jones admires cattalo heifers, born of longhorn cows by a buffalo bull.

ling Kansan, he announced in 1888 the arrival on earth of what he advertised as the world's first cattalo and the salvation of the Western livestock industry. However, when other cattlemen took a look at the hybrid, with its buffalo hump, goatlike beard and voice like a low-pitched pig grunt, they pronounced it to be nothing but a big mistake. And furthermore one of the barons, Charles Goodnight, added that it was not even new. For Goodnight himself had inadvertently become a cattalo breeder some years before when a pet buffalo bull of his named Old Sikes developed a strong romantic attachment for a number of Goodnight's longhorn cows.

It was difficult to see why either Goodnight or Jones cared who took

the credit for so misfortunate a beast. Besides being spectacularly ugly, the cattalo could not even survive—much less increase—as an independent species. The process of birth often resulted in either a dead calf or a dead mother. Male calves that lived were quite frequently sterile. Worst of all, the cattalo seemed to have lost so little of its ornery buffalo nature that even its most enthusiastic booster, Colonel Jones, had to admit it was "somewhat inclined to be cross."

In short the marvelous creature that Jones had once trumpeted as "the perfect animal for the plains" turned out to be a commercial flop. But cattalo experiments continued, and years later hopeful stockmen introduced a better range mongrel—the beefalo.

capital was lured to the plains by face-to-face confrontations with that fine old Western type, the silver-tongued American cattleman. Many of these fast-talking salesmen of the Western way went to Edinburgh, to Dundee and to the City of London and there found numerous capitalists who "didn't know a maverick from a mandamus," in the words of one historian, but lusted for more wealth.

One popular way of buncoing the Europeans was by giving a dubious tally, or book count, of the cattle for sale. Rounding up and actually counting herds on Western ranges nearly as big as Scotland itself was usually unthinkable; it would run off too much weight. So the buyers had to take the sellers' word—"all in favor of the vendor, and most disastrous to the buyer," ruefully observed the *Scottish Banking and Insurance Magazine*.

One huge outfit that was built almost entirely on wildly inflated figures was the Swan Land and Cattle Company, the occupier of a piece of Wyoming bigger than Connecticut, and commonly called, from its major brand, the Two Bar. The spellbinding central figure of this story was an authentic cattle baron, Alexander Hamilton Swan. Pennsylvania-born and well-educated, Swan had reached the valley of the Big Laramie River in Wyoming in 1873, after hitches as a farmer and stock raiser in Ohio and Iowa. Picking up a herd of cattle grazing on Chugwater Creek, he managed in 10 years to build three large cattle corporations with valuable waterfront holdings on Chugwater and Sybille Creeks. In typical baronesque style Swan arranged to graze his cattle on the public land between these tributaries of the Big Laramie.

"In our business we are often compelled to do certain things which, to the inexperienced, seem a little crooked," Swan once said—and there is no doubt that he gave prospective investors a false book count of his cattle. But his decision in 1883 to sell his holdings to Scottish investors was not conceived basically as a swindle. Rather, Swan knew that further expansion required fresh capital and that the cost of borrowing money in the United States was prohibitive. In getting the money Swan, like other barons, painted a boldly optimistic picture of his herd. Furthermore, he arranged a secure situation for himself. He proposed that he be kept on as salaried manager, and that he and some of his Wyoming partners should buy one sixth of the shares

of the Scottish company. Done, said the gentlemen in their musty offices at 16 Castle Street, Edinburgh, and the Swan Land and Cattle Company Ltd. was born. Said the prospectus: "The business of Cattle-raising in the Western States of America is now acknowledged to be highly remunerative."

The Scottish corporation bought out Swan for the sum of $2,387,675 and proceeded vigorously to expand. Swan and the Scottish chairman of the board acquired three small neighboring ranches that gave the company control over the entire courses of the Chugwater and Sybille. In 1884 they contracted to pay $2.3 million for 550,000 acres of Union Pacific land to the west, and since the sections of this purchase alternated with sections of government land, the company then held domain over more than a million acres, building its total range to 3.25 million acres.

By purchasing the herds of others Swan Land and Cattle came to own so many brands that it had to publish its own brand book for the information of its foremen. For a while the whole enterprise looked as solid and prosperous as promised. Cowboys fought to work for Alec Swan, who paid as much as $45 a month, provided a string of nine horses for each man and served rice-and-raisin pudding for dessert. The Two Bar became renowned as an outfit that "never shipped a steer until he was fat and smoothed up." Dividends for 1883, 1884 and 1885 averaged a fat 25 per cent a year — far higher than a cattle ranch normally could expect. And the work and cattle and profits were only part of the story. Once, for the benefit of the owners, Swan staged a three-day rodeo, one of the first anywhere, and a Two Bar cowboy, not yet famous, named Butch Cassidy entertained the Scottish and English visitors with his fancy pistol marksmanship.

But meantime, in Edinburgh, shareholder James Tait had been dourly — and quite correctly — contending that the original book count given for the company's cattle had been far greater than the cattle it actually received. Even more serious, the winter of 1886-1887 killed off a substantial number of the animals that really existed on the Swan spread. Eventually, in 1887, the board of directors sorrowfully declared that "after consultation with Mr. Swan, they have accordingly deemed it prudent and proper to write off . . . 200 bulls, 2,200 steers, and 5,500 cows."

Two years later Swan himself, who had been building up a personal financial empire on the side, went bankrupt in a house-of-cards collapse that shook both Wall Street and Edinburgh.

The scandalized directors of the company immediately dismissed Swan as manager and sent in a Scot named Finlay Dun to get to the bottom of the vexatious question that had been brought up in the 1887 report: "Do the numbers of Cattle on the books tally with the numbers on the range?" Dun's inspired solution was to have the cowboys paint a mixture of lampblack, varnish and turpentine on the left hip of every cow counted so as to keep tally. Chanted the cowboys: "Daddy Dun's a dandy/ But his paint won't stick!" And it didn't. By the time he counted a total of 29,008 head it was clear that rain and abrasion were erasing the mark on many animals. The buyers nonetheless brought suit against Swan, but the question of the count was never settled, for the judge threw the case out on a technicality. A fair guess is that the actual count of the original herd would have fallen short of the book count by 32,000. At the end of it all the Scots had indeed been swindled out of a good half a million dollars in beef money. But they had turned out to be far tougher and shrewder than Swan himself, who sank into poverty, while Dun and the others put the pieces of the cattle company back together into a solvent enterprise.

The Swan saga tells only a few of the hazards faced by foreigners who sank money into the giant Western cattle enterprises. One ranch suffered an epidemic of sunburned udders from light reflected off snow, and the afflicted cows would not suckle their calves. Cattle rustlers stole the foreigners blind, Indians set prairie fires on their rangelands, poisonous weeds appeared where none had ever grown before. And American weather seemed just awful. "When the winter has been good, the summer has been bad," complained the *Dundee Advertiser* in 1888. "When the drought has been on its best behavior, the blizzard has been violent all over the plains. The one thing that has not varied," the newspaper then concluded gloomily, "has been the downward run of prices."

Yet the foreigners persisted, and at the climax of the investment bonanza they created some of the greatest cattle spreads of all time. The Maxwell Cattle Company, Ltd., which straddled the New Mexico-Colorado border on 1.75 million acres, was so vast that the Atchison, Topeka and Santa Fe Railroad Company had to put in six stations on the track that crossed the property. The Texas Land and Cattle Company in 1885 owned and leased an area bigger than Long Island; some of its range later became part of the celebrated King Ranch. And the huge Matador Land and Cattle Company, Ltd. operated in Texas, Montana and Dakota under the management of a magisterial Scot, Murdo Mackenzie. Mackenzie kept his tight Caledonian hand on costs; one employee said that "we never buy a hobble rope on the Matador but they know about it in Dundee." Meanwhile, Mackenzie himself lived affluently in mansions in Denver and Trinidad, sent a son to Princeton and traveled widely. Mackenzie was, in fact, an exemplary cattleman who managed to ride out the boom and go on to something better. In 1911 he left the Matador to take on management of an even bigger ranch in Brazil.

If Mackenzie had a way with money, other foreigners had more flair. There was Danish-born Conrad Kohrs, whose background included stints as a ship's cabin boy, a Mississippi raftsman and a California gold miner. He got into cattle from the butchering end. Absorbing the old lesson that the man who sells to the miner generally makes more than the miner, he started

Clubs for the coyote country's gentry

No institution better symbolized the rise and the power of the cattle barons than the extraordinary Cheyenne Club that Wyoming ranchmen built in 1880 to give themselves the comforts befitting their status. The three-story mansard-roofed, brick-and-wood building (*below*) had wine vaults, two grand staircases, a smoking room, a reading room, a dining room, hardwood floors and plush carpets.

Limited by charter to only 200 hand-picked members, the Cheyenne Club claimed, with some reason, to have the finest steward in America. And its deft servants were recruited by founding President Philip Dater in Canada, where, under the British flag, the tradition of genteel service still flourished. "No wonder they like the club at Cheyenne," wrote Western buff Owen Wister, who was himself a Philadelphia clubman. "It's the pearl of the prairies."

No wonder indeed. Literally within earshot of howling coyotes, Sir Horace Plunkett — son of Lord Dunsany, who ran the E K ranch — could be found playing on the club tennis courts while yelling chess moves to two opponents on the piazza. In the meantime, Harry Oelrichs' $4,000, 16-passenger drag (the only rig so fancy anywhere west of the Mississippi) might be waiting at one of the club's 19 hitching posts.

Inside, members dressed for dinner on gala evenings in white tie and tails, which an old Nebraska member nicknamed "Herefords" in honor of the white-chested red-coated cattle. At dinner the members could savor such viands as caviar, pickled eels, French peas and Roquefort cheese, together with liberal quantities of suitable drink and tobacco. And woe to the supplier who skimped on quality. On February 13, 1882, New York's chic Park & Tilford got a stiff note: "The cigars are too dark. Send the lightest possible 500 Lazo Victoria." Later: "The Garvy Sherry lacked almost entirely fine bouquet. If you cannot send us the Garvy Sherry in good quality, omit that item."

Members were strictly accountable for their behavior: they were permitted no profanity, no drunkenness, no cheating at cards, no drinking in the reading room. And when Harry Oelrichs kicked a servant down the stairs the club kicked out Oelrichs. Ah, yes, exclaimed a reminiscing English member: "Cow punching, as seen from the veranda of the Cheyenne Club, was a most attractive proposition."

In a land of sod huts, the Cheyenne Club boasted a coal furnace and a dumbwaiter to carry food to the wood-paneled dining room.

vending beef to the gold diggers in Bannack and Virginia City, Montana. He acquired more and more cattle, took over a million-acre range in the eastern part of the state and was soon sending his wife to New York City every year for the season at the Metropolitan Opera House. Another swashbuckling foreigner, Pierre Wibaux, emigrated from France at the age of 25, settled into a sod-roofed hut on the Montana-Dakota border, grazed 65,000 head of cattle and finally built himself a house with carved woodwork, a billiard room, a wine cellar and—wonder of wonders—wallpaper.

One of the most exotic episodes of the whole cow-business saga was the brief reign of Antoine-Amédée-Marie-Vincent Mance de Vallambrosa, the Marquis de Morès, in the Badlands of North Dakota.

The Marquis took for his bride Medora von Hoffman, daughter of a rich New York banker, and they made a colorful and dashing couple. In three fast-paced years the Marquis built sheep and cattle ranches; a town, Medora, on the Little Missouri; a 26-room château with a French-English-German library and 20 servants; a $250,000 slaughterhouse; a refrigerator-car company, with ice plants at 12 points along the Northern Pacific Railroad; a string of stores in New York City to sell beef from the slaughterhouse; and a 225-mile stage line connecting Medora and the recent metropolis of Deadwood.

He also interested himself in gardening, dairying, pottery, gold mining and the tricky business of shipping salmon from the Columbia River to New York. For fun the Marquis and the Marquise went hunting. He once killed a bear with a knife; she, "skimming over the prairie at a gallop, an eagle feather in her hat" (according to biographer Arnold Goplen), picked off prairie chickens with a rifle—no mean feat. They traveled in their private Pullman or in a live-in hunting coach, with bed, table and drawers for silver. The Marquis often battled over range problems with his neighbor Theodore Roosevelt *(page 216)*—and then, lonely in his château, would invite him to dinner.

Every one of the Marquis' enterprises failed because each of them had a fatal flaw; the stage line, for example, failed to obtain a vital mail contract. This dashing gallant eventually went back to his native France, got involved in the ugly anti-Semitic politics of the Dreyfus era and met his death, ironically, at the hands of some casual Arab murderers in North Africa.

The luxurious life style enjoyed by the Marquis in North Dakota was far from unusual among the foreign investors, especially the Englishmen. They built what the British periodical *The Economist* described as "castles on the prairies," hired servants in red livery, traveled often to Europe. Moreton Frewen, part owner of the Powder River Cattle Company, saw to it that cut flowers were frequently sent to his ranch houses. One titled Englishman, invited to Christmas dinner by a Montana rancher, rode 30 miles through a snowstorm in his dress suit, arriving frozen but elegant.

It was English capital that produced the most impressive ranch of all, the XIT of Texas, in the Panhandle country lying west of Goodnight's JA. Covering over three million acres, the XIT used so much barbed wire that it had to buy staples by the carload. Strung along 200 miles of the Texas-New Mexico border, the ranch occupied parts of 10 counties. In fact, an old cowboy yarn says that the brand stood for "Ten in Texas"; more probably it was picked for utility, since it could be burned on with five strokes of a straight five-inch iron and was hard for rustlers to change. The XIT employed as many as 150 cowboys at once. They rode 1,000 horses, herded 150,000 head of cattle and branded 35,000 calves a year.

In the late 1880s the XIT, working in partnership with another cattle concern, put together a second ranch complex in the northern range that was almost as big as the original in Texas. This one, in Montana, sprawled over an area covering 200 miles by 75 miles between the Yellowstone and the Missouri Rivers. A long, long trail connected the two ranches, like the bar in a giant dumbbell. Thus, herds of XIT cattle could traverse no less than seven states—Texas, Oklahoma, Colorado, Nebraska, South Dakota, Wyoming and Montana —on the trail drive between their two giant pastures. This was the kind of security and control that any good cattle baron might long for. And there was unmistakable pride in the voice of XIT General Manager A. G. Boyce when, down on the Texas ranch, he issued to his northbound trail hands the order for what must surely have been the longest series of marches ever to begin and end on private property: "Keep your eye on the North Star, and drive straight ahead until you can wet your feet in the waters of the Yellowstone."

The major markets for the barons' cattle were stockyards such as this one in Kansas City, Missouri, which teemed with more than 100 acres of solid beef on any given day and handled more than half a million head a year in the 1880s.

This Dakota ranch house shows the signs of its owner's success. It boasts a side porch and a second story, plus a mechanical hayrake and mowing machine in the front yard. But the real luxury is the large quantity of the window glass.

3 | At home on the range

While a small number of cattle barons, dwelling luxuriously in walnut-paneled mansions, set one style for Western ranching, the mass of cowboys lived and worked around little family spreads that were the real backbone of the beef-cattle industry. Most of these small ranches did not achieve even the modest level of prosperity displayed by the Dakota outfit shown here. Ranching, particularly in its earliest days, was a grubby business, with no money for frills. The ranch buildings themselves often reflected both the owners' unending struggle to survive and their tough will to succeed.

Some families started living in covered wagons, others in a tent (overleaf). More commonly a family would begin in a one-room lean-to or a dugout cut into a hillside. Whatever their abode, they often slept on mattresses of feedbags sewn together and stuffed with Montana feathers, otherwise known as hay. Usually they stocked the ranch with 20 to 30 cattle at a total investment of perhaps $600. In time the house would graduate from dirt floors to plank, and the ranch might become a multidwelling spread. At any stage ranch life was grinding and lonely. Charles Goodnight's wife once confessed that when a friendly cowboy brought her three chickens she adopted them as she would human friends: "They were something I could talk to."

This is the beginning of a ranch near Miles City, Montana. While tents provide shelter, the men have nearly knocked together one building *(right, rear)* from their store-bought lumber. Even at this hand-to-mouth stage the family has managed to acquire one luxury—a bicycle-wheeled sulky.

Signs of prosperity appear in the yard of a Dakota spread. Pines have been planted as a windbreak, the women and babies have go-to-meetin' clothes and there are sleek horses (*left, rear*) to pull the farm gear.

This loosely built shack was suitable to the Arizona climate but had problems. The thatched roof leaked in desert cloudbursts and harbored tarantulas, scorpions, rats and snakes. Happily, the snakes ate the rats.

An embryo ranch like this tough bachelor setup provided few comforts. Inside there might be a wolfskin pallet for sleeping and some buffalo skulls for seats. The hide on the cabin corner probably served as a door.

The style of the Frying Pan ranch house in the Panhandle was Texas Traditional. The stout adobe walls and thick sod roof made a surprisingly comfortable year-round house, cool in summer, warm in winter and altogether dirt cheap. Often, as here, a flower or two sprouted from the rooftop.

A proper spread, complete with outbuildings, sprawls across a Northern upland valley. For the burgeoning horse herd there were pasture, a flowing stream and a corral (*background at right*); for the family and ranch hands a two-story house, a cookshack, bunkhouse, blacksmith shop and sheds.

79

The rugged pattern of the ranch hand's life

After a tour of the plains toward the close of the cowboy era, the celebrated journalist Richard Harding Davis observed: "The inhabited part of a ranch, the part of it on which the people who own it live, bears about the same proportion to the rest of the ranch as a lighthouse does to the ocean around it." This was a particularly deft description. The working area around a ranch rolled on endlessly, with the outfit's few buildings squatting forlornly in the middle of a grassy nowhere. As the pictures on the preceding pages show, the buildings often had a raw, unfinished look. Even after a ranch became settled and big enough to require the help of a fair number of cowboys the place continued to wear the aura of a camp, where comfort came far down on any list of necessities.

In this spartan setting the roughest place of all was where the hired hands lived, the bunkhouse. On many spreads, built according to the so-called saddle-bag plan, the bunkhouse was attached to a combination cookhouse and mess hall by a roofed breezeway or dogtrot, which served as a place to hang saddles, bridles and ropes, and to shelter the dogs. Most typically, however, the bunkhouse was a separate building, often just a shack made from weatherboard or cottonwood logs. In a few cases the cowhands themselves put in board ceilings over a single main room, creating an attic reachable by ladder. At the T-Anchor Ranch in Texas, during 1878, cowboy Harry Ingerton slept in an attic and pronounced it "the coldest place I ever saw." And the few blankets available did not always help much. "If I owned a ranch," grumbled cowhand Peter Wright, "I would buy these blankets and use them as a refrigerator in the summer." Sometimes the cowboys took the trouble to spruce up their quarters with a coat of whitewash on the walls, maybe a real wood floor over the dirt, buffalo robes or wolfskins for the bunks and perhaps a crude fireplace.

Whatever the design, there was one constant about these bunkhouses that made them instantly recognizable: the smell. The aroma that assaulted the senses of anyone walking in was a composite of sweaty men, dry cow manure, the licorice in chewing-tobacco plugs, old work boots and the smoke from lamps that were burning coal oil or perhaps even tallow rendered from the generous supply of skunks that scavenged around the ranches. There was a uniform look to these places, too, a chronic state of untidiness. Clothes were "hung on the floor," as one historian of the cowboy era said, "so they wouldn't fall down and get lost."

Astonishingly, some range hands found this atmosphere downright homey, and a few twangy choruses of "There's an Empty Cot in the Bunkhouse Tonight," delivered by hornyhanded balladeers like those at left, could actually bring a tear to an otherwise gimlet eye. To most cowboys, however, a bunkhouse was an acknowledged rural slum, where life was a constant low-key battle against filth and boredom. Cowpuncher Charlie Siringo recalled that his bunkhouse pals "made an iron-clad rule that whoever was caught picking grey backs [lice] off and throwing them on the floor without first killing them, should pay a fine of ten cents for each and every offense. The proceeds to be used for buying choice literature — something that would have a tendency to raise us above the average cowpuncher." The elevating literature that was purchased consisted mostly of picture magazines and mail-order catalogues. These were read, reread, passed along (at least among those men who were literate) and often ended up pasted on the walls and ceilings as wallpaper. Veteran hand John

Two cowhands strum a banjo duet outside their cabin in New Mexico. Other favored instruments in the bunkhouse were mouth organs, fiddles, guitars and jew's-harps.

A stern code for the XIT

In the turbulent early years of cattle ranching, cowboys had but one check on their behavior: loyalty to the rancher with whom they lived and worked. But when the big ranches came along, their absentee owners, needing to control scores of cowhands, brought in hard company rules limiting every aspect of life on the ranch. Below are only seven of the rules posted on the three-million-acre XIT spread in western Texas.

No employee of the Company, or of any contractor doing work for the Company, is permitted to carry on or about his person or in his saddle bags, any pistol, dirk, dagger, sling shot, knuckles, bowie knife or any other similar instruments for offense or defense.

Card playing and gambling of every description, whether engaged in by employees, or by persons not in the service of the Company, is strictly forbidden.

Employees are strictly forbidden the use of vinous, malt, spirituous, or intoxicating liquors, during their time of service with the Company.

Loafers, "sweaters," deadbeats, tramps, gamblers, or disreputable persons, must not be entertained at any camp, nor will employees be permitted to give, loan or sell such persons any grain, or provisions of any kind, nor shall such persons be permitted to remain on the Company's land under any pretext whatever.

Employees are not allowed to run mustang, antelope or any kind of game on the Company's horses.

No employee shall be permitted to own any cattle or stock horses on the ranch.

It is the aim of the owners of this ranch to conduct it on the principle of right and justice to everyone; and for it to be excelled by no other in the good behavior, sterling honesty and integrity, and general high character of its employees, and to this end it is necessary that the foregoing rules be adhered to, and the violation of any of them will be just charge for discharge.

Hendrix remembered the case of a cowboy who spent an entire winter alone in a shack papered with old newspapers and farm journals; fighting mightily against ennui, the man read the north, south, east and west walls, "and was just starting to read the ceiling when they called him to headquarters."

This puncher was lucky. Cattleman Dennis Collins was once stuck with nothing to read "except a patent-medicine pamphlet, and I had read that so often and so thoroughly that I had some of the symptoms of seven different maladies that were therein pronounced fatal." Numberless other hands passed the time memorizing the labels of tomato or condensed-milk cans.

Packs of ancient, greasy playing cards got the boys through many an evening — with a lookout posted close to the door if the ranch happened to have a stuffy Victorian owner like the one cited at left, who disapproved of everything but work, sleep and maybe prayer. The stakes during the marathon poker matches (dominoes was another popular diversion) were often wolf scalps, redeemable in bounty money. Rarely did the bunkhouse suffer an infusion of what might be called culture. One ranch hand whose education had been a good cut beyond that of the common cowboy used to amuse his buddies — up to a point — by quoting the Scottish poet Robert Burns by the yard.

Most efforts at uppishness in the bunkhouse were shot down. If a cowboy tried to impress the other hands with a particularly big word, someone was likely to shout, "Where'd it go — there it is!" and then draw his gun to blast away at the dark corner where the extravagant phrase was presumably flapping around. Such random gunplay was a bunkhouse norm, both because of the boredom and because many cowboys were barely more than kids for whom guns were a favorite toy. One evening at a ranch near Trinidad, Colorado, the hands got to looking at magazine pictures that had been pasted to the walls. Soon, out came the pistols. The first shot got Benjamin Franklin square in the eye, reported one cowhand who took part. Another cowboy decided: "That pretty girl's nose is too long," and proceeded to snick off pieces of it with well-placed shots.

Despite the discomfort and boredom, cowboys managed to accept the raw-edged routine of bunkhouse life and the basic rangeland philosophy that underlay it. For every cowhand was aware that a ranch was set up for

A cowboy's bunk was his private corner of the world. The man who slept in this Wyoming bunk was the prosperous owner of a rifle, a double-barreled shotgun, a pair of warm angora chaps, a new hat and barbells.

the care and well-being of cows, not people. When he was not killing time around the bunkhouse he knew that he would be spending most of his hours and months tending cattle or enduring dozens of other dirty or monotonous chores that bore little resemblance to any glamorized vision of cowboy life.

Out on the range cattle had to be watched and worried over to keep them healthy—and even alive. Throughout the summer, for example, cows by the thousands had to be doctored for blowflies. These insects laid eggs in open wounds, such as fresh brands or castrations. The eggs developed into screwworms—maggots about three fourths of an inch long—which inflicted agonizing pain, and sometimes death, on the animals. To daub the wounds and kill the screwworms the men

carried bottles containing a powerful mixture of carbolic acid and axle grease, among other ingredients.

These crude remedies occasionally turned out to be more lethal than the ailments. A cowboy named J. W. Standifer got orders to treat a bunch of cows suffering from a skin disease similar to the mange. He did, by dousing them with kerosene from a garden sprinkling can. This was the standard cure, and it might well have worked, except that one cow ran through a branding fire that turned it into a living torch. The cow fled back to the others and ignited the whole bunch. Twenty head died, some after lingering for two or three days.

One particularly rough job on the range was pulling cattle from bogholes, where they tended to wander in the spring looking for water or trying to escape swarm-

A photographer's magnesium flash lights up the faces of eight ranch hands in their crudely decorated cabin. The newsprint wallpaper was mainly for warmth, but it also provided reading matter. Over the newspapers these cowboys have plastered other bunkhouse embellishments: cattle-breeding charts, postcards, demure 19th Century pinups, a map, cartoons and even a photograph festooned with mourning tassels.

ing heel flies by wallowing in deep mud. The cowboys pulled them out with ropes snubbed around their saddle horns. An old cow bogged for a long time usually reached solid ground too weak to stand up, and might simply lie there and perish. On the other hand a young steer trapped only briefly would come out fighting and angrily turn his horns against his rescuers.

Another rugged rangeland chore was dehorning, a procedure sometimes performed on longhorns to keep them from goring each other. Puncher S. R. Cooper got a taste of it at the XIT in Texas. In a bedlam scene he and 20 other men dehorned 1,100 freshly purchased cattle that were forced out of a corral one at a time through a narrow chute. With most of the animals the men used a saw to cut the horns, but the harder horns of the old bulls had to be chopped off with an ax.

In summer, when the sun baked the treeless rangeland, cattlemen had to keep a steady fire watch. A blaze could sweep over entire counties, killing cattle and wiping out the grass. To curb the fires cowboys got behind plows and made firebreaks—sets of furrows 75 to 200 feet apart, with the grass in between purposely burned off. Foreman Ira Aten estimated that in a single summer he had plowed 150 miles of firebreaks. But the range was too big to keep it completely safe, and a blaze could start on any dry summer day.

One afternoon a puncher at Charles Goodnight's ranch in the Texas Panhandle saw smoke boiling up to the south and raced toward it. When he arrived at the scene he found a gang of men beating at flames with wet gunny sacks, slickers and brooms. When the fire refused to go out he and the other men attacked the blaze by a grisly but effective method: they shot a big steer, skinned him on one side and tied ropes to two legs. Then a pair of riders on either side of the fire line dragged the bloody carcass over it to quench the flames, like moving an eraser across a blackboard. The horses had to change sides frequently, or the one trotting on the burned patch might have been crippled by the charring of his hoofs.

As fire or drought or overstocking by hungry cattle made one range or another unusable, the herds had to be moved on to better grasslands. The problem of finding adequate grazing ground became increasingly acute —and a more onerous chore for cowboys—as the cattle business flourished. On the XIT, cowboy J. S. Ken-

yon recalled working day and night to drive 30,000 hungry, thirsty cattle to a fresh range from one that an inattentive foreman had allowed to become critically overgrazed. And in 1885 Montana baron Granville Stuart ordered his men to move 5,000 head from the drought-stricken Judith Basin to the wetter Little Rockies, all without running off any fat from the marketable steers—and after first culling out the bulls so they could be kept on the home range for breeding.

Cattle drives to new ranges often had many of the troubles of the long drives to market, including labor problems as well as the hazards of trailing cattle any distance. Trail boss S. P. Conrad mailed the following bleak report of his efforts to move some cattle across the Bitterroot Mountains in Montana: "I went as far as the Summunt & Made up my mind that we could never drive the Cows with Their calves & returned & sold Them [the calves] at $4.50 per head." Having virtually given away the calves, he then was able to get the rest of the herd to Missoula, Montana, still in the middle of the mountains—but most of his trail crew had quit. "I think it is impossible to get men worth a dam," he wrote in high exasperation. "Bill Owenby left when we most needed him & all of the old crew goes soon the cattle look first rate but we had a hell of a time we nearly all came through barefoot it is terrible on horses. I apprehend no Trouble I intend to hire a full crew & kick out every son of a Bich that has the belly ache."

In later days the coming of windmills and barbed wire largely eliminated any need to move cattle from range to range. A rancher would fence off an area to keep the animals from wandering off and to provide them with an adequate supply of water in a windmill-pumped tank. But though the cowhands were then spared a great deal of hard driving, the mills and the wire provided a new set of duties.

"A whole lot of sorry things can happen to a fence," one oldtimer said. Riders called pliers men went out to patrol the fences, equipped with a pouch full of staples, a roll of spare wire, and a tool that was both nippers and hammer. A man usually was assigned 10 or 15 miles of fence. Besides repairing wire he often had to reset the "deadmen," buried boulders to which were attached guy wires that kept the fence taut but which tended to wash out in storms. On any given round of fence patrol, too, a pliers man might have to chivy

Some recipes from the autocrat of the kitchen

A ranch's cookshack was a private realm ruled over by a cantankerous autocrat. As permanent member of the outfit he wielded even more power than the itinerant cooks who filled in on roundup and on the trail *(pages 164-171)*. Aloof from the rest of the men, he slept in the cookshack rather than in the bunkhouse, and he made certain the hands showed proper respect—which he sometimes enforced with the broad end of a skillet.

The root of his authority, of course, was that he provided the one element that (together with sleep) a cowboy most cherished. And woe to the ranch whose cook served up bad food, for top hands would not stay at such a place. A first-class cook, however, kept the men as fat and happy as ranch hands ever got. Here are five typical cowboy dishes, for which variations were created on the trail, that men like jaunty John White *(right)* of the N Bar Ranch in Montana fixed with supplies bought by the rancher or scrounged by the cook himself.

Sonofabitch Stew

2 pounds lean beef	1 set brains
Half a calf heart	1 set marrow gut
1½ pounds calf liver	Salt, pepper
1 set sweetbreads	Louisiana hot sauce

Kill off a young steer. Cut up beef, liver and heart into 1-inch cubes; slice the marrow gut into small rings. Place in a Dutch oven or deep casserole. Cover meat with water and simmer for 2 to 3 hours. Add salt, pepper and hot sauce to taste. Take sweetbreads and brains and cut in small pieces. Add to stew. Simmer another hour, never boiling.

Cook John White glowers from his lair.

Cowboy Beans

2 pounds pinto beans	4 tablespoons sugar
2 pounds ham hock (or salt pork)	2 green chilies (or to taste)
2 onions, chopped	1 can tomato paste

Wash the beans and soak overnight. Drain, place in a Dutch oven and cover with water. Add remaining ingredients and simmer until tender. Sample the beans while cooking. Add salt to taste and water as needed.

Sourdough Biscuits

1 cup sourdough starter	1 tablespoon shortening
1 teaspoon each of salt, sugar and soda	3 to 4 cups sifted flour

Place flour in a bowl, make a well in the center and add sourdough starter *(above, right)*. Stir in salt, soda and sugar, and add shortening. Gradually mix in enough flour to make a stiff dough. Pinch off dough for one biscuit at a time; form a ball and roll it in melted shortening. Crowd the biscuits in a round 8-inch cake pan and allow to rise in a warm place for 20 to 30 minutes before baking. Bake at 425° until done.

Sourdough Starter

2 cups lukewarm potato water	2 cups flour
	1 tablespoon sugar

First make potato water by cutting up 2 medium-sized potatoes into cubes, and boil in 3 cups of water until tender. Remove the potatoes and measure out two cups of remaining liquid. Mix the potato water, flour and sugar into a smooth paste. Set in a warm place until starter mixture rises to double its original size.

Red Bean Pie

1 cup cooked, mashed pinto beans	1 cup milk
1 cup sugar	1 teaspoon vanilla
3 egg yolks, beaten	1 teaspoon nutmeg

Combine ingredients and place in uncooked pie crust. Bake at 350° for 30 minutes or until set. Make meringue with the leftover egg whites; spread on pie and brown in oven.

Vinegar Pie

1 cup sugar	5 tablespoons vinegar
2 tablespoons flour	
1 cup cold water	2½ tablespoons butter
4 eggs, beaten	

Combine sugar and flour. Add the rest of the ingredients and place in a saucepan. Cook until thick and pour into a prepared pie crust. Bake in a 375° oven until the crust is brown.

weak, starving cattle to a haystack or pick porcupine quills from some sad calf's nose. Sometimes in drought or cold a calf would die, and the fence riders, attracted by the mother's bawling, would have to rope and tie her, then milk her distended udder to ease the pain.

Other men were assigned regular patrols to check on the screeching and all-too-fallible machinery of windmills. The primary task for mill riders — usually they rode in pairs — was to scramble up the ladders bolted to the mill's tall legs and coat the primitive bearings and gears with grease. Standard mills were 32 feet high, but the men at George Littlefield's Yellow Houses Ranch in Texas faced a truly dismaying climb when they greased one mill. It rose as high as a 13-story building to catch the wind above the canyon walls.

Frequently as the riders approached a mill its big wheel would be whirling wildly, and they would know that the sucker rod, which normally transmitted the pull of the windmill crank to the plunger deep in the well casing, had broken. Then they would hitch horses to a block and tackle, haul out the jointed rod, fish up the plunger from the well, repair the break and start the mill again — all the while surrounded by milling cattle bawling out their thirst. Such repairs could be dangerous work, for a cowboy bowled off the top by a swinging vane might be injured or killed.

If a man did get hurt windmill tending — or saving a bogged steer or getting kicked by a horse or in any of a score of other mishaps common to his hard trade — he could expect very little in the way of formal medication. Doctors were scarcer than Latin scholars on the range, and medical treatment was often amateurish improvisation. A cowhand named Steve Stephens fixed a sprained ankle in a few days by wrapping it in brown paper and soaking it with vinegar. In Arizona, Evans Coleman suffered a deep cut along his hairline from the hoof of a rearing horse. He claimed he made it as good as new by applying a gummy poultice of Climax, his favorite chewing tobacco. At one New Mexico ranch a man who was running a fever and complaining of a pain in his side received a drink of Thribble H Horse Liniment mixed with hot water and was made to sleep with his head to the north. Only serious injuries merited going for help — and then the help might be primitive. Texan Arch Sneed gashed his thigh to the bone when his horse ran into a fence, and Doc Hed-

rick, in Dalhart, sewed up the wound without benefit of an anesthetic. He simply had his office boy, who weighed 200 pounds, sit on Sneed's head.

Around the ranch house itself, cowboy work tended to be less taxing and sometimes downright undignified, especially if it had to be done on foot. Over a three-week stretch Texas cowhand Blue Stevens did nothing but gather dried cow manure for fires. C. H. Hanbury, on the XIT Ranch, was equally far removed from the image of the tall-in-the-saddle cavalier when he was assigned the task of building traps for turtles that had overpopulated a lake used to water livestock. One Colorado puncher, W. H. (Lasso Bill) Sears, even sank to the abysmal level of milking cows and raising chickens, although he at least had the satisfaction of turning a personal profit: "I picked six good milk cows out of the herd of range cattle and drove them into the corral and milked them twice a day. I had to rope these cows every time I milked them, snub their heads close to a post and then tie their hind legs together before they would submit to being milked. I made butter and sold the extra butter, milk and buttermilk, also eggs, to passing immigrants. I had a flock of chickens at the ranch and they furnished me several dozen eggs a day."

Farm chores, always unwelcome, became an increasingly common cowboy activity as the cattle business expanded and grew modernized. Some hands spent months on end getting in hay and other crops. One big Texas spread had 800 acres under cultivation, some of it in wheat, corn and melons, but most of it in hay. A cowhand on the ranch, Lee Landers, recalled with a certain rueful amazement that he once created "the longest haystack ever seen on the Rito Blanco Division" — 70 steps in length.

The slowest time around a ranch was winter, the one season when there was little work of any kind. By late November two of every three ranch hands were laid off until the spring roundup and summer trail drives brought new demands for cowboys. Most of the unemployed men housed up with bachelor buddies in town and took temporary jobs, such as bartending or blacksmithing. Others rode off for days or weeks at a stretch to participate in one of the unique customs of pioneer country: grub-line riding — i.e., riding from ranch to ranch picking up free meals and doing odd jobs. Unlike the so-called professional chuck-line rider, who was typically an unknown saddle bum, the grub-line man was a respectable cowhand who honestly had nothing to do at the moment. Owners of outlying ranches, starved for the sight of a friendly face, welcomed the grub-line rider as a source of news and fresh stories. If by chance no one was home when the grub liner came by, he walked in anyway. Ranchers did not lock their doors, and a hungry rider was free to enter any house, feed himself from the bacon and flour, and bed down.

Most of the winter chores that cowboys did perform were on the order of maintenance and repairs, along with a fair amount of assorted drudgery that had been put off at busier times of the year. Firewood had to be gathered; the men dragged tree trunks with ropes made fast to their saddle horns. Texan J. W. Standifer recalled once being assigned to "cutting dead cottonwood into stove wood. It was like cutting sponge—every time my ax hit it bounced back." At the Goose Egg outfit in Wyoming, cowpunchers were assigned to haul stone two miles from a quarry to build an eight-room house for the manager. And on a ranch in the Dakotas the boys were set to mining coal from a small seam on the spread. In a classic piece of make-work Texan Bob Haley spent an entire winter rendering the suet of 11 slaughtered beeves for tallow. He reported that the stuff gave "a purty good light" in lamps. Furthermore, he said, sourdough biscuits could be rolled in it just before baking for extra flavor.

There were two wintertime tasks that no one took lightly. One was the necessary and grueling business of going out from time to time to be sure the cattle were not starving or freezing to death, or both. Cattle had a stubborn, mindless tendency to stand, shivering and hungry, in deep snow rather than attempt to find food. Bundled in their bulky buffalo coats, men on horses tramped out trails and paths to hillsides where wind had blown snow off the grass—then returned to drive the cattle to the cleared spots. The cowboys also had to chop through snow crust and ice so the cattle could drink, because most cows lack the instinct to eat snow for moisture. Often the marooned cattle were themselves crusted heavily with snow, their eyes frozen shut and their muzzles dripping icicles.

When the cowboys rode out after a blizzard they frequently found cattle that were dying or already dead from the cold. If this happened, the hands usually tried to salvage a small part of the animal's value—the hide. But they had to work quickly. "The only cows we could skin were the ones yet with circulation," explained cowhand Arch Sneed, assigned to the cattle-skinning detail on the XIT spread. "They were down and couldn't get up. We would cut their throats and skin them while yet warm. The ones which had been dead for some time were frozen so hard that we couldn't possibly skin them."

The other demanding winter assignment—and the only one that held any real excitement or reward—was wolf hunting. In cold months, when the pickings were lean among natural game on the range, the wolves became particularly bold in stalking cattle. Moving in packs, they would disable a cow by severing the hamstrings in its hind legs; then they moved in to finish off the cripple. R. M. Dudley was hired by a ranch in Texas to shoot wolves at a salary of $35 a month plus the $5 a scalp bounty offered by the county government. The ranch, in addition, provided him with food, four to eight horses, two rifles, a Colt .45 and all the ammunition he needed.

The Wyoming ranch where A. B. Snyder worked kept Russian wolfhounds to run down the predators; other outfits used greyhounds, deerhounds and staghounds. Cowboys, riding to the hounds like roughhewn gentry, would overtake the pack and gun the wolves down. Lee Landers, like many another cowboy, once caught a wolf with his lariat: "I didn't have anything to kill him with but my rope; so I doubled it up and beat the wolf to death."

The most effective tactic against the predators was to get the she-wolf and pups in their den. At a ranch in Texas the cowboys wriggled into long, narrow wolf tunnels, pushing candles and six-shooters in front of them, and fired away when they spotted the glow of candlelight reflected in the animals' eyes. Cowhand Charlie Orr tried this sort of attack once and missed his first shot. The frantic she-wolf, rushing to escape, jammed herself in the tunnel on Orr's back. She finally scrambled her way out, but at great cost to Orr's skin. Another cowboy who had been standing by shot the wolf, then dug out the lacerated Charlie.

No matter what kind of chores they were assigned, most cowhands preferred to be near the ranch rather

Line-camp duty in winter was the loneliest part of the cowboy's year. Here, at a camp on the Pitchfork Ranch in Wyoming, a hand saddles up after a snowstorm, when the temperature may drop to 30° below.

than patrolling the back country. One reason was that around the ranch a cowboy might have an occasional chance to at least look at a woman. In almost every case she would be the owner's or the foreman's wife, to be treated with the most elaborate and distant respect. But in a country where the male-female ratio was about 10 to 1, and the distance between individual females might be anywhere from 50 to 100 miles, the very sight of a woman—no matter if she was someone else's—was something of a treat.

At least once a year, winter or summer, even this pleasure was denied when cowboys drew the utterly monastic duty of line riding. Most large Western ranches were too big to be manned from their central buildings alone. Like small nations, they needed outposts. The Millet Ranch on the Brazos had such outposts spotted every six or eight miles around the 60-mile perimeter. In the days before barbed wire (and sometimes in the days after it, if the boss was a wire hater or had fence-cutting neighbors) the line riders patrolled between their stations, forming a kind of living fence around the owner's range, holding in their ranch's strays and chasing the neighbor's cows off the home grass. Of course, the cows had to be found before they could be shooed back where they belonged, and a line rider's days were spent mainly cutting for sign—that is, picking up the trail of a cow that had strayed away.

In addition to his ceaseless efforts at cattle containment, the line rider performed such multifarious duties of guardianship as keeping cows away from alkaline water, watching out for rustlers, and hunting or poisoning wolves, mountain lions and even eagles, which sometimes attacked calves. He was also expected to brand any cow missed at roundup time and to take note of pasture conditions for the boss's information. On a ranch located near a rail line a hand would be assigned to patrol the tracks, chasing cattle off the right of way and keeping a record of cows that were run down so that a carefully itemized bill could later be presented to the railroad.

Life at the line camps was, not surprisingly, more primitive than in the lowliest bunkhouse. Most outlying camps consisted of a one-room shack of sod or logs, or sometimes a mere dugout scratched from the side of a hill. "We dug an open-topped rectangular hole into the South side of a slope near water," recalled John Young of Texas. "Thus the back wall and a part of each of the two side walls were formed by the ground. The remainder were made of logs chinked with mud. The flat roof [of dirt-covered logs] butted against the hillside, but a line of mounded earth prevented water from running off the slopes onto it." A blanket or an old cowhide usually served for a door.

The line camps were generally manned by one or two hands, and after a few weeks on line even a pair of men tended to get very lonely. In one Montana dugout a visitor in 1886 found a scrap of diary that read: "May 6th—arrived here. Lonesome as hell, but a good supper. Buffalo hump and onions." That brief entry described 10,000 evenings in line camps all across the West. Cooking seemed a principal hedge against boredom, and some cowboys had a real flair for it, although culinary techniques were crude (pie dough was often rolled with a whiskey bottle and coffee was made by the old-time, range-proved recipe—"a handful of coffee to a cup of water"). As a rule cowboys on line-camp duty ate only twice a day, rarely packing any food on horseback—except perhaps a can of tomatoes.

"When I went into winter camp, I always took plenty of novels and tobacco, and usually a cat," reported Jim Christian, a line rider for the J A Ranch in the Panhandle. "A cat and a briar pipe were lots of company when a fellow spent months shut off from the world. Of course a puncher would drop in for a meal or a visit once in a while, or maybe I would meet a puncher now and then while riding; but I have gone for weeks at a time without seeing a soul."

Christian was one of the rare cowboys who actually enjoyed being alone and looked forward to line duty. "I loved to ride to a steep ledge, view the canyon at sunrise, to smell the dewy cedar, and listen to the mocking birds," he said. "I learned to know the trees, shrubs and flowers in their seasons, and the signs and legends belonging to each. I have robbed the eagle's nest for sport, and fed wild turkeys and quail the bread and beans from my table. I delighted in a plunge at the big spring, formerly a watering place of the Indians. The hoot of the owl and the howl of the coyote were music to my ears through the long night. My comrade was my horse. A fellow could spend lots of time petting, currying and fooling with a horse."

Such attitudes, however, were rare. Most range hands would have agreed with the description of cowboy historian Ramon Adams, when he described line duty as living "the life of a buck nun." And they could not get back to the home ranch fast enough. Once there, they were ready to blow off a little steam, which many of them did in characteristic cowboy fashion—that is, with a lot of crude vigor. One rough form of fun was riding any unwilling creature at hand—oxen, mules or cattle. "It's real fun to feel the cow's hide roll back and forth with each jump they make," reported R. M. Dudley. Horse racing was another diversion, especially in spring when the hands captured and broke new mustangs (pages 98-103) to add to the mounts they already had in the ranch's common pool of cow ponies. "The cowboy is usually under the impression that he has at least one race horse in his string," wrote an Englishman who toured the West. The races were brief, because the short-legged mustangs, like quarter horses, were best at dashes. Often cowboys raced against Indian ponies and the Indians were even keener on the accompanying bets than the punchers.

Somewhat less sporting was the special event called pulling the chicken, learned from the vaqueros. It was described by a Texas newspaper, The Tascosa Pioneer: "A lusty young rooster was buried in the earth, his head only being left above ground, and the young men and boys dash by, one after another, and as they pass the rooster each man swings himself down from the saddle and reaches for its head. The chicken naturally dodges more or less and renders it no easy matter to catch him. Finally secured, however, by a lucky grab, the body is brought out by a jerk which generally breaks the neck."

In their outbursts of bruising, brutal fun, cowboys did not spare each other. A favorite way of whiling away idle hours was to call a kangaroo court into session and try some hapless cowhand on a trivial or preposterous charge, such as stuttering or boasting. The accused stood no chance of acquittal in the bunkhouse court-

Two groups of cowboys turn out for a porch party and stiff little stag dance. At the Archdale Ranch in Montana (top) they sit through a Fourth of July dinner, and on the Lazy S in Texas two men—one heifer-branded with a frilly apron—dance under the eye of a young ranch wife and baby.

Among the luckiest men in Texas were these XIT cowboys. They were not only able to enjoy a swim but also
managed to find eight girls for the seven men—in a frontier
region where women were usually in a 10-to-1 minority.

room, since the puncher assigned to defend him was purposefully inept and the judge and jurors relentlessly hostile. After the inevitable verdict of guilty was announced (to loud applause) the cowboy acting as a judge dreamed up a suitably humiliating penalty. The transgressor might be tossed into a creek to purge him of his grievous sins. Often the sentence was even rougher. Many a victim of a kangaroo court was forced to bend over a wagon tongue and endure a painful spanking with a pair of chaps.

Once in a great while, perhaps at Christmas or the Fourth of July, some semblance of civilization would come into the cowboy's life, and he would be invited to the main ranch for dinner with the boss and wife, or even to a dance. At the smallest ranches dances tended to be sad little affairs with a few fiddles and no women. In a noble attempt to liven up such occasions one or two cowboys would allow themselves to be what was known as heifer-branded; they would put on an apron or tie a handkerchief to their sleeve to indicate they were dancing the female part.

More rarely — and happily — there would be a genuine fandango, a huge party with wine and real women and all the trimmings. Cowboy Eb Jones attended rancher Fred Dupree's wedding party for his daughter, Marcella, at the Dupree spread on the Cheyenne River in 1887. There were 10 solid days and nights of dancing. One hundred whites and 500 Indians consumed 20 gallons of whiskey, a keg of wine, 30 beeves and four buffalo. Near Paducah, Texas, the 3 D ranch hands built an outdoor platform big enough for four dance sets, with dressing tents nearby. The favorite waltzes were "Over the Waves" and "A Bird in a Gilded Cage." For the Valentine Dance at the huge Matador spread one year, the cowboys showed up both in range dress (battered Stetsons and flannel shirts) and fancy dress (white buckskin vests and watch chains braided from a sweetheart's locks). Flaming cedar logs warmed the scrubbed-down bunkhouse against the cold. Everybody stopped dancing at midnight for a supper of ham, turkey and chicken. But then the fiddler picked it up again, fast and tricky:

> *Weave 'em up and weave 'em down,*
> *Weave 'em pretty girls round and round....*

And the dancing did not end until the break of day.

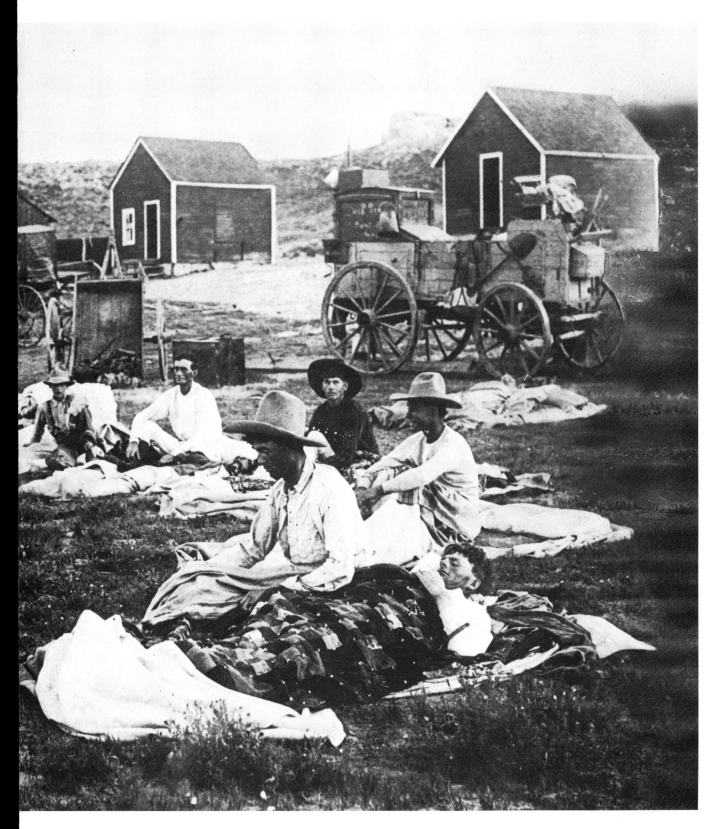

Ranch hands bed out for the night at the W. D. Boyce Cattle Company in Kansas. In summer cowboys often would not sleep in bunkhouses, which were usually hot, crowded and ridden with bedbugs and lice.

Bronco buster Lee Warren ropes a bay gelding as it pounds around the corral.

Forging the cowboy's essential tool

The basic piece of equipment the cowhand used in working cattle was a plains mongrel called the cow pony. Half wild and wholly ornery, this sturdy animal—like the one being roped below—was treated by cowhands about the way a modern farmer treats his truck: with just enough care to keep the thing running, but with no time to spare for pampering or affection. Most of these cow ponies came from the open rangeland and were an odd collection of wild mustangs (a term derived from the Spanish word *mesteño,* meaning "stray") or mustangs interbred with U.S. Cavalry thoroughbred remounts and Eastern-bred work horses. There

they roamed free till about age four, living on bare survival rations of grass and rarely growing beyond a modest 12 to 14 hands and 700 to 900 pounds (today's Western horses commonly stand 14 to 16 hands high and weigh well over 1,000 pounds).

In the late spring the men came out to corral the untamed four-year-old ponies and slam them through a traumatic, nerve-shattering tour of basic training that lasted no more than four to six days. The process was called breaking, or busting, and either name was appropriate; for the object was quite literally to break the animals' wild spirit through lessons of fear and respect for

the cowboy that the horses would never forget. Sometimes the buster was a particularly saddleworthy local cowboy. More often he was a specialist who traveled from ranch to ranch, working for five dollars a head to gentle (the cowboy euphemism) the green mounts selected to join the remuda that year.

Such a specialist was Lee Warren, whose running battle with a new bunch of ponies at the Bow and Arrow Ranch in Montana appears in the rare and authentic pictorial record on these pages. Warren was a typical contract bronco buster, full of bruises and old sprains, as tough and vulnerable as the wild horses that he saddled. The photogra-

pher who captured Warren's difficult workout was L. A. Huffman of Miles City, Montana, and he jotted down a detailed preamble to this visual record: "While we waited for the horses," he wrote, "Warren took stock of his outfit. Just a plain, ordinary, cow-saddle, bridle, and lariat, spurs, quirt, and some short pieces of grass rope for the cross-hobbling." Then, Huffman observed, came a distant cry of "Hy-ar they come a f-o-g-g-i-n'," and a group of raw broncos was herded into sight.

"Swiftly across the wide flat, flanked by a half a dozen well-mounted riders, the little band swings in a wide circle, leaving adrift behind it a long ribbon of dust. The big gate is flung open, and the day's work is corralled." From that point on, Huffman's pictures tell the story of one buster's grueling, sweaty, dusty morning, as he saddled and rode six wild horses.

Warren began by roping each bronco, then snubbing it to a post (or throwing it if necessary) to put on the bridle. Next came the saddle blanket topped by the 40-pound saddle—and it was no mean feat to swing a heavy saddle shoulder-high with one hand while holding a rearing horse with the other. Finally came Warren himself, and that is when all gut-jarring hell broke loose for both the horse and the buster. The buster always won, for the rougher a horse behaved the rougher the treatment he received in retaliation from the rider's quirt, spurs and rope end. The reason for the brutality of bronco busting was not sadism but basic economics. "If a buster was getting fifteen bones a head instead of five, and all the time he needed for a bunch like this," Warren told Huffman, "horse fighting would be a heap safer for horses and men." But it was not, because ranch owners refused to pay for the extra time. Or, as Warren summed it up: "Bosses won't stand for a fifteen-dollar finish on a thirty-five-dollar horse."

Not long after these pictures were made, however, buster Warren was reprieved from his hazardous profession by a higher power. He got married, and his new bride prudently demanded that he climb off the broncos and settle down to a far safer role—deputy sheriff.

Feet braced, a captured horse pulls gingerly against the choking effect of a snubbed lariat, as buster Lee Warren tries to put on a bridle.

Bridled and hobbled but still full of fight, a blaze-faced cow pony ducks away from the saddle blanket in Warren's right hand.

Another horse bucks at the first tightening of the cinch. The stirrup is hooked over the saddle horn to get it out of the way.

Fighting to throw off the saddle, a horse, cross-hobbled by ropes on its forefeet and one hind foot, tugs Warren around the corral.

Warren twists the ear of a bronco, counting on the pain to distract the animal long enough for the buster to swing aboard.

By quirting the bronco furiously every time it bucks, Warren beats in the lesson that disobedience brings instant retribution.

To teach a pony to ignore unexpected sounds and motions, Warren hazes it with a rain slicker, then rides to a standstill.

On a Western saddle each part *(identified on the diagram at right)* evolved to meet a specific cowboy need, from the horn for roping to the broad stirrups in which the cowboy stood when he was riding down steep slopes or trotting along the trail.

The functional beauty of the saddle

The single piece of equipment that the cowboy was fussiest about was his saddle. And small wonder. For months at a time he sat in it all day and sometimes half the night as well. And when he finally lay down to rest at the end of a long day's work he pillowed his head on it. So indispensable was it to his life and livelihood that the phrase "he's sold his saddle" came to mean of a cowboy that he was finished in the profession.

Unlike the horse, which was supplied by the employer, the saddle was the cowboy's own personal property. A saddle like the typical Western rig shown at left, turned out in 1875 by master craftsman E. L. Gallatin of Denver, cost a cowhand a month's pay or more. But the $30 or so was money well spent, for the saddle could serve him well for as much as 30 years or even longer.

The Western saddle, as it evolved on the plains (*pages 106-107*), was a direct descendant of the 16th Century Spanish war saddle, pictured above, on which the Spanish conquistadors rode into Mexico. This war saddle (itself descended from one devised by the Moors a few hundred years earlier) weighed up to 40 pounds, had a wooden frame, or tree, was well padded and was covered with brocaded silk velvet.

The pommel at the front of the saddle is at left in the illustration; the cantle, at the back, was sharply curved to prevent the rider from sliding off. They were made of ornately chased silver, as were the long plates descending from the pommel on either side. The plates served two purposes: they shielded the rider's thighs and prevented an enemy lance from getting under the rider and unseating him. The saddle had stirrups, not shown, that hung low; the rider sat with his legs hanging almost straight down.

When the war saddle moved into cattle country in the early decades of

A 16th Century Spanish war saddle held a lancer secure between its pommel and sharply curved cantle, at right.

the 19th Century, the cowhands kept the tough wooden tree that was its foundation, and they retained the general notion of a high pommel and cantle. But from there on they made a number of drastic changes. The curved cantle was tilted well backward for the rider's comfort and lowered for easier mounting and dismounting. The ornate velvet gave way to long-wearing, readily available leather. The high metal pommel was modified in size, tilt and material until it became the horn needed to secure a lariat. And the metal thigh guards, or braces, disappeared altogether. If a cowboy wanted anything extra to steady himself in his seat, he rolled up his slicker or some other piece of the gear that he carried and tied it into place with the leather strings that hung from the saddle.

Carefully crafted and lovingly maintained, a fine saddle was at least as important to the horse as to the cowboy. A rider with a gentle hand and a good rig could travel 70 miles in one day and still have a healthy horse. But a thoughtless tyro in a poor saddle could make a horse sore in an hour's time.

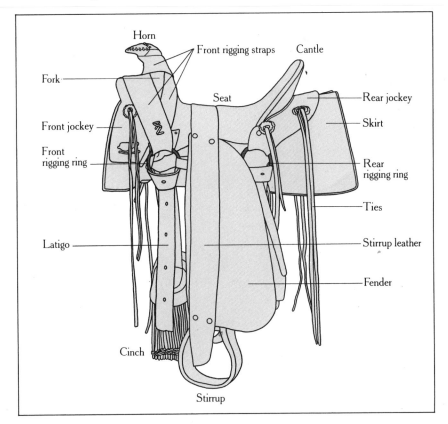

California mission saddle, circa 1830

The first true American cowboy saddle was developed by the vaqueros. The saddle's slim horn, or pommel, held the rawhide lariat *(page 125);* the stirrups were made of hollowed-out wood, and the early cowboys covered them with leather casings, called tapaderas, which shielded the rider's feet from cactus thorns.

Texas saddle, 1850

When the cattle business moved to Texas the elaborate skirt disappeared, and the leather-bound wooden horn became thicker and sturdier for heavy-duty roping. The stirrups were made of wide steam-bent wood — stronger and more durable than hollowed wood. The fenders protected the rider's legs from the animal's sweat.

BALANCE POINTS ON THE SADDLE RIGGING

The location of the rigging rings, through which the saddle was tied to the horse by canvas or cordage bands, was critical to the balance of the saddle. Yet the rings' position varied widely from region to region. Texans preferred the stout double rig *(far right)* for roping — while Mexicans felt that any good vaquero could easily balance a single-cinch rig by shifting his weight backward when a roped cow pulled against the saddle horn.

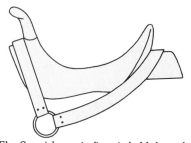

The Spanish, or rimfire, rig held the saddle, with the cinch circling the front of the horse's belly. But in roping the rear tended to rise up, throwing the rider.

Denver saddle, 1875

By the 1870s the saddle had become longer, and all of its frame-work was now covered with leather. These big saddles were a boon to cowboys, who found they provided a steadier, smoother seat. But they weighed about 40 pounds, and this bulk, combined with the length, tended to rub sores on the backs of horses.

California saddle, 1880

The classic cowboy saddle evolved on the West Coast. Shorter and lighter by 10 pounds than the Denver, it was easier on the horse. The slim horn, made of either wood or metal, had returned, and the saddle frequently had fancy leather tooling — an innovation intended less for decoration than to help hold the rider in place.

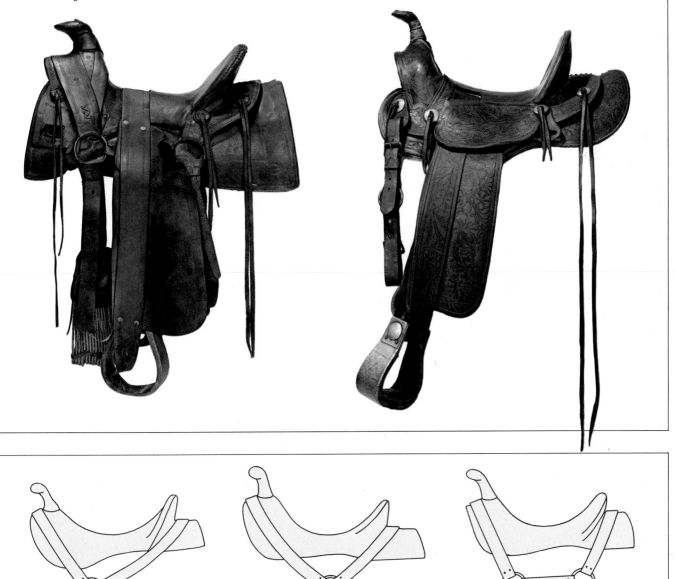

The three-quarter rig gave the saddle bet-ter balance whenever the cowboy was roping. Occasionally, however, the cinch could slide forward, loosening the saddle.

The commonest single-cinch arrangement for light or occasional roping was the center-fire rig, which could be counted on to hold steady under lariat pressure.

A double-cinch rig was eventually de-vised for heavy roping. The rear cinch provided the saddle with balance, but nev-er pulled so tight as to hurt the horse.

The spade

The spade, which was painful with any but a gentle touch, had a sharp raised plate that lay across the horse's tongue.

The ring

Circling the horse's lower jaw, the ring pressed a sensitive nerve. A curb under the jaw also helped control the horse.

The half-breed

On this bit a gentler port, shaped like a rounded A, replaced the spade. The bit had a chain, which acted as a curb.

The curb

The simplest and most humane bit, the curb, had a low port. Leather reins were buckled directly to the bit.

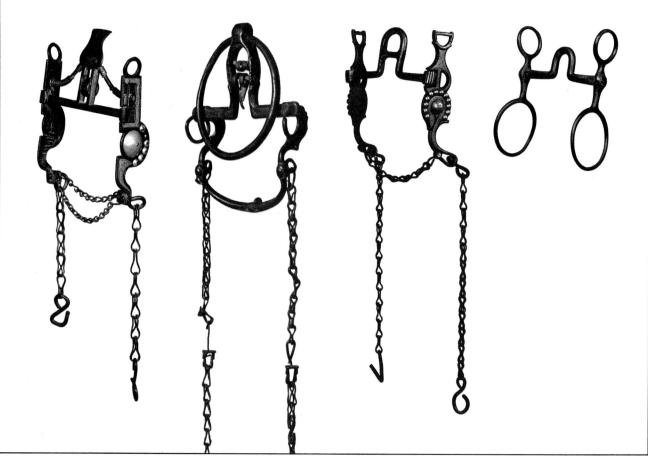

The cowboy controlled his horse by manipulating reins attached to a bridle made up of headstall and bit. Like most other pieces of cattle-country technology, the bridle came to the range from Spain via the California missions. The early bits were fierce looking and could tear a horse's mouth if roughly used. But a skilled cowhand knew how to use such a bit without punishing his horse; instead, the slightest backward pull on the cruel-looking metal helped him stop the animal. To guide his horse, he usually relied on a flick of the reins on the side of the animal's neck.

The most popular bridle combined the curb bit with the split-ear headstall. The cowboy first worked the bit into the horse's mouth and then slipped the stall over the ears, which held the rig in place.

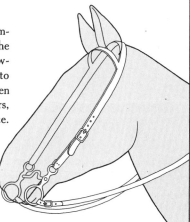

The California
Made either of woven horsehair or of leather, depending on the rider's preference, this bridle was held in place by a brow band across the horse's forehead.

The split-ear
A cowboy could easily improvise this simple, common headstall by splitting his own belt in half with his knife. The splits went over the horse's ears.

The hackamore
Requiring no bit, the hackamore could be used to break a sensitive horse. A properly trained horse would respond to the slightest touch of the reins.

4 | Roundup time

The critical moment for every rancher occurred twice a year, at the spring and fall roundups. That was when his men rode out into the rangeland to harvest the cattle—and he found out just how much he was worth in terms of beef on the hoof. Then, too, depending on the region and the time of year, there were other critical chores to be done. In spring the men traditionally went out when the grass first turned green. In Texas this was generally during April, and on the Southwestern range the prime purpose of the roundup was both to brand new calves and to gather the mature beef for sale to drovers who would trail the animals north.

In Montana and Wyoming, where the grass might not turn till May or June, few if any cattle were brought in for shipment in spring. Instead, the work emphasis was on branding and especially on returning strays that had wandered from their home ranches. Then during fall the Northern cattlemen held another roundup, when the mature beef was driven to shipment centers. In the Southwest the fall gathering was primarily a mop-up of animals missed in the earlier roundup. But on any part of the Western range, from the first sign of spring, there was rarely, if ever, a time when cowboys were not out gathering cows. As the wife of one ranch manager remembered, the chuck wagon and roundup hands who went out to the range in April often did not return "till the wagon made tracks through four-inch Christmas snow."

Wyoming range hands gather a bunch of bulls, steers, cows and calves into a milling, bawling circle in a spring roundup. Once the animals had settled down they would graze so placidly that two or three men could hold them together.

111

With the herd assembled, a cowpuncher clutching his broad-brimmed sombrero separates out a cow and her unbranded calf. Most mother cows stayed close to their calves, moaning in alarm, or in the case of an occasional feisty longhorn, making a threatening charge at the approaching cowboy.

113

Passing up one calf whose mother has made a protective stand in front of it, a cowboy on the Matador Ranch in Texas uses his lariat to capture and haul a plunging, battling yearling across the roundup ground toward the branding fire.

115

At a branding fire in a corral near Cheyenne, Wyoming, the work of a spring roundup comes to a climax. At right, two hands hold a calf while a third brands its side and another man cuts a notch in an ear for added identification. At left, a roped calf skids through the dust for its turn at the fire.

Harvesting the annual crop of cattle

Roundup time had come to the northern range: and for a couple of days in mid-April 1886 Miles City, Montana Territory, became the whooping, clattering, tail-tossing, cowboy capital of the West. The reason for all the bustle was the annual meeting of the Montana Stockgrowers Association, attended by 175 members. Along with the heavyweight local cattlemen came out-of-territory ranchers from as far south as Texas, from as far west as Washington plus a few from over the Canadian line. Barons were there, men like John Clay, Granville Stuart, Conrad Kohrs, Pierre Wibaux, the Marquis de Morès. So were representatives of the top officials of the cattle-shipping Northern Pacific Railroad and of the St. Paul stockyards. All of them had come to Miles City not only to treat themselves to a big convention blowout, but also to plan the hard, intricate work that would need doing on the range that spring.

The blowout came first. A military band from nearby Fort Keogh led the opening-day parade, and the association's officers and their ladies followed in carriages. Then, in dust and tumult, came more than a hundred cowboys, high-spirited and whooping, many clad in new pearl-gray California pants from the Orschel Brothers Clothing Store right up the street.

The festive mood held through the convention: the opening luncheon lasted so long that the cattlemen did not buckle down to their afternoon business sessions at Miles City's new and commodious roller-skating rink and civic center until 4 o'clock. And the "concluding exercises," according to the florid report of the *Weekly Yellowstone Journal and Live Stock Reporter,* "were

of a terpsichorean character." At the Stockgrowers Ball in the spacious dining room of the Macqueen House, military officers from the fort, in braid and dress swords, danced till midnight to the music of a six-piece orchestra; their partners included the comely half-Indian daughters of cattleman Granville Stuart. Meanwhile, along the town's rough streets, the cowboys bellied up four deep at saloon bars or hovered over poker tables the whole night long. At institutions such as Turner's Theater short-skirted girls called box rustlers wheedled cowboys into going upstairs for wine at five dollars a bottle, or back to discreetly curtained rooms behind the stage for other pleasures.

In spite of all the frolic the cowmen managed to enact much important business. None of it was more important than setting up the 1886 Montana roundup, one of the most extensive in the history of the cattle industry. In its sweep and complexity this great roundup served as an exemplar of all the problems, the strategy and the techniques of roundups as they occurred in the high time of the Old West.

During the early years of the cattle business roundups had been informal, individualistic and often strictly private affairs. In the Spanish territories of Mexico and California a ranchero would stage what he called a rodeo —not an exhibition of riding and roping but, as the Spanish word actually signifies, a surrounding, designed to locate scattered stock in rough country. Sometimes without even bothering to seek out their cattle, the Mexicans would plant tall, highly visible poles coated at the bottom with salt and tallow, and the cows would come home by themselves to lick the delicacy.

The early roundups in brushy southern Texas were even more informal. There, ranchers often went out by themselves to look for their stock, just as Appalachian farmers had been doing in cow hunts that dated back to the 18th Century. "Those old-time ranchmen were

Bundled against an early snowstorm, a cowpuncher out on fall roundup rescues a weakened, motherless calf that he found stranded on a high range in Wyoming.

The 17 districts designated in the spring
roundup of 1886 covered roughly a third
of Montana. The dark gray area north of
the Yellowstone River was District 8, fo-
cal point of the story told on these pages.

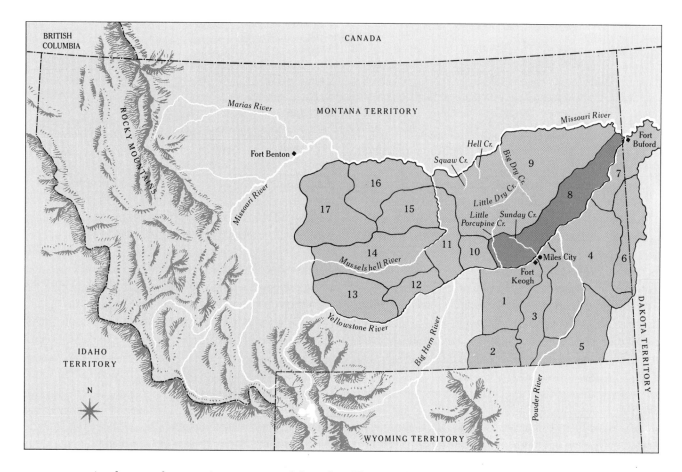

content to simply cow hunt twice a year and brand
their calves," said one Texas cowboy, almost contemp-
tuously. Later, finding that cattle from different outfits
sometimes mixed together, local ranchers united to drive
in their various brands for sorting out. And on some occasions groups of as many as 20 to 25 Texas range
bosses joined in a kind of cooperative roundup. In
1880, for example, winter storms mixed up cattle so
badly that 80 men and 10 wagons lined up on the
southern borders of Palo Pinto and Parker Counties,
west of Fort Worth, and for 30 days worked north in
five-mile strips to throw together a massive herd from
which each owner picked out his own cattle.

Such occasions were exceptional in the Southwest.
The cowmen of that frontier region had no end of space
in which to roam about when they felt crowded; if a
new neighbor settled within 15 or 20 miles of an existing camp or ranch, the original inhabitant could, if he
wished, simply pick up and move on to less crowded
country. And on the dry, sparsely vegetated plains of

Texas and the Southwest, cattle tended to group themselves around water holes and rarely strayed across the
intervening parched country to join other herds. Most
Southern ranches, especially enormous spreads like the
XIT, needed only to search their own holdings to find
their cattle — a job that remained more of a cow hunt
than a formalized roundup.

In the North the situation grew to be quite different.
There, mass roundups of cooperating ranchers became
the rule. The main reason for the difference was the
burst of cattle-business speculation that brought enormous herds of cattle onto the lush feeding grounds of
the northern range. After 1880 the land became overstocked and overgrazed, forcing cattle to cross divides
and mingle with other herds to find new grass and
water. Every rancher went out to sift every other rancher's range to find his own cows and drive them back
home. Steers were kept on a dead run for days, or even
weeks. This chasing of cattle ran off tons of salable beef
and weakened some animals so badly that they could

not survive the winter. It also opened many opportunities to rustlers, who could prosper in the confusion.

Out of this intolerable commotion grew the need for cooperative herding and branding. To some extent cooperation extended well beyond the roundup season. For example, Montana and Wyoming cowmen agreed among themselves not to gather cattle on any of their ranges between November 15 and the beginning of the spring roundup. Or if they did, they would give neighbors notice and let them inspect the gathered herd as a protection against misbranding, particularly by ambitious small-scale operators.

By the spring of 1886 the problem facing the cattlemen assembled in Miles City was almost as vast and complicated as a major military campaign. North, east, south and west of Miles City, in an area as big as Pennsylvania, nearly every coulee, gulch and box canyon contained cattle, for a total of more than a million. As at all roundups — even the smallest — these animals had first to be gathered together. Next the increase in new calves would be tallied and branded. At the same time most of the males among them would be castrated to make them gentler (a relative condition, considering the wildness of some steers) and to help them gain weight on the range. Ailing stock would be doctored, and some healthy ones would be dehorned. Finally all the strayed cattle would be separated into individual groups and driven home — perhaps the most monumental job of all, since no less than 4,000 different recorded brands were to some degree mixed together.

The difficulty of finding all this stock was compounded by both the size and the diverse character of the territory to be scoured. At any given moment, any given man glancing around any given range might see nary a cow, or at best only a few. In 1885, the year before the big Montana roundup, a tongue-in-cheek story in the *Colorado Springs Gazette* had announced that Colorado's ranchers hoped to solve their own roundup problem by importing from Cambridge, Massachusetts, a telescope powerful enough to read brands on cattle 150 miles away. The Montana stockmen of 1886 might have wished for such a wonder, but neither they nor anyone else had it.

At the Miles City meeting they cut up the range into 17 districts, some of them as big as Rhode Island or Connecticut but all considered by Westerners to be small enough for one roundup group of about 50 to 100 men to screen. No straight lines defined the borders of the districts; instead, the borders followed watercourses and divides in the pattern shown in the map on the opposite page.

At the eastern end of the pattern lay District 8, a 130-by-30-mile swath of land extending along the north shore of the Yellowstone River, and bounded on the north by the divide between the Yellowstone and the Missouri. With its mixture of terrain — it was made up of broken land in the west and flat plains in the east — the district typified the varied activities of the entire roundup. Some of the most powerful outfits of the northern range would be working District 8: the Circle Dot, the N Bar N, the L S, the J Lazy J, the Bow and Arrow. The area also contained 12,000 cattle and 300 horses of the L U Bar, a new ranch stocked by four herds driven up from Texas the year before.

The night the convention ended, the L U Bar's foreman, a fine horseman named Waddy Peacock, headed back to the ranch to get things ready. With him was a young Texas trail hand, 18-year-old Luke Sweetman, whom Peacock had hired to help with the spring work. After a 65-mile ride the two men bedded down in one of the L U Bar's two desolate gray-shale houses to rest up for the long weeks of work to come. In later years Sweetman would recall those weeks with detailed clarity, and his written recollections of the 1886 roundup form the basis of this account.

As it turned out, the start of the roundup was postponed over a month for lack of rain; not until late May did the range green up enough so that the cows could graze out of the ravines and hidden bottom lands and the gathering could begin. At the L U Bar the men utilized the delay to repair saddles, to line up good strings of horses — breaking some — and to overhaul the chuck wagon, grease its big wooden hubs, load the mess gear and choose a stalwart four-horse team. Finally Peacock, Sweetman and half a dozen other cowhands, along with the L U Bar cook and his wagon, set out for the designated meeting place of District 8, near Miles City. They went at a walking pace so as not to tire or excite their cavvy (a term derived from the Spanish word *caballada,* meaning a band of saddle horses; on the Southern ranges and on the Texas range and trails such a band of saddle horses was generally called a remuda).

The daily strategy of a typical spring round-up focused on a moving chuck wagon from which the men fanned out in the morning and to which they circled back with the cattle for sorting and branding each afternoon.

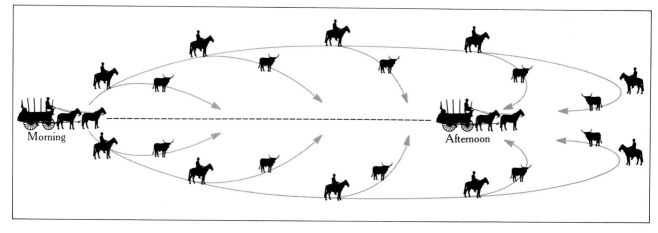

Down Sunday Creek the nine men rode for three days, until they reached the benchland on the north bank of the Yellowstone across from Miles City — which had been placed off limits to prevent pleasure-seeking cowhands from straying. The benchland and lowland beneath teemed with nearly a hundred men and more than 500 horses — a pool of manpower and horseflesh cooperatively assembled by the ranchers, big and small, of District 8. Half a dozen other wagons were there, in dispersed camps, with as many as a dozen or so men attached to each. Each wagon fed not only its own crew, but also hands sent by participating ranches too small to own a wagon. To the men and wagons with home ranches in District 8 there were added other cowboys called reps (for representatives) from ranches outside the district who would retrieve their outfits' far-strayed cattle. They arrived singly or in pairs, each driving a string of horses, some of them loaded with bedrolls.

Here on the riverbank occurred another reunion, cruder than the one in Miles City back in April, but typical of roundup time on the northern range. Some of the men had ridden up from the Powder River in Wyoming, others down from as far as the mouth of the Musselshell, along the Yellowstone from Fort Buford in Dakota and over the trail from the Big Horn River. An old hand like Waddy Peacock could throw his arm around the shoulders of cowpunchers he had known on many a past drive and roundup. The air echoed with greetings: "If it ain't…!" and "Well I'll be!" Men with names like One-Eye Davis or Original John shouted friendly insults at friends named Curly

Kid or Bean Belly. The commonest type was the Montanafied Texan, who had come up the trail in the preceding 8 or 10 years and learned to stand the cold; but, as always in the West, there were also blacks, Mexicans, a scattering of Easterners-turned-range-hands and a few others out playing at being cowboys.

One strong-faced man, jogging everywhere in his big silver-bangled Mexican sombrero, was Tom Gibson, good-humored yet authoritative foreman of the J Lazy J. The stockgrowers' convention had picked him as captain of the District 8 roundup, and as he studied his men and measured their talents, he let most of them relax with a couple of days of high-mettled fun. While the cooks took their heavy wagons by ferry across the Yellowstone to the stores of Miles City for supplies, the cowhands who had assembled for the roundup went swimming, staged foot races, twirled ropes.

As they had done at their bunkhouses on long, empty winter afternoons, the men might convene kangaroo courts to rule on meaningless or ridiculous offenses. At roundup time, though, such courts had a special tang and savor; they were not held simply to relieve boredom, but to enhance the excitement of the roundup itself. A convicted cowhand — and every accused man was convicted — might be condemned to ride bareback on a wild young steer picked from the first day's roundup, or to break a notorious bucking horse from the pack of some neighboring outfit. More mildly, he might be compelled to hand over part of his precious tobacco as a fine for his offense, but he knew that when the roundup began in earnest his fellow punchers would share their stores with him as long as there were any.

The rowdiest sport was racing horses. The entries

ran between jammed rows of onlookers, afoot or mounted, who closed in behind the racers yelling and shooting pistols. Some of the cowboys had one or two horses of their own and raced pony against pony, the winner taking both. Nights the men wandered from wagon to wagon, testing the various cooks' specialties, finding friends or jawing with strangers, yarning around campfires. With discipline temporarily relaxed, some of the hands sneaked off to Miles City to drink at the Cottage Saloon; others crossed the street to Charlie Brown's establishment, where the owner kept a pot of Mulligan stew on the simmer ("Just help yourself") and let the boys sleep off their hangovers on the floor; and still others dallied with such floozies as Cowboy Annie and Connie the Cowboy Queen, who sported a $250 dress embroidered with the brands of every outfit from the Yellowstone to the Platte.

On the third night, however, the roundup crews got all the rest they could; most of them, in fact, stretched out on the ground before the lingering dusk of May had darkened into night. They knew that for the next six weeks, at least — or for as long beyond that as the roundup lasted—they would never get enough sleep. And they were right. A few hours after the men dozed off, the L U Bar's night wrangler whipped the ranch's horse band out of the still-black night. Soon, for the first of many mornings, the L U Bar cook roused his crew in the darkness with a call that began in a trill and ended in a roar: "Come, boys, get up and hear the little birds singing their sweet praises to the Lord God Almighty; *damn your souls, get up!*" They breakfasted, not hungry, while the horses sniffed the campfire smoke. Then Sweetman flung a loop over the neck of a wiry buckskin, a horse that he himself had ridden up the trail from Texas the year before. With Peacock leading, the L U Bar boys rode off to where Captain Gibson, gathering all the men and foremen around him, gave out the orders of the day.

Gibson's overall strategy was to divide his forces between the eastern and western halves of District 8, because the area was far too big to be combed by one set of men, wagons and horses. In both the east work and the west work the men would carry out certain identical tasks. Along with the routine chores of gathering and branding, they would divide their herds into different groups to facilitate the returning of strays to their home ranges. Strays belonging to ranges ahead of the roundup's path would form a growing day herd driven along with the wagons and horses and subsequently distributed according to ownership. Strays from ranches behind the line of march would be the responsibility of the reps, who would string along with the roundup until they had as many of their own brand as one man could drive home alone.

On this first day, though, everyone stayed together and gathered in the cattle grazing close at hand. The start happened to be on the range of the Bow and Arrow Ranch, and by custom Gibson turned his authority for the day over to that ranch's foreman, Buck Merritt. It fell to Buck, when the herd was gathered, to ride and select the first calf of the roundup. He smoothly roped the bounding beast, dragged it to the fire and applied a basic tenet of cowboy lore to the problem of choosing a brand: he would let the calf's already branded mother tell him what brand to use. For a cow loves her calf, and when that calf is roped at roundup the cow informs the men by wild-eyed bawling that the calf is hers. This simple fact was one of the bases of the range-cattle ownership system, and Buck Merritt used it now. Holding fast to the struggling calf he had picked out, he read the brand on the flank of its hovering mother and shouted: "Bow and Arrow!" Two of the boys wrestled the calf down, and Loring Rea, the Bow and Arrow's manager, did first honors by burning his brand into the little animal's side.

The next calf Buck roped was attended by a bawling mother with the brand of the Mankato Cattle Company, way to the south; cow and calf obviously had swum the Yellowstone. "Tarantula!" yelled Buck, for that was what cowboys thought Mankato's script-M brand looked like. The Mankato rep brought up a hot iron with his company's brand and stamped it onto the calf. Next came a calf from the L U Bar, also a long way from home; an L U Bar man branded it. The fourth calf already had some indistinct brand. Buck, suspecting hocus-pocus on the part of one or the other of the small-scale ranchers standing by, coolly said to one of the men around him, "Better teach your calves to quit sucking at Bow and Arrow cows," and stamped the animal with his own brand. By the end of the afternoon the air around the fire was acrid with the smell of burned hair from the hides of several hundred calves.

On roundup in Montana Territory during the 1880s, cowboy E. H. Brewster pays out a loop in his lariat big enough for a longhorn.

The indispensable art of roping

From the earliest moment in the morning—when he went to the remuda to catch out his day's mount by slipping a rope around its neck—the cowboy was rarely out of reach of his lariat. Snugly coiled, it hung from his saddle whenever he mounted up. On the trail he had it ready to drop over the horns of a rebellious herd quitter or to pull out a bogged cow or wagon. And the knout end was a convenient whip for a balky horse or steer. At roundup time he used the rope to catch calves or stray cattle for the branding iron. Sometimes he even made his rope function as a crude adding machine, totaling up the newly branded animals by shifting a coil of

the lariat from one hand to the other for every hundred head.

A lariat was not just any piece of rope. It was made of carefully braided rawhide or twisted grass and had to be stiff enough so that when a cowhand like the one at left paid out a broad loop and then sent it flying toward its target the loop stayed flat and open. Moreover, the lariat had to be strong enough to take the wrenching shock of a roped 1,200-pound steer yanking it as taut as any blue-water fishing line. A lariat could be dangerous, too, in inexperienced hands. One Texas greenhorn who got tangled up in loose coils found himself lashed to the side of his

pony upside down, a target for the horns of the steer he had just roped.

Most cowboys spent a fair portion of their leisure time practicing with the rope, refining their skill and fooling around with fancy casts. But woe to the cowboy who got too enamored of his lariat and busted cattle unnecessarily or used the working day as an occasion to try out his trick roping, for he risked being fired. For practical purposes a cowboy had to know only two catches plus one potentially lethal variation *(pages 126-127)*. With these basic catches, and a smart, willing cow pony, he became the master of the Western plain and of its four-legged creatures.

THE ELEMENTS OF A CATCH ROPE

For ordinary roundup work like calf catching most American cowboys used a grass rope averaging 40 feet in length. At the head of the lariat was an eyelet called a honda, through which the main line of the rope slid to form a loop usually four feet or more in diameter. To toss the lariat, a cowboy grasped both the main line and the loop in his throwing hand *(as at right)*, with the honda about a quarter of the way down the loop for balance. In his other hand he held the coiled remainder of the rope, letting out extra line with his thumb and index finger. The last two fingers of the same hand held the reins in order to guide the cow pony through the quick stops and turns of the roping sequence.

Two kinds of ropes and hondas

The lariat introduced by the vaqueros was made of braided rawhide and was so easy to throw that the average length for one was 60 feet. But it was expensive and a little delicate, and most Americans turned to tough grass. The grass rope was also more practical in that it could easily be knotted to form the honda, while rawhide usually had to be spliced around a piece of cowhorn.

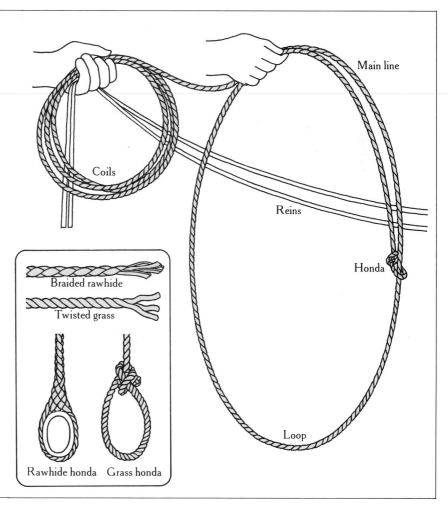

Coils

Braided rawhide

Twisted grass

Rawhide honda   Grass honda

Main line

Reins

Honda

Loop

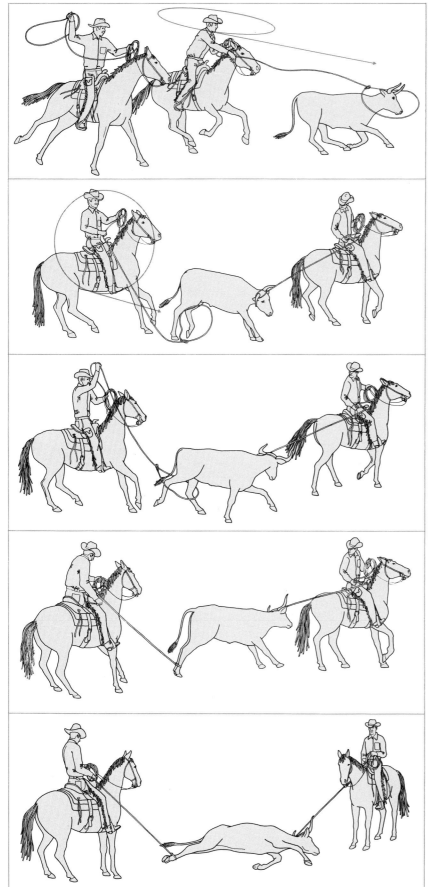

The most common ways of roping were head and heel catches. For a calf one was enough, but with a steer cowboys might team up and use both. Here the lead cowboy makes an overhand toss for the head.

Pulling the loop tight around the steer's horns, the lead cowboy reins in his pony. Another cowhand then rides up behind to make a heel catch, using a sidearm cast to slip the rope under the animal's hind legs.

The second cowboy secures the heel catch by pulling his rope up and back to take out the slack and draw the loop tight. Often in the speed of this maneuver a heel catch might snare only one of the steer's legs.

While the lead roper rides ahead slowly, the second cowboy stops his pony so that the steer is stretched out and topples over. If only one leg has been caught, a cowboy on foot must throw the steer to the ground.

Once the steer is down, other hands can move in to brand it. The riders can even dismount and do the work themselves, leaving their ropes tied to saddle horns while the ponies lean back to hold them taut.

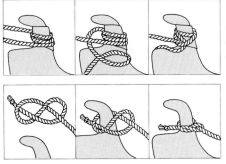

Dallying to hold a calf or steer
Men working in open country held a roped animal by taking a few turns, or dallies, around the saddle horn. When dismounting they locked the rope with a half hitch.

Hard and fast for rough country
In brushy or rocky terrain, where a loosened dally might mean a lost calf, range hands kept the near ends of their ropes tied hard and fast with a figure-8 knot.

THE BRUTAL BUSTING OF A HERD QUITTER

A savagely effective variation of the head catch was used to bring down a steer trying to break out of the herd. The cowhand gallops up behind the steer until he is close enough to drop a head catch over its horns.

Having caught the steer's horns and pulled the slack out of the loop, the cowboy then flips his rope over the animal's flank. Next, he spurs his pony until he is riding at full speed almost directly parallel to the steer.

Now the cowboy turns his pony at a 45° angle away from the steer's path. His rope twists the animal's head back and lifts its hind legs, flipping it over and reversing its direction in a violent corkscrew somersault.

The dazed steer, finding itself facing the herd, would generally get up and trot back to it meekly enough. But occasionally it did not get up at all, for busting did injure or — sometimes — even kill an ornery steer.

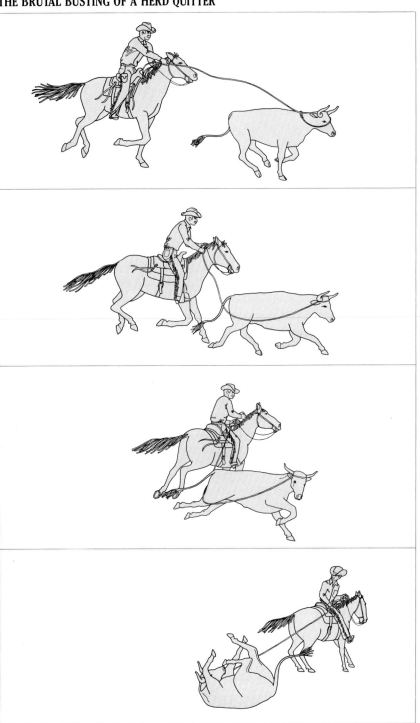

After the relatively easy work—and rough ceremony—of the first day was over, the roundup army divided and the really tough work began. The bigger half of the crew, including the L U Bar wagon, pulled out across the hills and over Sunday Creek to sweep the eastern part of the range as far as the confluence of the Yellowstone and the Missouri. Luke Sweetman, who left the fullest written record of the roundup, did not share in the chores of this so-called east work nor did any other journal-keeper. However, it is fair to assume that Tom Gibson himself took charge of the east range, using wagons from the N Bar N, J Lazy J and Bow and Arrow outfits as well as the L U Bar. And if, as was likely, the east work had the dimensions of other four- to ten-wagon roundups of the time, it included over 60 men with 400 or more horses. Together they gathered herds of 2,000 to 3,000 cattle at a time. With so many men Gibson could throw out a circle of riders covering 700 square miles or more, with the outermost men driving cattle to a relay of hands, who took them on for branding and sorting. And the operation could afford little luxuries, such as tents for the cowboys in rain or cold, a choice of dishes at dinner and even a full-time hand to cut all the firewood—a chore usually rotated among tired men just off their horses.

By contrast, the west work was a one-chuck-wagon affair. To take part in it Luke Sweetman left his home L U Bar wagon, for he had been given the job of repping —a significant token of trust for a cowboy only 18 years old—with the L S Ranch's wagon, the mobile nucleus of the west work. No doubt the men also had a bed wagon, which held bedrolls along with branding irons and other tools. Under the L S foreman, Al Popham, the west-work expedition moved out upstream along the Yellowstone.

Every morning about 3:30 the cook served sowbelly, hot biscuits and coffee. Then the wrangler drove the cavvy into a crude rope corral formed by two heavy lines that were tied at their inner ends to wagon wheels and supported at their middle and outer ends by three-foot forked sticks. As the ponies milled and dodged, each rider roped—from his designated string of six—a good, long-legged distance horse and threw on his saddle. In predawn darkness Popham mapped out the plan of the day's campaign by drawing on the ground with a

When the cowhands went on strike

To most range hands, the bedrock of the cowboy creed was loyalty to the home ranch, coupled with spartan acceptance of every kind of hardship from broken bones to coolie wages. But in March 1883 hands from three large ranches in the Texas Panhandle near the town of Tascosa did the unthinkable: they walked out on strike. Twenty-four men signed the original strike notice (below), but their number quickly grew to about 200, amid dark rumors of range burning and fence cutting. Alas for labor solidarity on the range; the cowboys quickly gambled, guzzled and danced away the strike fund in the saloons of Tascosa. Worse yet, the town was full of drifters willing to work for the standard wage of $30 a month. And that was the wage most of the dissidents accepted, as the strike collapsed and they straggled back to their old jobs.

We, the undersigned cowboys of Canadian River, do by these presents agree to bind ourselves into the following obligations, viz:

First: That we will not work for less than $50. per mo. and we farther more agree no one shall work for less than $50. per mo. after 31st of Mch.

Second: Good cooks shall also receive $50. per mo.

Third: Any one running an outfit shall not work for less than $75. per mo.

Any one violating the above obligations shall suffer the consequences. Those not having funds to pay board after March 31 will be provided for for 30 days at Tascosa.

Thos. Harris	J. A. Marrs
Roy Griffin	Jim Miller
J. W. Peacock	Henry Stoffard
J. L. Howard	Wm. T. Kerr
W. D. Gaton	Bud Davis
B. G. Brown	T. D. Holliday
W. B. Boring	C. F. Goddard
D. W. Peepler	E. E. Watkins
Jas. Jones	C. B. Thompson
C. M. Hullett	G. F. Nickell
A. F. Martin	Juan A. Gomes
Harry Ingerton	J. L. Grissom

stick. He picked a roundup ground at the center of the day's work, and as soon as he did so the chuck wagon made for that place at a smart trot, with the cook cracking his whip and the wrangler driving the cavvy to the rear. Then Popham divided his mounted men into two bands of a dozen each to scour the left and right halves of the terrain ahead.

As the sun threw its first long shadows across the range, the leader of each band led his men out of camp. If the country was flat the men would ride at an angle to the chuck wagon's route, then go parallel to it and finally curve back toward it. Every couple of miles the leader would tell off—that is, station—a rider, so that the two groups together would block out a circle about 20 miles in diameter (*page 122*). Within an hour or two after their departure puffs of dust on the rim of the circle showed that the riders were beginning to find and chase cattle. In theory—and on flat plains in practice—the men with cattle in hand would all head back for the center along lines like the spokes of a wheel, driving and concentrating the scattered cattle, each man coming nearer the next so that by weaving their horses back and forth they could make a cowproof net.

But the country northwest of the Yellowstone River was broken in many places by high, open hills, and the work usually was far less precise and geometrical than the ideal. In going out of or coming into a patch of hills, one rider would often follow the bottom of the branch of a creek while the next rode the ridge between two branches. Getting to the most distant points on the circle required speed; with a change of horses, cowboys riding on circle often logged 35 miles in the morning and as much again in the afternoon, some of them at a lope or gallop.

In this fast, rough riding along the creeks, horses skidded down the hills on their haunches or jumped from ledge to ledge. Cowboys spurred their mounts to spook cattle out of patches of brush or to look into steep-sided ravines, or to top a bench or foothill. The surprised cows usually tossed their tails in the air and agreeably trotted off toward the roundup so that presently little bunches were running together. The bigger the bunches, and the faster they grew, the better, for bosses believed that the real test of a cowboy on roundup was how effective he could be in rousing every last cow out of broken country. They reserved their most intense ha-

tred for stingy ranchers who sent to the roundup second-rate cowboys poorly mounted—men who would not, or could not, work the draws and pockets, thus greatly increasing the number of unrecovered strays. The crew of the west work was happily free of such characters. Some of Popham's men drove back hundreds of cattle apiece, and the collected herd at the end of each day was usually more than a thousand.

As the day herd rumbled near to the wagon, the LS men had to wait for the inevitable milling to die down and for the cows to seek out their calves. Meanwhile the cowhands looked over the gather to see what curiosities it might contain. The bulk, as a rule, were cattle belonging to whatever patch of land the roundup happened to be on, for the line riders of the ranch that owned this land had been doing their best all winter to keep their own brand together. Nonetheless, many cattle inevitably had strayed, some from neighboring districts, a few from clear down in Wyoming.

As soon as the cattle had settled and the whole crew had ridden up to the chuck wagon, ravenous from the morning's ride, the men took their main meal. On roundup the crew generally ate better than punchers on other jobs. By an unwritten law a rancher killed one of his own beeves when the operation was working his land. A good chuck-wagon cook would barbecue the fresh beef, having already spent the early morning preparing an assortment of puddings and pies. After they ate, the men dashed the dregs of their coffee cups on the canvas that covered the water keg so that evaporation would make the contents cool. And every once in a while some merchant's so-called band wagon might catch up with the roundup, whereupon the scene at the chuck wagon became quite festive. In that spring of 1886, for instance, Orschel Brothers sent out one such wagon from Miles City, equipped with hats, gloves, underwear, knickknacks—and a little whiskey.

But these respites could never last very long, for the hard work of the afternoon still lay ahead. After the meal the wrangler again corralled the entire cavvy. This time Sweetman and the others took ponies especially trained for roping and for separating out, or cutting, certain cows and calves from the main herd. These were the most responsible and skillful horses on the range. The best cutting ponies were so alert and intelligent that their riders had little need of reins. In fact, a rider

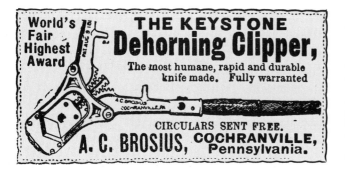
would often drop the reins to the saddle horn and steer his mount with knee pressure alone, aware that over-guidance might distract the horse and break its concentration—which was intense. As soon as the man showed the pony what calf or steer he wanted to pull out of the herd the horse's ears began to twitch, and its eyes would stay glued to the pursued animal while it was being chased toward the branding fire. For the most part both the horses and riders worked as unobtrusively as they could to keep the herd still and the calves with their mothers.

"A horse that knows what is wanted goes quietly through the herd while you are looking for your brand," wrote a Montana cowman named Reginald Aldridge in 1884. "Then, when you have singled out your animal and urged her gently to the edge of the herd, he perceives at once which is the one to be ejected. When you have got her close to the edge, you make a little rush behind her and she runs out; but as likely as not, as soon as she finds herself outside the herd, she tries to

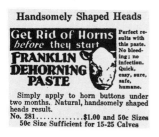
get back again, and makes a sudden wheel to the left to get past you. Instantly your horse turns to the left and runs along between her and the herd so that she cannot get in. Then she tries to dodge in behind you. The moment she turns, your horse stops and wheels around again, always keeping between the cow and the herd till she gives it up and runs out to the cut, where you want her." To aid the work still further, the cutting horse might also encourage the flight of a chased animal by biting it.

The cutting out of a herd followed strict rules of precedence, the same rules that had been observed on the

very first day of the roundup back near Miles City. Whatever outfit seemed to have the most cows in a herd (usually the outfit that owned the range being worked) got first cut and sent in two or three men to haul out its calves. Then Popham judged which brand was the second most numerous, and that outfit's cowboys moved into the herd. And so on. Finally, the reps were waved on to pick out any remaining strays and to chase them as close as possible to the branding fire.

When the calf or unbranded steer got reasonably close to the fire the pursuing cowboy unlimbered his rope *(pages 124-127)* to capture it. A calf might be roped for branding in either of two ways. Ideally, if very close to the fire, it was roped by the hind legs and dragged to the branding iron side-up and all ready. Otherwise it had to be head-roped and then grappled to earth. The bigger steers were team-roped. No matter what animal or which technique was used, roping was the most dangerous single job on the roundup. A line carelessly dallied around a saddle horn could nip off a man's thumb or fingers as some steer pulled the rope taut. In the hurly-burly, men went crashing to the ground with their mounts; others fell off their horses. On a New Mexico roundup one unlucky hand even went over a cliff when a roped steer plunged over the precipice so fast that the horse went with it. But the rope hooked on a stump, and when the dazed cowboy looked up from the gully he saw both horse and steer, suspended side by side, rotating gently.

Such occurrences were happily uncommon, and the

men assigned to branding waited in the dust and heat by the fire for the roped animals to be brought up. "You would have to holler to make a man hear you, that was right at you, and before you got your mouth shut again it and your throat would be filled with dust and smoke from the burning hair," recalled S. R. Cooper, a Texas cowboy. If a calf came in head-roped, a flanker dashed out from the group of half a dozen men

around the fire and walked down the taut rope until he got a hand on the noose at the neck. Then he flipped the rope off, reached over the calf's back, grabbed a fistful of loose skin on the side and pulled, at the same time kneeing the near foreleg out from under the scared animal. Down went the calf with the wind knocked out of it, and while the man who threw it sat on its head, another pushed the underside hind leg forward with a booted foot and pulled the topside hind leg with his hands. Thus the calf's skin lay stretched smooth for the iron and his scrotum, if it was a male, exposed to the cowboy's knife for castration.

The branding fire, fueled by wood dragged up from the creek bed with a rope hitched to a saddle horn, was only campfire-hot, for irons heated beyond a dull red burned too deep and set hair afire. An even brand, one that took off the outer layer of skin and left it the color of a new saddle, was thought to be about right. When the brander pressed the iron home the calf usually loosed one loud and anguished "baw-w-w-w!" — for branding hurt. "I told one fellow," said D. J. O'Malley, a Montana cowboy, "if he would sit in his bare skin on a red hot stove for a minute he could form a pretty good idea as to how a calf felt when a hot iron was putting a brand into his side." The pace of the branding was fast; the average was about 300 calves an afternoon. One Marias River, Montana, crew in 1885 branded 130 calves in an hour, supplied by just two cutters hauling the beasts out of the herd.

As the work proceeded, the branders ran into various minor problems on the markings — and solved them promptly. If an L U Bar calf accidentally got an L S brand, the crew righted things by branding the next L S cow's calf with an L U Bar. Then they gave both babies proper jaw brands that would clarify for later range riders or buyers why a calf might appear to be sucking the wrong mother. Sometimes a cow turned up with a brand no cowboy knew, but Popham had the Montana Stockgrowers' just-published brand book with him and could look up the unfamiliar marking. Among the branding irons were stamps for all the well-known local ranches, and curves and straights for copying others. Thus cowmen hundreds of miles away would have marked for them — and eventually brought home by reps — stock they did not even know they owned.

At the moment of branding, cowpunchers often cut

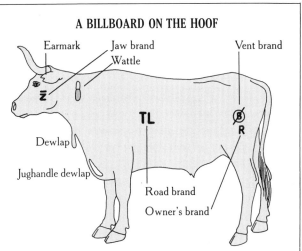

A BILLBOARD ON THE HOOF

A range cow was often a walking billboard of marks from hot irons and sharp knives. These marks could appear almost anywhere on the animal, but the locations shown here were common. From its first owner it often got a hip brand (and a jaw brand if the original was unclear or incorrect). A trail driver later marked its side with a road brand. A subsequent purchaser might mark out (or vent) the old hip brand and burn his own nearby. Since brands were hard to read in herds, cattle also bore knife cuts (wattles, dewlaps or earmarks) on their necks, throats, briskets and ears.

an earmark on a calf as an additional way of identifying the animal. The ear could be notched or cropped on the top, bottom or end in more than 200 variations known by such names as "under bits," "over hack," "sharp" and "steeple fork." To make still another mark of identification, some cowmen also sliced the dewlap, the pendulous skin under the cow's throat, so that a fold hung down a couple of inches.

Though it was not a necessary part of the roundup job, the men at the fire were always prepared to undertake some rough-and-ready doctoring of any infected animals that turned up. They were not vets, but they could and did treat lump jaw, sores or open wounds with a variety of salves and ointments. They might also need to do a little judicious dehorning. Long horns on a rambunctious steer could endanger other animals, while misshapen horns could curve backward and injure their owner, and the crew stood ready to meet these problems with clippers, ax or saw.

As the afternoon wore on, branded, doctored and dehorned cattle scampered away from the fire. At the fire itself, cutoff scrotums and parts of ears, tossed into a bucket and later counted, served as an added check on the number of cattle that had been branded. But the primary responsibility for this figure, and for the totals of individual brands, fell to a full-time tallyman, who penciled marks into a notebook. The marks might appear mystifying to a layman, but this served as a quick and easy inventory list to a cowhand. In the District 8 roundup the tallyman had the further task of selecting eight promising baby bulls for every 100 heifers; these bulls were spared from castration in order to ensure an adequate supply of future sires.

Toward the end of each afternoon's branding, small bunches of guarded cattle formed around the main, or day, herd, which was kept together to move on to the next day's roundup. One of these bunches contained the local range's branded calves and their mothers, both carefully prevented from returning to the main herd. And there was also a bunch of throwback steers, cows and calves being held until they could be driven back to their own ranges, which the roundup crews had already passed by. Holding the cut—that is, circling these bunches—was irritating work, because the gregarious animals kept trying to join the big herd. Frequently the riders had to race after a bolting steer and turn him back. One trick in keeping each of the cuts together was to find some placid cow willing to stand quietly in a cut and serve as a nucleus.

When all the calves and mothers had been cut from the herd, an unidentifiable calf or two often remained as a kind of orphaned residue. These leppies, or dogies —calves lost by their mothers or temporarily separated from them—were mavericks, or mavericks in the making. And in the fast-profit atmosphere of Northern ranching in the mid-1880s, mavericks were immediately taken in hand as potentially marketable beef. Popham and his men branded such calves with the mark of the range upon which they were found (some cattlemen's associations branded mavericks with the association brand and then auctioned them for money to pay association expenses). Finally the riders cut out branded steers and heifers that belonged on the local range. Yelling and firing six-shooters, the punchers drove these cattle, along with the newly branded calves and their mothers, away from the line of march so that they would graze on their own land.

Toward the end of each afternoon the wagon moved on to a night camp, and after the branding was done the crew and the cattle of the main herd jogged toward this camp through the slanting sunlight. While a few men circled the herds, the others ate their final meal of the day after 15 or more hours in the saddle. A few unlucky riders prepared to guard the cattle in shifts through the night, and the rest of the crew bedded down.

A cowboy's bed was his own private retreat on the range. As Will James reported, it was likely to contain tobacco sacks, cigarette paper, buckskin and leather, a marlinespike, perhaps a picture of the cowboy's girl, some old letters, magazines, shirts, underwear, socks, a clean suit, an extra pair of boots, soiled clothes, a spare cinch and a rope, all weighing as much as 150 pounds. Laid in soft grass on dry, cool ground, a bedroll could be a cozy place. The prairie nights could be beautiful, too, their sounds soothing. "You can even hear the ponies bite off the short, crisp grass and chew it," recalled one Wyoming cowhand.

However, like any sleep-out, nights on roundup tended to be better in the remembrance than in the actual experience. On hard ground, cushioned by no more than a soogan (quilt), sleep was brief and likely to be broken. Near prairie sloughs in late spring, men half suffocated with tarps over their heads to fend off mosquitoes (these insects could settle so thickly on a roan gelding as to make him appear gray; and, flying away, leave him streaked with blood). Unfortunately, the tarp —seven feet wide and 16 feet long so that it wrapped around to serve as both top and bottom of the bed —might keep out oxygen but it never kept out driving rain. This meant that after any real downpour every man was sleeping in soaked blankets.

Whether the night had been cold or damp or both, the hands on that roundup of 1886 invariably woke to a day that was coming on to be scorching hot. Working every creek through endless burning days (the weather shaped up as a full-scale drought later in the year), the men recalled that the year before their problem had been steady rain, mud and floods, and complained bitterly: Wasn't the weather ever just right? Of course, it wasn't. In hot weather, by noon or late in the day, a far-swinging rider was plagued by thirst. "I have many times been glad to lie down and take a few swallows from an old cow track, made in the mud sometime previously and still holding a few drops of moisture," said

The heraldry of the branding iron

Arizona cowpuncher Evans Coleman once remarked that he knew cowhands "who could neither read nor write, but who could name any brand, either letters or figures, on a cow." A brand was the key to ownership in a business where ownership was everything. Many cattlemen, in fact, named their ranches after their brands and held the symbol in as proud esteem as did any knight his crest. Branding was an ancient practice before the first cow came to America. Certain 4,000-year-old tomb paintings show Egyptians branding their fat, spotted cattle. Hernando Cortés burned crosses on the hides of the small herd he brought with him to Mexico. The vaqueros passed the custom on to U.S. cowboys, who developed and refined their own calligraphy.

On any 19th Century ranch the greenest cowhand quickly mastered the three major elements of the branding alphabet *(below)*. He learned to read the components of a brand in correct order: from left to right, from top to bottom, or from outside to inside (a T inside a diamond translates as Diamond T, not T Diamond). In time he could pick out any one of hundreds of markings in a milling herd; a good cowboy, said Coleman, could understand "the Constitution of the United States were it written with a branding iron on the side of a cow."

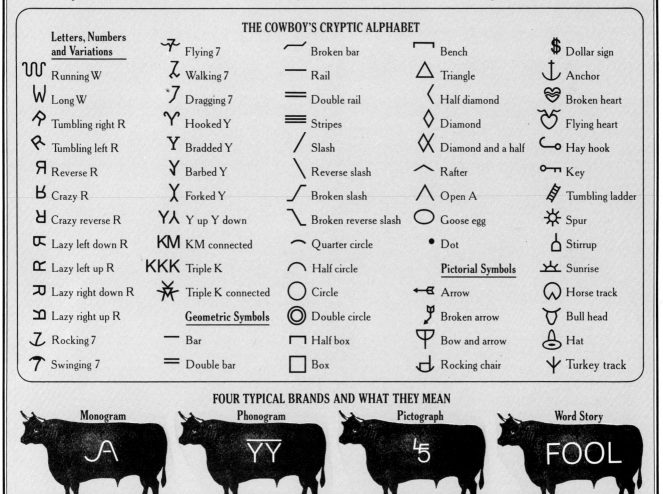

THE COWBOY'S CRYPTIC ALPHABET

Letters, Numbers and Variations

Running W	Flying 7	Broken bar
Long W	Walking 7	Rail
Tumbling right R	Dragging 7	Double rail
Tumbling left R	Hooked Y	Stripes
Reverse R	Bradded Y	Slash
Crazy R	Barbed Y	Reverse slash
Crazy reverse R	Forked Y	Broken slash
Lazy left down R	Y up Y down	Broken reverse slash
Lazy left up R	KM connected	Quarter circle
Lazy right down R	Triple K	Half circle
Lazy right up R	Triple K connected	Circle
Rocking 7	**Geometric Symbols**	Double circle
Swinging 7	Bar	Half box
	Double bar	Box

Bench	Dollar sign
Triangle	Anchor
Half diamond	Broken heart
Diamond	Flying heart
Diamond and a half	Hay hook
Rafter	Key
Open A	Tumbling ladder
Goose egg	Spur
Dot	Stirrup
Pictorial Symbols	Sunrise
Arrow	Horse track
Broken arrow	Bull head
Bow and arrow	Hat
Rocking chair	Turkey track

FOUR TYPICAL BRANDS AND WHAT THEY MEAN

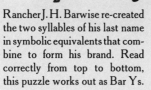

Monogram

Charles Goodnight's simple and famous JA brand spells out the initials of his partner John Adair. The running curves have a practical purpose: sharp angles tend to blotch and blur the brand.

Phonogram

Rancher J. H. Barwise re-created the two syllables of his last name in symbolic equivalents that combine to form his brand. Read correctly from top to bottom, this puzzle works out as Bar Ys.

Pictograph

A gunslinger turned rancher arrived in the West with nothing but two .45-caliber pistols to his name. Later, when he made good as a cattleman, those two guns were memorialized in his brand.

Word Story

"A man's a fool to raise cattle," said Texan T. J. Walker, and he took the word for his brand. Fun-loving cowpunchers with running irons would sometimes rope his bulls and change the F to a B.

Cowboys on roundup often carried notebook lists of the brands and earmarks likely to be found on cattle. This 1886 roster recorded the various brands from three neighboring ranges in northern Montana.

one Colorado hand. He drank as well from drying water holes "that would become thick with hair and dead animals, and also with all kinds of insects and refuse."

The west riders on the great Montana roundup of 1886 also had a special problem of sorts. Day after day a silent crew of six-gun-toting cowboys ghosted along right behind the roundup's line of march. This was the STV outfit, to which the Montana Stockgrowers Association had denied participation in the roundup because it had put 3,500 Texas cattle to graze on ranges north of the Yellowstone that were already close to the point of being overgrazed.

Boycotts like this took place all over the West as big cattlemen who had grabbed government land tried to prevent smaller newcomers from doing the same — or from sharing in grazing rights. In 1883 the 20 outfits that divided up the 3.9-million-acre Musselshell Range in Montana published a notice reading: "We consider the said range already overstocked; therefore we positively decline allowing any outside parties or any parties locating herds upon this range to join us in any roundup." The General Land Office agent for the region wrote Washington that this tactic was "quite as effective as fencing the entire tract." And when Texas cowmen asked the federal government to establish a national cattle trail running from Texas to the northern ranges, the Northerners flatly vetoed the project. Said a Montana newspaper, slangily but to the point: "We-uns just got pie enough to go around, and ain't got none to spare for you-uns. See?"

Such tactics did not always work. The attempt to boycott the STV outfit at the 1886 Montana roundup failed, because the STV's owner John H. Conrad of Fort Benton, Montana, decided to ignore it. He instructed his boys to follow the L S wagon within easy sight. Each afternoon, as the official roundup cast loose the herd that had been cut, STV punchers, who had been watching the work motionless on their mounts, looked over the freed cows and invariably found a few of their cattle. With even greater effrontery, STV men followed the roundup's cowboys on circle. When, for example, Sweetman, out cattle hunting, found one of the STV brand, he had no alternative but to drive it away, and the STV man, shadowing him, took it under control. Thus, without belonging to the roundup, the STV outfit benefited from it. As Sweetman observed, there was no real way to prevent a man from riding a rod or two away from the circle, "especially when he is armed." And in any case, he added, "It all happened on Uncle Sam's land."

At Little Porcupine Creek, the western border of his assigned sweep, Popham joined the roundup wagons for District 10, and moving together they both worked north for a few days.

Gradually the roundup doubled back toward the range of the L U Bar. Luke Sweetman found many cattle of his own brand, and during the hard-riding days he pushed them back over the hills toward home. On balance, he enjoyed the prestige and independence of repping; reps felt that they had more fun and met more people than other cowboys did.

Soon the L S wagon got to the divide between the Yellowstone and the Missouri, broke off from the District 10 gang and threw in for many days with the roundup of District 9. Together the two groups searched the Big and Little Dry Creeks and all their tributaries. As part of this work, Popham sent a crew with pack horses northwest to the Missouri tributaries called Squaw Creek and Hell Creek, which ran through country too rugged for a wagon. As Sweetman later recalled it, in the stiff rhetoric of his mature years, the men "penetrated those variegated, inaccessible nightmares of disturbed earth and brought out cattle that had not even been seen by man for over two years."

With this final task the men of the west work had finished their duties for that spring of 1886. And a formidable achievement it had been finding, roping and branding a fair share of the total of more than a million head. In the fall, beginning about September 1, the whole roundup process would be repeated, partly to gather and ship the marketable beef, partly to brand any calves that might have been missed in the spring. Indeed, if too many calves had been missed, the ranchers might decide to hold a second roundup right away. However, the range hands in the west were smugly certain that no foreman would be calling them back to District 8 this spring. For what a bunch of skilled cowpunchers could do, these men had done. In cowboy argot they had "covered the dog" — that is, they rousted out every single head of cattle from the tough territory assigned to them. It had been, as Luke Sweetman was proud to record in his journal, "a perfect job."

5 | The long, long trail

To the cowboy of the Old West, nothing was more challenging, or miserable, than the unique and short-lived phenomenon called the long drive. It was the climactic event of his working life, the chance to prove his prowess by chivying great herds of longhorns from the home range, where beeves were worth four dollars, to a point of sale where they might bring $40 a head.

The high time of the drives lasted only about 20 years, from the end of the Civil War to the mid-1880s. In that brief era 10 million cows walked the trails from Texas to railheads in Kansas and Missouri. Many of these went farther, into Wyoming and Canada, to be sold as brood stock rather than as beef for Eastern food markets.

A small herd might number no more than 500 head; the biggest ever to hit the trail included 15,000 animals that moved out of Texas in 1869. And once during the spring floods of 1871, when a great many herds got jammed up at a river crossing, no fewer than 60,000 head of cattle were crowded together into a single milling, mooing mass. Whatever the size of the herd, each drive seemed to generate its special measure of toil or trouble. Steers would drown in sinkholes at the river crossings. Indians constantly tried to beg or steal cows. Settlers drove the herds from their fields with guns. A clap of thunder might set off a stampede during which half a dozen calves would be trampled. There was rarely enough water for the cattle and never enough sleep for the weary cowhands. When one cowboy commented on this his trail boss snarled, "What the hell are you kicking about? You can sleep all winter when you get to Montana."

A drive of Herefords plods through the snow under the eye of a Wyoming cowpoke, bundled in his goat-hair chaps and sheepskin jacket. This photograph was taken after 1900, when chunkier shorthorn cattle had replaced the longhorn.

Plunging down an embankment, the Spur Ranch's thirsty herd wallows into a stream near Roaring Springs, Texas. On long drives through the driest country cattle could smell a watering place when they were still 10 miles from it.

The cattle drive: a hard way to earn a hundred dollars

First light on the prairie on a June night in 1879. On the Chisholm Trail beyond the northern Texas border the eastern glow reveals a chuck wagon surrounded by sleeping forms and one man — the cook — at work with pots and pans. The silence breaks: the cook bellows his daily predawn warning that if the cowboys do not rise he will take bacon, beans and biscuits and throw them into the creek.

One of the hands, a 19-year-old redhead named Baylis John Fletcher, stirs, sits up in his undershirt and groans. Getting up is agony on this particular morning, for it has been barely three hours since Fletcher came off his shift as night guard over the cattle. Like all cowboys on the trail he never seems to get enough sleep. Besides his grogginess, Fletcher's ankles still ache with the inflammatory rheumatism that he picked up lately, he believes, from drinking gyp water, the heavily alkaline dregs of a prairie stream. His lower legs are swollen so badly that he has to slit the sides of his boots in order to get them on.

Out in the dying night the two men of the last guard still ride their opposite circles around the bedded herd of 2,500 cattle. Fletcher and the other five newly roused cowboys pull on their pants and boots, wet their faces with water from the spigot of the barrel on the wagon, dry with a community towel and button on wool shirts. Some — including Fletcher, who was taught to be neat by the maiden aunt who raised him — even go so far as to comb their hair.

The trail boss, George Arnett, a former Confederate soldier and Indian fighter, decides that today he will drive the herd to the South Canadian River, which bi-

His bandanna pulled over his mouth as a mask against choking dust, a cowhand riding behind a trail herd keeps stragglers moving with stinging flicks of his rope.

sects, on a west-east course, the Indian Territory separating Texas and Kansas. It is still only quarter past 5, with the boys swallowing the last of their hot black coffee, when the sun rises, the refracted light making it appear to be coming up from a hole in the dead-flat horizon. The wrangler, who has been out gathering up the mounts, drives them into a corral even more temporary than the ones used at roundup: in this case two cowboys stretching ropes tied to the wagon's wheels. Each man catches out a horse for the morning either by roping it or simply walking up and slipping on a bridle. Two of the cowboys ride out to relieve the men of the last guard. The men who have just been spelled gallop up to gobble their breakfast and to change horses.

Now the cattle are getting lightly to their feet in the one swift, graceful motion peculiar to the longhorn. Normally the hands move the cattle right onto the trail at dawn to take advantage of the cool air and also to keep the animals from walking in dew-laden pasturage, which tends to soften their hooves. But Mr. Arnett (the men always call the boss "Mister") is pleased to see that on this particular morning the buffalo grass is pretty dry, and he rules that the herd will be allowed to graze, while drifting north, until 9 o'clock.

Into the chuck wagon the men throw their billowy bedrolls, tarp-enclosed quilts. Then, with the smoke-blackened Dutch ovens clanging like dissonant bells, the cook — a Mexican named Manuel García — stows the chuck box at the back end of the wagon and drives off through the cattle toward the noon rendezvous that Arnett, riding ahead of crew and herd, will find.

At 9 the men begin to throw the cattle on the trail by closing in on the broad drift of animals and squeezing them into a ragged line of march: "Ho cattle ho ho ho ho." The cowhands on the rear and sides hold firm, chasing back any strays and pressing the rest; the men in front make an opening up the trail. This is a mixed

Cowboys on a drive advance in formation as shown in this diagram. While the trail boss rode ahead to scout for water and pasture, the cowhands rotated among the other positions.

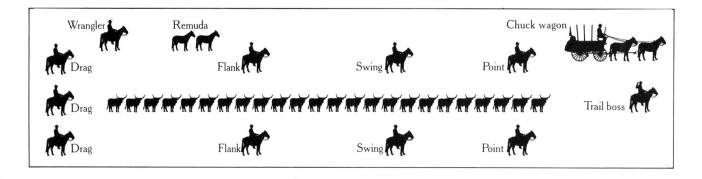

herd of cows and calves, which tends to drive poorly because the mothers and young wander around looking for one another, calling in mournful groans like the notes of a pipe organ. To make the drive more orderly Arnett has brought along a few steers as leaders. These now move naturally to the head, and the cows and the calves fall in. The column narrows to a dozen head, lengthens, then stretches into a two-mile line four or five abreast.

Fletcher rides on the left flank of the herd this morning. The men have found it fair to take turns at the various positions (above) designated to keep control of the moving cattle, the worst job falling to the drag riders, who come at the rear, breathing dust through bandannas as they harass lame cattle and weak, orphaned yearlings to make them keep up. By the end of the day the herd will be 10 or 12 miles closer to its destination in southeastern Wyoming, where it will be sold as brood stock, having grown fatter on the rich prairie grass as it worked its way north.

This early summer morning marked the second month and five hundredth mile for Fletcher and his fellow hands on the grandest and most grueling adventure the cowboy life offered—the long drive. They had started from southern Texas, where the natives chattered in Spanish accents and the air smelled of salt from the Gulf of Mexico. In another 700 miles they would be in Wyoming, where pine-scented winds tumbled down from the snow-covered crest of the Rockies. At trail's end in Wyoming they would have been in the saddle every day for four months, having sweated through a formidable, perilous, whole-souled experience that turned smooth-faced youngsters like Baylis John Fletcher into fully breveted cowboys. For more than two thirds of the 1,200-mile journey, they

were to follow the main north-trending route of the cattle drives, the old Chisholm Trail.

The Chisholm was named after a Scotch-Cherokee trader, Jesse Chisholm, who had carved out part of the path as a straight, level wagon road, with easy river fords between southcentral Kansas and his trading post on the Canadian River. It had opened as a cattle trail in 1867; in five years more than a million head had gone clumping and bawling up the road, which by then had been trampled in places to a width of 200 to 400 yards and had been cut by erosion below the level of the plains it crossed. Beside it lay the bones of cows killed in stampedes and of calves shot at birth because they could not keep up with the drives. There were the bones of humans, too, interred in shallow graves—a drowned man pulled out next to a river crossing, or an early-day trail hand or settler cut down by Indians. Every man who set out knew the risks and knew that on the trail he was considered less valuable than the cows he drove. "Look out for the cows' feet and the horses' backs and let the cowhands and the cook take care of themselves" was the trail bosses' slogan.

Yet the cowboys went eagerly, many of them no more than boys testing themselves against the unknown as other young men had always done by going off to war or shipping out before the mast. Never mind that to the profit-motivated cattle barons the long drive was only a means of moving masses of beef to market at the cost of a mere penny or so per mile per head. Never mind that the harsh realities of trail life could degrade a man to the point of forcing him to lick horse sweat from a saddle when the chuck wagon ran out of salt. And never mind, either, that in return for three to four months of dust, thirst, blisters, cold and danger the cowboy received a paltry $100 in hard wages—barely the price

Before starting on the long drives, cattle bosses
picked up handy trail guides offered free by the
various Western railroads as a means of pro-
moting their profitable beef-hauling business.

of a new hat and a fancy pair of boots. There were, of course, some compensations: the comradeship of the trail, the epic sight of great brown rivers of cattle on the move (on a single day in 1883 a trail hand standing on a mound near the North Platte River saw, in a sweep of the horizon, the dust of 28 herds), the satisfaction of passing the toughest test in the trade and per- haps, too, a proud awareness of being part of something fundamental and grand. It was challenges and emotions such as these, coupled in some cases with the sheer necessity of finding a job—any job, no matter how hard—that drew onto the trail youngsters like the "Texas lad of pioneer days," as Bay- lis Fletcher described himself.

Fletcher hired out in the spring of 1879. His em- ployer was a celebrated and enterprising Texas drover named Tom Snyder, who usually rode with his herds but for this drive had hired Arnett as trail boss. Snyder was a pious and cautious man. He did not allow his trail hands to curse. Nor did he want his cattle sloppily handled, so he hired cowboys at the ratio of 1 for each 250 head of cattle, even though some drovers thought that 1 for 400 was enough. Wages ran around $30 a month "and found" (that is, with food) for cowboys; less than $30 for the lowly horse wrangler, who dou- bled as a clean-up and errand boy for the cook; $100 for the trail boss; and something in between for the cook, in recognition of his role as den mother to the hands. To carry the crew Snyder had bought a remount herd, or remuda, of 80 horses at $15 each. He had also supplied a wagon, to be sold along with the horses and cows in the North.

The 10-man outfit had picked up the 2,500 cattle —an average-sized trail herd—the first week in April at Green Ranch just north of Corpus Christi. As the hands swung into the final preparations for the drive, chasing strays and rooting out reluctant cows from river- bottom thickets, Fletcher began to take careful note of the duties and details of the trail crew's life. Later his recollections were published in a memoir that survives

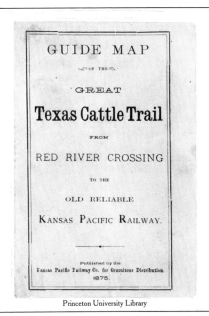

GUIDE MAP
OF THE
GREAT
Texas Cattle Trail
FROM
RED RIVER CROSSING
TO THE
OLD RELIABLE
KANSAS PACIFIC RAILWAY.

Published by the
Kansas Pacific Railway Co. for Gratuitous Distribution.
1875.

Princeton University Library

as a remarkable account of the drudging day-by-day adventure of the long drive.

When, as Fletcher reported, all the cattle were finally in hand, the men headed them through a chute and, poking a smoking iron between the rails, burned in a road brand—in this case a T L—to mark them as trail cattle. This trail branding was a prudent custom developed by drovers who frequently moved herds made up of cattle from several ranch- es with differing brands. The added road brand on their side marked them as belonging to a single, legit- imate trail herd rather than a mixed bag of rustled strays.

On the night before Fletcher's bunch pointed the cat- tle north, they hired some Mexican guitar pickers and staged a rollicking stag dance at the ranch, each cow- boy waltzing, as Fletcher later wrote with amusement, "in the warm embrace of another wearing spurs, leather leggings, and broad-brimmed sombreros."

The next morning, April 11, they were launched on the long drive's first leg—a 50-day, 400-mile trek just to get out of Texas. The start was by no means smooth. Second day out, while the herd was being cautiously guided through the streets of Victoria, a splenetic old woman flapped her sunbonnet at the passing cattle to keep them off her roses, whereupon the lead steers stam- peded back against the followers, who scattered at a dead run. Longhorns flashed in every street, and the cit- izenry vanished indoors as the cows rushed and dashed without direction. No one was hurt, but it took Arnett and his boys a couple of hours to stop the cattle, line them up and get them marching again. As often hap- pens with trail cattle, this initial stampede made them spooky. That night, they stampeded by fits and starts from midnight until almost dawn, with every cowhand in the saddle and thoroughly exhausted by morning.

It was a bad beginning made worse a few nights later. Fletcher and his night-guard partner, in dereliction of duty, were dismounted and warming themselves around a fire when suddenly the bedded cattle jumped to their feet and took off in another rumbling stampede.

The two cowboys cringed behind an oak, around which the steers divided so closely that they raked the bark off with their horns. When the cattle had passed, Fletcher got on his horse, galloped to the head of the stampede and turned the leaders back so that the herd took the shape of a rotating wheel, which gradually slowed and stopped. Next morning 100 cows were missing. Four hard-looking men rode up and offered to find the cattle for one dollar a head. George Arnett, guessing correctly that he was dealing with the men who had started the stampede, offered 50 cents. The men accepted, but managed to bring back only 60 head. Arnett's trail scouts brought in another 20 strays, leaving 20 cows that had been successfully — but unprovably — rustled.

The following Saturday night the herd stampeded while bedded down in one of the corrals that southern Texas ranchers rented to trail herders in settled country. This time there were no rustlers or any other apparent cause. The cattle just ran, breaking out of the corral and giving all hands one more grim night in the saddle. In the melee Fletcher lost that proudest of all cowboy possessions, his hat. Next day he found a country store that carried hats, but the sanctimonious owner would under no circumstances sell a hat on the Sabbath. So Fletcher went bareheaded — an almost unendurable state for a cowboy — until the next day, when he finally got a replacement.

It was well that he did. Two weeks later, with the herd in central Texas, the sky opened up with a cannonade of hailstones as big as quail eggs, pelting birds and rabbits to death and raising welts on the men so bruising and numerous that later the skin sloughed off. The storm caused the herd to drift off the trail and scatter; the whole crew had to ride in front of the drift and press the animals back into line. Meanwhile the remuda stampeded, two horses disappearing for good. This was the only hailstorm of the trip, for which Baylis Fletcher was duly grateful. Working out on the treeless prairie, with no natural shelter to hide under, cowboys dreaded hail; a man could take shelter only by quickly dismounting and covering his head with his saddle. Hail was only one of the harsh-weather hazards. Another was snow, for a blizzard sweeping down from the North could hit south Texas as late in the year as May. One such storm in 1874 struck a drive with such savagery that all 78 horses in the remuda froze to death.

Four days after the hailstorm the herd approached Fort Worth, the biggest town (1879 population was 6,500) on the Chisholm. Drummers for the outfitting stores downtown rode out to greet the herd and try to sell chuck-wagon groceries to the boss. Encouraged by the other cowboys, one of the older hands met the first salesman to arrive and, pretending to be the trail boss, accepted blandishments of cigars and whiskey. By prearrangement another hand then galloped up, yelling at him, "The boss says come on you lazy cuss and get to work, or he'll turn you off at Fort Worth." The cowboys yelped with glee at this rare and precious success in buncoing a city slicker. Boss Arnett, who was watching from the sidelines with a quiet smile, made it up to the drummers by buying two months' provisions.

The next 100 miles north of Fort Worth were easy, three weeks of good grass and quiet weather. But then loomed a barrier of critical significance to every cowboy driving north from Texas: the Red River. Like most of the other half a dozen major streams on the Great Plains, the Red River flows west to east. The main cattle trails went north and south. These inconvenient geographical facts forced the cowboy, usually pictured as dry and thirsty and covered with alkali dust, to spend many hours half naked and up to his neck in brown water, trying not to lose any animals in crossing. Or cowboys. For these rivers all had headwaters in the distant Western mountains, where unseen storms could, without warning, send floods surging across the trail fords. A river six inches deep might rise to 25 feet in a day's time. With good luck big rivers like the Red were usually low enough to be waded. The cowboys hated deep water. Few were good in it; many could not swim at all. And they took only scant comfort from the fact that their cow ponies were strong swimmers, capable of striking across the deep spots with a man clinging to the pommel or even sitting in the saddle.

The Red River represented special hazards — physical, geographical and psychological. Here the men and cattle left the protection of the law of the state of Texas and entered The Nations, the Indian Territory (now eastern Oklahoma) settled by Cherokees, Creeks, Seminoles, Choctaws and Chickasaws, and crisscrossed by several of the notorious warrior tribes, most notably the fierce Kiowas and Comanches. Here, at the rough border village of Red River Station that squatted on the

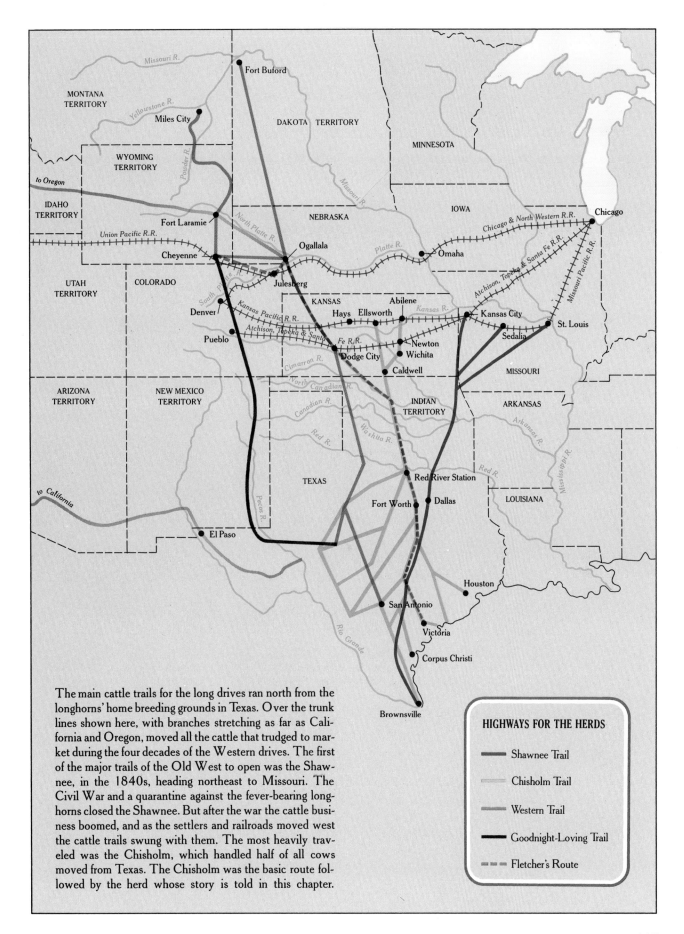

The main cattle trails for the long drives ran north from the longhorns' home breeding grounds in Texas. Over the trunk lines shown here, with branches stretching as far as California and Oregon, moved all the cattle that trudged to market during the four decades of the Western drives. The first of the major trails of the Old West to open was the Shawnee, in the 1840s, heading northeast to Missouri. The Civil War and a quarantine against the fever-bearing longhorns closed the Shawnee. But after the war the cattle business boomed, and as the settlers and railroads moved west the cattle trails swung with them. The most heavily traveled was the Chisholm, which handled half of all cows moved from Texas. The Chisholm was the basic route followed by the herd whose story is told in this chapter.

HIGHWAYS FOR THE HERDS

— Shawnee Trail
— Chisholm Trail
— Western Trail
— Goodnight-Loving Trail
--- Fletcher's Route

145

Running blind alongside cattle stampeded by a nighttime thundersquall, a cowhand gallops toward the head of the herd to turn the animals by riding in against the leaders.

147

Texas bank at the easiest ford, the boss weeded out any bad actors in the crew and hired new hands. And here, most particularly, was the river itself, underlaid with quicksand, the streamside trees bearing tangles of driftwood in their high branches, marking the high water of past floods. A scattering of rude graves near the Station held the bodies of men who had been killed while attempting to make the crossing.

A trail boss tried to ford or swim his herd across a river like the Red in the same formation used on the trail. Some of the cows seemed to take downright pride in their swimming—"proud as swans," as one cowpuncher said. "All you can see is the tips of their horns and the ends of their noses." Even calves plunged fearlessly in, their little heads next to their mothers.

But it was a rare crossing that went smoothly. Quicksand often mired the cattle. In such a plight a cow might sink millimetrically for a day, until at last its nose went under. Usually, however, the cowboys were able to rescue the trapped animal by a difficult and risky procedure. Because the cow's extended legs stuck like anchors in the quicksand, cowhands had to burrow around each leg, double it at the knee and tie it. Thus trussed, a cow could be pulled out by four or five horses roped to the horns, or by the raised wheel of the

chuck wagon used as a capstan with the rope turned around the hub. If in the process a truss broke or slipped, the animal might come out of the quicksand with a whole leg pulled off. Then the only recourse was to put the maimed creature out of its agony with a bullet.

Once past the quicksand and into deep water the cattle might panic or start to mill, turning into a turbulent confusion of horns and heads and bodies pushed under, with many of the animals threatened by drowning. This happened during the 1871 season when the Red River was so badly flooded by the spring thaw that 60,000 head of cattle had jammed the Texas bank waiting for a chance to cross. A cowhand who was there described it: "The litter of heavy brush and broken trees sweeping by gave you the feeling that, for hundreds of miles, everything that grew had been plucked out by the roots and sent swirling and bobbing down." At last this man's impatient boss pushed his herd into the choppy, red-brown water. Halfway across they went into a mill, swimming in a circle. The cowboy stripped to his underwear, swam his horse to the mill and jumped "right onto the cattle. They were so jammed together that it was like walking on a raft of logs. When I got to the only real big steer in the bunch on the yon side, I mounted him and he pulled for the shore." The herd followed,

Leaders of the long drives

"Our leaders were a pair of prairie steers named Broad and Crump," recalled cowhand Alonzo Mitchell, in deference to a pair of canny longhorns that had walked like drill sergeants at the head of a drove going up the Chisholm Trail to Kansas. Such bovine leaders were common on a drive. Indeed in virtually every herd the first day out a few dominant steers marched instinctively to the lead and stayed there. The other cows followed—across gullies, through rivers. Trail hands freely conceded it was the lead steers' initiative as much as the cowhands' prodding that kept the animals moving.

At the railhead these longhorned

Pied Pipers usually went the way of the other cows—straight into the loading pens headed for slaughter. A few, however, proved so valuable on the trail that they were spared to lead again. Best known was Charles Goodnight's Old Blue, which during eight seasons led some 10,000 head to Dodge City. En route he wore a bell around his neck the sound of which other cows soon learned to follow. At night Old Blue would wander freely into camp and mooch handouts from the doting cowboys. After his last drive he retired to a comfortable pasture, and when he finally died at age 20 his horns were mounted in the Goodnight ranch office.

to the everlasting luck of the trail boss, for the mass of cattle remaining on the south bank all stampeded. It took the 350 men in the other trail crews 10 days to cut the mixed cattle into the more than 30 original herds backed up there.

Fletcher and the TL herd caught the Red River when it was low and fordable but still ready to mete out a measure of trouble. In midcrossing, with the herd moving nicely and the river apparently mastered, the cook stopped his wagon to fill the water barrel. The whole rig promptly sank to its axles in quicksand. The draft oxen, straining and twisting, ripped off the wagon tongue. Turning carpenters, the cowboys cut a cottonwood pole and sloshed into the water to bolt it to the wagon as a substitute tongue. Then they borrowed two more yoke of oxen from another outfit waiting at the crossing. Together the six straining animals managed to drag the wagon across, while Baylis Fletcher and the other cowboys lined out the herd on the far bank for the drive through the Indian Territory.

As a reasonably well-educated young fellow, Baylis Fletcher knew everything about Indians that could possibly be learned from having read the novels of James Fenimore Cooper. Like other cowboys, he had seen or heard of an occasional trailside mound headed by a nameless board reading, "Killed by Indians." Rustling by Indians was still fairly common. At night the Comanches, particularly bold, would creep toward a herd, then suddenly stand up and wave buffalo blankets to stampede the cows. Later they would make off with some of the scattered animals. James Baker, another Texas cowboy who went on the long drive in 1870, wrote this account of a typical Indian raid: "We were aroused last night by the guards and found Indians running thru camp yelling and shooting. They stampeded our herd and in the confusion that followed got 15 of our horses, leaving us only 5, looted our wagons, stealing all of my expense money. We spent the day gathering up the cattle and, with part of the men walking, managed to drive them . . . a distance of 15 miles."

Though by 1879 the Indian hazard had waned, Baylis Fletcher was excitedly aware that they were heading across 300 miles of wild and lawless land belonging to savages, many of them still hostile. So he took his Winchester carbine, which had been stowed in the wagon along with the outfit's other firearms, and stuck it into his saddle scabbard. The other boys strapped on their six-shooters and rubbed them bright.

"We marched on now, armed to the teeth for savage foes and wild animals," Fletcher wrote. For a time they

The anatomy of the chuck wagon

The mother ship for trail drives was a broad-beamed, sturdily built vehicle that carried virtually everything 10 men might need on a prairie voyage lasting as long as five months. Credit for the ultimate design of the wagon belongs to cattle baron Charles Goodnight, who in 1866 rebuilt for his trail crew a surplus Army wagon, picked primarily for its extra-durable iron axles. To the basic wagon bed, where bulk goods such as foodstuffs and bedrolls were to be stored, Goodnight added three already customary trail-drive appendages: on one side a water barrel big enough to hold two days' supply of water; on the other a heavy tool box; and on top bentwood bows to accommodate a canvas covering for protection against sun and rain.

But the innovation that made the Goodnight wagon unique at the time, and a useful prototype for all self-respecting wagons that followed, was the design and installation of a chuck box. Perched at the rear of the wagon, facing aft, it had a hinged lid that let down onto a swinging leg to form a worktable *(side view, below)*. Like a Victorian desk, the box was honeycombed with drawers and cubbyholes *(rear view)*. Here—and in the boot beneath—the cook stored his utensils and whatever food he might need during the day. A typical arrangement is shown on these pages, with the most convenient niche occupied by the coffeepot and the whiskey bottle, the latter being in the cook's sole charge as medicine (to which cooks were partial). Above them is the "possible drawer," a combination first-aid kit and catchall, holding everything from calomel to sewing needles. The design of Goodnight's wagon proved so practical that cattle outfits all over the West imitated it, using redesigned farm wagons and Army vehicles. Inevitably the idea went commercial and became a standard item for major wagon builders, including the well-known Studebaker Brothers Manufacturing Company, which sold chuck wagons for $75 to $100.

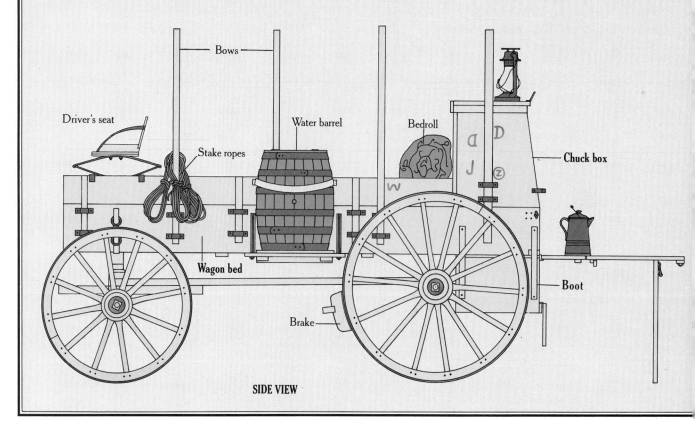

SIDE VIEW

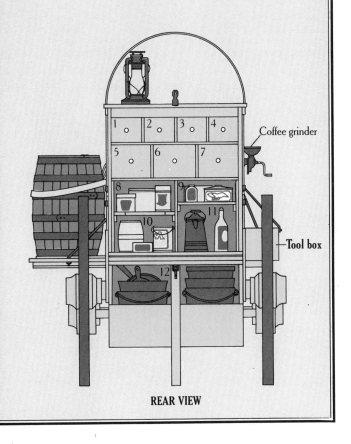

Wagon Bed	Tool Box	7 *Possible drawer:*
bedrolls	shovel	castor oil
slickers	ax	calomel
wagon sheet	branding irons	bandages
½-in. corral rope	horseshoeing equipment	needle, thread
guns, ammunition	hobbles	razor, strop
lantern, kerosene	rods for pot rack	8 salt
axle grease	extra skillets	lard
extra wagon wheel		baking soda
salt pork	**Chuck Box**	9 vinegar
raw beef	**and Boot**	chewing tobacco
		rolling tobacco
Bulk storage:	1 flour	10 sourdough keg
green coffee beans	2 sugar	matches
flour, pinto beans	3 dried fruit	molasses
sugar, salt	4 roasted coffee beans	11 coffeepot
dried apples	5 pinto beans	whiskey
onions, potatoes	6 plates, cups,	12 skillets
grain for work team	cutlery	dutch ovens
		pot hooks

Coffee grinder

—Tool box

REAR VIEW

trailed along safely, seeing no hostiles. In frustration they kept up a running fusillade at rabbits and rattlesnakes. Then, on a mid-June morning after having crossed the South Canadian River, they spied riding in a circle around them . . . Indians! The chief approached. Fletcher, taking a wary stance as the Deerslayer might have, bent to catch the warrior's fierce words.

"Mebbe-so white chief give Injun some beef?" the Indian begged. "Injun mighty hungry. Squaw mighty hungry. Papoose mighty hungry."

Alas for romance, this confrontation was typical of most encounters on the trail between cowboys and Indians. Even in the early days the desire of practically all Indians was to get money, horses or cattle—whether by threat, theft or begging. On the old Shawnee Trail, the Cherokees charged tolls of 10 cents a head for crossing the Indian Territory and mounted a well-run police patrol called the Cherokee Light Horse to see that the money was forthcoming. Less civilized in their approach were the Comanches, who would come thundering at a trail herd in a fearsome mass charge. When the terrified cowboys had run for their lives the Comanches would get down to the real business of the day—butchering and feasting on cattle.

In an effort to avoid any such trouble, trail bosses usually tried to meet the Indians halfway and buy them off by giving away a few cattle. One foreman reported that appeasement could become almost a full-time chore: "We struck Indians by the thousands [but] managed to keep peace by giving them a beef every day."

This was a sound strategy, the only question sometimes being: whose beef? One trail boss, named Bill Jackman, happened to pick up a fat, stray steer with the brand of a Texas neighbor named Ike Pryor. Bill intended to take the steer to Pryor, who was known to be a few miles ahead. Suddenly 40 Indians galloped up and handed Bill a note.

To the trail bosses:
This man is a good Indian; I know him personally. Treat him well, give him a beef and you will have no trouble driving through his country.

Ike T. Pryor

No man ever had a clearer invitation to be generous. Bill cut out Pryor's steer and turned it over to the Indians without a twinge of conscience. Unfortunately

A trail boss gives the cattle sign to an Indian by imitating horns with his upraised arms, indicating that the brave may take an animal to eat from a herd crossing Indian land.

153

Fletcher's boss had no strays to give away, so he ordered the men to cut out one of the T L steers. Then he lent the Indians some pistols to fell the animal. They killed it, skinned it at once and ate while the flesh was still twitching, the animal's warm blood running down their chins. After this encounter with ferocious redskins, Fletcher—with rueful reflections on the vanished era of James Fenimore Cooper—put his Winchester back into the wagon, and the other boys sheepishly unstrapped their guns.

In the days that followed, the drive fell into the normal routine of the trail. During the early morning the cattle grazed as they drifted a couple of miles northward. Once thrown onto the trail, they covered another four or five miles in the course of the morning. Arnett, galloping off ahead, would find good noonday pasture where no other outfit had yet stopped or bedded down. The point men would watch Arnett until they saw him ride a circle and stop broadside to the herd, his horse's head indicating the direction for the cattle to turn. At about the same time a curl of smoke showed that cook García and the wagon had arrived, and dinner—as cowboys called the noon meal—was being prepared. During the noon stop the cattle rested or grazed, the men eating in shifts so that at least two riders were always out keeping an easy watch, or "loose herd," over the cattle. In an hour the herd would be back on the trail.

These afternoons in Indian Territory passed almost hypnotically, the prairie unfolding before the trail riders in a slow, majestic panorama. For mile upon mile the cowhands could see nothing but an undulating expanse of seared brown grass. Dust rose in choking clouds. The only sounds were the muffled crack-crack of the cows' ankle joints, the steady thudding of hooves, the occasional clatter of long horns swung against each other. Sometimes a cow, bawling and worried, turned and trotted back against the line of march, looking for her missing calf.

Always close to the T L herd was its remuda, walking along under the eye of the wrangler, who drove them by day, kept an eye on them at night, rounded them up in the morning and brought them into jury-rigged rope corrals whenever the cowboys needed a change of mounts. This occurred two or even three times in a day, since the cow ponies, though quick on their feet and hardy enough to live on a little water and

Lullabies for jittery cows

Many cowboy ballads originated as a means of quieting stampede-prone cattle at night. Composed impromptu by cowhands riding around the herds, the often atonal songs took their rhythm from a horse's gait. Some had mournful tunes but no words and were termed "Texas lullabies." Others had standard verses that, like those excerpted below, became favorites.

Little Joe the Wrangler

*Little Joe, the wrangler, was called out with the rest;
Though the kid had scarcely reached the herd,
When the cattle they stampeded, like a hailstorm
long they fled,
Then we were all a-ridin' for the lead.*

*The next morning just at daybreak, we found where
his horse fell,
Down in a washout twenty feet below;
And beneath the horse, mashed to a pulp, his spur
had rung the knell,
Was our little Texas stray, poor Wrangling Joe.*

The Old Chisholm Trail

*I'm up in the mornin' afore daylight
And afore I sleep the moon shines bright.*

*No chaps and no slicker, and it's pouring down rain,
And I swear, by God, that I'll never night-herd again.*

*Oh, it's bacon and beans most every day—
I'd as soon be a-eatin' prairie hay.*

*I went to the boss to draw my roll,
He had it figured out I was nine dollars in the hole.*

*I'll sell my horse and I'll sell my saddle;
You can go to hell with your longhorn cattle.*

range grass, could take only four or five hours of hard riding at a time and stay in good shape.

Though the herd was still just halfway to Wyoming, the pace of the drive remained purposely relaxed, for the essence of good trailing was to make the cattle gain weight. "Your profits depend on moving them along quiet and easy," explained one boss, adding: "You've no idea how easy it is to knock a dollar off a beef." Longhorns, though too lean and stringy to be classed as the best of beef, accommodated themselves relatively well to trail driving. Their long-legged stride and steel-hard hooves helped them over the great distance. But on the Western trails, even these tough creatures were driven with a light hand. "Folks didn't really drive cattle —they moved 'em," explained one old cowhand. A boss like George Arnett tried to ease the cows along in the gentlest way — some restraint on fast-stepping leaders, some pushing of the cripples and the sore-footed cattle in the drag. Moreover, the trail bosses made shrewd use of the animals' need to reach water. Some drivers chose bed-grounds near watering places, a tactic that made the cattle move briskly along late in the afternoon when they could sense there was water ahead. Others watered for two or three hours at noon and bedded on high ground, where there was no water nearby to which the cattle might drift. Whichever method he chose, scouting water was a major chore for any boss; it might keep him in the saddle for 30 to 40 miles at a stretch, riding sometimes a full day ahead of the herd.

During this particular year on the Chisholm Trail, however, there was no need to ride far to learn anything. For the route itself was heavily traveled, and communication was surprisingly efficient for hundreds of miles around. Freighters, driving heavy wagons south along the trail, traded news of weather and Indians. Cowboys from other herds, looking for lost horses, let the TL men know with great precision which herd was ahead of them and which behind. And for a detailed, day-by-day prediction of what lay just ahead, Arnett could have relied, if necessary, on a map and accompanying trail guide published by the Kansas Pacific Railroad to attract droves to its shipping points.

A typical entry for one stretch of trail the outfit traveled in late June described the terrain on either side of the Cimarron River, which the herd was just about to cross for the first of several times as trail and river braid-

ed back and forth across each other through the northern half of the Indian Territory.

Trail from King Fisher Creek over level upland prairie. Water on west side of trail. Camping ground two miles beyond the ford, north side of stream. Abundance of wood and water.

What the guide did not mention was that at the next crossing, four days beyond, the river water was fouled from an enormous deposit of alkali. Arnett knew that a long drink of such water might kill his cattle. Yet it would be hard to prevent the herd, thirsty from a dry day, from stopping to drink while fording. He could think of only one recourse: deliberately stampede the cows across. The men kept the cattle under a tight hold right up to the riverbank; then, on a signal, they waved and rattled their ponchos or rain slickers to spook the herd. The cows took off on a splashing run right through the river and out on the other side. Once across, the animals tried to double back, and the riders had to battle all night long and part of the next day to get them moving ahead again.

About 5 o'clock each afternoon, the herd neared a place that Arnett had chosen to be the night's bed-grounds. He would signal the spot by waving his hat slowly around his head, and the side riders would spread apart to give the herd room to turn toward him. Meanwhile the cook was opening up the chuck box on his wagon and kindling a fire for supper. Surprisingly for this broad, barren-looking plain, there always seemed to be plenty of fuel. During the day's travel each time the herd crossed a creek the cook and the wrangler picked up bits of brush and broken limbs from the cottonwoods that grew by the watercourses, tossing the fuel into a calfhide suspended under the wagon. Farther up the trail, in even drier terrain, this calfskin hammock would carry dried cow or buffalo manure, dubbed "prairie coal," because when lighted with bacon rind for kindling it burned with a fine, hot flame. Collecting the stuff required gloves; there was a scorpion under almost every cow chip.

Over his fire cook García boiled the beans that were his monotonous specialty—"Pecos strawberries," the boys called them. For meat García almost always served fried bacon, or "overland trout." Though literally surrounded by cattle, cowboys on a drive rarely ate beef. "Killing a beef on the trail was a great waste, as only a small part of the meat could be eaten before it spoiled," Fletcher explained in his journal. But the T L crew did kill one fat yearling stray that had joined up with the herd, and the cook broiled "an abundant supply" for the trailhands' supper.

Killing a young cow provided not only beef but also the ingredients for the gourmet dish known as sonofabitch stew for which there were nearly as many recipes *(page 87)* as there were range cooks. On the trail it was likely to contain cut-up heart, testicles, tongue, liver and (for flavor) marrow gut, which is the semi-digested contents of the tube connecting the ruminant's stomachs. Only in settled territory did a cowboy get anything approaching a regular diet of fresh food—and not then if the local farmers were antagonistic. If they were friendly the boss might strike a bargain: the herd bedded down on a farmer's pasture; as payment for the resulting cow chips the farmer would provide eggs and vegetables. Other times the outfit might offer a new-born calf, a windfall for the farmer—and for the cowboys, who otherwise would have had to shoot the animal because it could not keep pace with the herd.

In his memoir Baylis Fletcher noted in great detail the routine of a typical night on the trail. As the light failed, the men of the first night watch—dusk to 10—bedded down the cattle by circling the herd for half an hour in a diminishing spiral. Then one of the guards reversed his course to establish the opposite circle routes of the regular night guard. Fletcher went over to the remuda and picked out his own prized night horse, Happy Jack. Leading him to a spot about halfway between camp and the near arc of the night-guard circle, Fletcher staked him out to a steel picket pin. He also hobbled a spare horse, tying the forefeet together with a rawhide thong to keep the animal from straying. Then he headed back toward the center of camp, listening with half an ear to the slow, sentimental sound of the guard singing the interminable songs that cowboys made up, or learned as lullabies, to calm restless cattle through the long night. One cowhand from another outfit used to play his fiddle to the herd as he rode, and he swore that the cows took special pleasure in his own two favorites, "Dinah Had a Wooden Leg" and "The Unfortunate Pup." Baylis himself hummed Presbyterian hymns; they

Cattle raiders: rough stuff on the trail

This illustration, showing Texas cowboy J. M. Daugherty being whipped by border ruffians, is a dramatic depiction of one of the trail's hazards. Too dramatic, it never happened that way. However, the engraving—produced in 1873 for promoter Joseph McCoy's book *Cattle Trade of the West & Southwest*—was based on a real event.

What did happen was rough enough. On a drive to Sedalia, Missouri, in 1866, Daugherty's point man was shot and 500 longhorns were stampeded by armed men calling themselves Jayhawkers, after pro-Union guerrillas who had marauded the Kansas-Missouri border

Faked drawing of Daugherty's whipping shows the 16-year-old victim as middle-aged.

seemed to have a quieting effect on the cattle.

When Fletcher returned to the campfire the night was fully dark. The other cowboys had all finished eating and were squatting in a group trading yarns. Several rolled cigarettes and smoked in slumped exhaustion. Two of them argued inconclusively over whether the person burning brush on the moon (a surmise based on its orange tint this night) was a man or a woman. One fellow played his harmonica; another polished a new verse for the best-known of night-guard tunes, "The Old Chisholm Trail." Fletcher, too tired to sing or to talk or smoke, unrolled his tarp and quilts, made a pillow of his pants and shirt and fell asleep in an instant. Doubtless the others soon followed. For the twin demands of night guard and early rising kept the men from ever getting more than six hours' sleep.

At midnight a cowboy from the second watch waked Fletcher with a low-voiced word; a man was not supposed to touch or shake another when waking him for fear of startling the sleeper (and perhaps getting shot by someone who had bedded down with a gun nearby). Fletcher, refreshed by his brief nap, got right up and mounted Happy Jack. As he rode out to start his turn,

the cattle, which had risen to their feet at the changing of the watch, were lying down again, and the stars were bright as only prairie stars can be. A glance at the Big Dipper assured Fletcher that he had been wakened almost precisely at midnight. Very few cowboys carried watches, and the stars had to serve as the timepieces of the trail *(page 161)*.

On nights when the skies were cloudy, the cowboys depended on their horses to quit on time. One night horse was a Texas pony named Old Sid, who would under no circumstances walk a watch more than two hours. If for any reason Sid's rider had to stay overtime, the cowboy would have to ride into camp, dismount, wait a couple of minutes and then climb aboard again. This seemed to convince Sid that he was starting a new turn rather than being overworked on the old one.

A good night horse had other talents, too. Its eyes were sharper than those of a day horse, so it could find a lost cow or pick its way safely along gullied land in inky darkness. It was calm, not inclined to shy at shadows or sudden noise. It could gallop at night without putting a foot into a prairie-dog hole. And it could handle cattle boldly in case of a stampede. This was a critical

during pre-Civil War days. Daugherty himself was captured, but after debating whether to kill him by hanging or flogging, the Jayhawkers let him go because he was only 16 years old.

Daugherty and his crew had run afoul of an outlaw version of the toughest trail hazard faced by the Texans: angry farmers who, shotguns in hand, tried to bar the oncoming herds. The farmers' motives were often legitimate, since longhorns did trample croplands. Worse yet, they often carried the Texas fever, a virulent disease fatal to the settlers' Northern-bred cattle.

But ingenious ruffians also used the farmers' grievances to gouge the cattle drovers. Gangs like the one at left were, in many cases, just cattle rustlers who exploited the fever scare to intimidate cattlemen and steal from their herds.

Though the worst abuses occurred in Kansas, the game went on in other states as well. In Colorado in 1869, 50 men, proclaiming their fear of the Texas fever, stampeded 1,600 longhorns and made off with the strays. During a confrontation in 1869 the redoubtable Charles Goodnight tried to reason with blockaders, then unlimbered his own Winchester and threatened, "I've monkeyed as long as I want to with you." With that he took the cattle through.

All sorts of other extortionists tried to leech the drovers. Back in Texas, where state inspectors checked departing herds for stolen cattle, both real inspectors and fake ones often demanded—and received—bribes. Other officials called trail cutters, appointed to ensure that drovers did not keep strays

from other ranches, frequently carved out extras for themselves from a passing herd. And hoodlums pretending to be trail cutters would stop herds, get the drop on the point men, then stampede and steal the cattle.

However, the worst of the trouble focused on the Kansas border. Though incidents declined during the '70s, by 1880 the dirt farmers had become so adamant about the longhorn-bred Texas fever that practically all Kansas was off limits to the trail herds. Confronted in 1885 by a Winchester blockade of short-tempered border guards, a drover delivered himself of a sarcastic order that eventually became a slogan for trail bosses on the long drive: "Bend 'em West, boys. Nothing in Kansas anyhow except the three suns—sunflowers, sunshine and those sons of bitches."

Swathed and huddled against the bite of a Montana blizzard, ranch hands on the northern range keep their cattle moving away from the wind so the animals will not freeze.

ability, for on the trail nighttime was stampede time.

Nights of lightning and rain, with the air full of tension, seemed to tighten the cattle's nerves to the point of stampede. And then a cannon shot of prairie thunder would set them off. But even on clear, tranquil nights in the back of every herder's mind was the uneasy thought that a thousand things could make the cattle rise and run. Some of these things were ordinary, even trifling —a coyote's yelp or a horse's whinny, a startled jack rabbit or a jumping deer, the rattle of cooking pans, the flare of a match as a cowboy lighted a cigarette. One herd was spooked in daylight when a hen from a settler's cabin flapped across the trail; the cattle, when finally rounded up, refused to pass that cabin again. On another drive a shred from a cowboy's pouch of chewing tobacco lodged in a steer's eye, setting off a raging charge that resulted in the death of two riders and the loss of 400 cows.

Occasionally the mass of animals would take off for no reason at all. A herd that had broken once or twice was likely to go again and again (conversely, a herd might go the length of the trail without ever stampeding). In a number of herds half a dozen troublemakers might take a "chronic fright, from which they never do recover," wrote Joseph McCoy, the articulate Abilene cattle entrepreneur. "They would rather run than eat, anytime. The stampeders may be seen close together at all times, as if consulting how to raise Cain and get off with a burst of speed." McCoy held that "it is actually economy to shoot down a squad of these vicious stampeders." A few cowmen tranquilized stampeders by sewing shut their eyelids; by the time the thread rotted, in about two weeks, the animals were considerably meeker.

Oddly, when the cattle stampeded they uttered no sound at all. A trail hand sleeping off-watch would suddenly be aware of a deep rumbling, a trembling of the sod beneath him. He would know that the cattle were off, and as the trail boss bellowed, "All hands and the cook!" the crew would run, stumbling through the dark to mount their night horses for a blind dash toward the point. The longhorns, though angular and ungainly to look at, ran with surprising speed, their hooves pounding and their horns clashing as they thundered along. A stampeding herd looked, in the words of one cowboy, like a "tempest of horns and tails," and Charles Good-

night testified that stampeding cattle gave off bodily heat that "almost blistered the faces" of the men who were riding on the lee side.

Two or three cowboys, usually the best riders, spurred hard to get out in front of the stampede. Then, depending solely on "the sureness of the horse's feet to keep from changing hells," they reined back to try to slow the charge. Meanwhile other hands at one side of the point pressed in to turn the herd. If the cattle refused to turn, the cowpunchers flailed their slickers in the faces of the leaders, or fired six-shooters into the ground close to the stampeders' ears. The leaders might dodge and go down and other cattle trample them at heavy cost in dead steers and broken horns and bones. After three or four terrifying miles the cattle usually began to circle, then mill. For the hands this was one of the most dangerous times, with the cows jammed together so that a trapped horseman might be jostled from his mount. At the end of one stampede near the Blue River in Nebraska, when the milling cattle had stopped and had drifted back to their bed-ground the horrified cowboys came upon the remains of a comrade who had fallen to the ground beneath the circling crush of hooves. Nothing was left but a gun butt.

But while the cattle were still in the full run of a stampede they rarely hurt men. Normally the charging cattle would split around a fallen rider. However, cowboys rarely cared to test this trait and on many occasions took prudent refuge behind the chuck wagon. One cowboy, caught in a stampede, fell from his horse onto the backs of the running cattle and was carried along for a quarter of a mile till he finally rolled safely off to one side. Another shaken but unhurt victim of a stampede in Kansas in 1874 was a settler living in a dugout house; the cattle caved in his roof, and 800 pounds of cow landed feet up in his bed.

Usually the only harm done on a stampede was to the animals—and the cattleman's profits. In a four-mile run on a hot night a beef could lose up to 50 pounds, and a spooky herd would arrive at the railhead looking mighty stringy and unpalatable to its buyer. Worse yet, it might be minus a fair number of cows; in the thunder of a stampede cattle bruised, crushed and gored one another. In the worst stampede in history, in July 1876, a big herd plunged into a gully near the Brazos River in Texas, the leaders crushed by those behind; when it

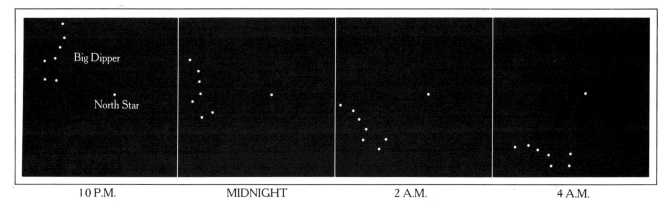

10 P.M.   MIDNIGHT   2 A.M.   4 A.M.

was over 2,000 steers were either dead or missing.

The luck of the T L crew was such that the herd gave up stampeding altogether after its first week in Texas. By the end of June the herd was about to make its last crossing of the Cimarron River, where it marked the end of the Indian Territory and entry into the sovereign state of Kansas. As they approached the river Fletcher spotted on the far side what seemed a random strewing of buffalo skulls, and they reminded him of a wagon driver he had passed along the trail. The man had been a buffalo-bone collector, a symbol of the fast-changing life on the prairies. Wandering across the plains, these gypsy tradesmen picked up the chalky remnants of the buffalo slaughter of the early 1870s and sold the bones to manufacturers of all manner of things, from fertilizer to bone china. In earlier days, when buffalo still roamed the plains, hundreds of cows would sometimes mingle in a drift of buffalo and be gone forever. One trail boss stopped his cattle in 1871 and watched incredulously as a mixed herd of thousands of buffaloes, horses, elk, deer, antelope, wolves and cattle crossed the trail — a peaceable kingdom on the plains.

Now there was nothing left of the huge buffalo herds but the bones, yet here at the Cimarron River the bones spoke with a special significance. Beginning at the north bank, the line of skulls, one placed every half mile, marked a cutoff leading to Dodge City, 175 miles southwest of the old Chisholm trailhead in Abilene. This new route had become necessary a few years before when the government of Kansas, under pressure from settlers, excluded all Texas cattle from the east-central part of the state. And well they might.

"There was scarcely a day when we didn't have a row with some settler," reported a cowboy named Bill Poage. "The boss was arrested twice in one day for trespassing. A settler would plow a furrow around his claim. According to the laws of Kansas, this was a fence. Any loose stock that crossed it was trespassing, and the owner was liable for damages." Most such claims were settled out of court, for the trail bosses knew they had no chance before a Kansas judge and would hand over to a farmer anything from 50 cents to $100 rather than risk the loss of time and additional money of a court appearance.

The new cutoff, though free of farmer trouble, confronted the T L herd with an ordeal that every trail rider dreaded: a dry drive, a grueling 100-mile push from the Cimarron to the Arkansas over virtually waterless country. At the T L herd's normal trailing speed, 100 miles would have taken eight days. But Arnett knew in that time the parched cattle might be dying or dead. He worried particularly about the cows, which would panic if they thought their calves were suffering. He decided, therefore, to make the dry run in four days of double-speed driving.

The herd went on the trail at sunrise July 1, rested and grazed during the noonday heat, then marched on until after sundown. The harsh routine was repeated the next day and the next. But the T L's luck held; a providential rain squall provided a few puddles along the trail to relieve the cattle. And by the time they reached the Arkansas River near Dodge City they were able to water without overdrinking.

Had it not rained, two possible consequences awaited the T L cattle — or any herd driven to places distant from water. First, the cattle might turn ungovernable after three or four days without water, and the crew would discover that the animals had gone blind, a com-

The number of cows trailed out of Texas rose dramatically
for the first five years of the great drives, then dropped due
to a market glut in 1871 and a depression two years later.

mon effect of thirst. Or second, the cattle, no longer able to smell water ahead, would turn back to the last drinking place they could remember —perhaps three or four days behind them—and many would perish.

The worst dry trail drive in the West was the one cattle baron Charlie Goodnight had pioneered *(page 48)* from the Concho River in western Texas to the Pecos River in New Mexico, 80 miles of desert and greasy sunshine, hotter and even more barren than southern Kansas. The strategy for this ordeal was to water the cattle at the Concho at 11 o'clock in the morning and then press forward for some 60 hours, with brief rests at morning and midnight. The men lived on black coffee. At the end of the grueling drive the bone-tired cowboys, who on occasion rubbed fiery tobacco juice in their eyes to stay awake, had to summon the energy to keep the lowing, piteous animals from stampeding to the Pecos once they had smelled its water about 10 miles away. At the river, some steers charged over the bank and killed themselves, some trampled others to death, some overdrank and died. But most waded in until half covered, moaned, waited half an hour before drinking and then drank only a little, stood another hour in the stream, drank some more and came calmly out to graze.

After a dry drive trail bosses ordinarily let a herd lie over for a couple of days, grazing and watering, while the men rested. And so did the TL's Arnett at an old cow camp just across the Arkansas River. Not far from the spot, in plain sight of the cowhands, sprawled Dodge City, described by one romanticizing chronicler as the "beautiful, bibulous Babylon of the trail." Babylon it was not. Beautiful it was not. But bibulous it surely was, the first place in many hundred miles where a man could wet his throat with something more potent than chuck-wagon coffee. However, true to the Sunday-schoolish style of all drover Snyder's trail drives, Arnett allowed Fletcher and the boys only a few hours to visit

Box score for the big years

1867	35,000
1868	75,000
1869	350,000
1870	300,000
1871	600,000
1872	350,000
1873	405,000
1874	166,000
1875	151,618
1876	321,998
1877	201,159
1878	265,646
1879	257,927
1880	394,784
1881	250,000

Dodge, and then just during the day, when the pleasure parlors were in low gear and the trail crew's main form of entertainment was gawking at the piles of buffalo bones that awaited shipment. Having thus been spared by their employer's morals from all temptation to drink, gamble and dance with floozies, the TL crew put the herd back onto the trail on July 6 for the last leg of the drive, 380 miles through Kansas toward Wyoming.

A few days out of Dodge the crew passed the carcass of a horse killed by lightning and, next to the horse, the grave of his rider. Astonishingly, lightning was one of the commonest causes of death on the trail. Four men were killed and three seriously burned by lightning on the Chisholm Trail in three years. On the Salt Fork in Kansas a cowboy grimly recalled lightning that "would hit the side of those hills and gouge out great holes in the earth like a bomb had struck them, and it killed seven or eight cattle in the herd back of us." Said yet another vivid account: "It first commenced like flash lightning, then came forked lightning, then chain lightning, followed by the peculiar blue lightning. After that show it rapidly developed into ball lightning, which rolled along the ground . . . then, most wonderful of all, it settled down on us like a fog. The air smelled of burning sulphur; you could see it on the horns of the cattle, the ears of our horses and the brims of our hats. It grew so warm we thought we might burn up with it."

At such times, reported a young cowpoke named John Connor, "the horses stuck their heads between their knees and moaned and groaned till I decided the end of time had come. So I got down off my horse and lay flat on the ground and tried to die, but could not."

At the first rumble and flicker of an approaching storm cowboys fearful of being struck might take off their metal spurs, hide their knives and in extreme cases even throw away six-shooters. To these cautious tactics Fletcher and the other TL boys added a pious touch: they cut out even private profanity during lightning storms, on the theory that cussing was disrespectful and therefore invited sudden destruction from the controller of the elements.

Whether by divine restraint or the simple good luck they had enjoyed most of the way, the TL crew weathered July's thundersqualls with no casualties to either men or livestock. However, they had one last bizarre fright before swinging westward out of Kansas. Near the town of Oberlin, on the Sappa River, settlers hurrying past on the trail greeted them with a fearful rumor: the Cheyennes were on the warpath and had scalped some homesteaders. On every hand people were fleeing to the towns and forts. As a safety measure the boys voted to sleep hidden among the trees away from their wagon. The dark hours passed with no attack. Next day the TL outfit met the boss of a horse herd headed for Ogallala, Nebraska.

"Seen any Indians?" the man asked the TL cowboys in a strangely unconcerned tone.

"No."

The boss laughed. "We are the only Indians in western Kansas," he said. Then he explained. Like many another livestock drover he had become thoroughly fed up by the homesteaders continually harassing the herds and refusing to let them graze. It had occurred to this cheeky horse herder that "all we had to do to depopulate the plains" was to start stories about marauding Indians. So he had. The TL men, sheepish at having been deluded but glad to have the settlers out of their path, pushed their cows through to the Nebraska border.

Now Fletcher's outfit was on the last leg of the journey, an easy run through the valley of the Platte River and then on to Wyoming. As they moved westward the land rose until the herd was traveling at an altitude of four thousand feet. Though the noon sun still bore down with enervating force, the air was turning cooler, the nights becoming almost too chilly for Texans reared in the humid climes of the Gulf Coast. With little more than 100 miles to go, they branched off the Platte Valley and began following a section of an old Mormon trail that paralleled a Platte tributary called Lodgepole Creek. Along the route Baylis Fletcher could see the weathered residue of the Mormons' terrible journey. Twenty-three years before, several thousand emigrants had come this way, pushing their baggage along in handcarts since they were too poor to afford wagons and draft animals. Incessant blizzards had struck the trekkers; disease ravaged their exhausted bodies, and Indians attacked them repeatedly. Now broken, abandoned fragments of the carts littered the roadside, and at intervals the herd passed some of the graves of the 200 people who had perished.

After a few more days' travel the Lodgepole Creek Valley narrowed to a canyon hemmed by two pine-clad cliffs. And soon thereafter the trail led through a streamside town appropriately named Pine Bluffs and marking, at long last, the border of Wyoming. A local foreman met the outfit and instructed Arnett to turn over the cattle at a ranch 20 miles north of Cheyenne, where the herd would be taken in hand by the Swan Brothers Cattle Company, one of the most powerful outfits in the West.

For Baylis Fletcher and the others, tired, bearded, shaggy haired and dirty, the great journey was nearly over. On the morning of August 12, 1879, the final stretch of trail emerged from the Lodgepole Creek canyon onto a broad plateau lying at 6,000 feet above sea level. And there, strung out in a distant line of stone and snow, lay the grandest sight of Fletcher's life, the Rocky Mountains, 100 miles distant. "I feasted my eyes for several days on the backbone of America," he wrote.

On August 15 the drive pulled up at the Swan Brothers pasture, where Arnett's men gave over the cattle. Another livestock company bought the saddle horses — including Fletcher's favorite, Happy Jack — and yet another picked up the wagon and other loose trail gear. With a quickness almost painful the TL outfit had lost all symbols of its identity, and for the men the magic of sharing a great experience was dissolving. Using a letter of credit on a Cheyenne bank, Arnett gave each man his pay, $100 apiece more or less, depending on old obligations and loans or other debts picked up on the trail. The boys scattered through Cheyenne to splurge on shaves, haircuts, baths and new clothes. Thus refurbished, they could hardly recognize one another on the streets. Fletcher, too taken with Wyoming to leave right away, hired out with a local outfit for a short drive in the high country. He enjoyed it, an easy chore after the ordeal of pushing 2,500 head of longhorns across one third of the United States. Then one day he went abruptly to the Union Pacific rail depot and bought a ticket to Texas. The odyssey of the long trail was over.

All the comforts of a horse-drawn home

On the drive or at roundup, home base for the cowboy was a circle with the chuck wagon at its center. The radius of the circle was short—no farther than a man felt like walking after supper to roll out his bedding. The chuck wagon itself served as a rolling commissariat, crammed full of everything from bedrolls to spare bullets. At mealtimes, on the ground next to the wagon, gathered a rough and sweaty crew that for more than one cowboy was the closest approximation to a family he might have during his working life.

Though range hands took their orders from a foreman or trail boss, the president pro tem around the chuck wagon—and the key to a contented crew—was the cook, whose job on the range was twice as demanding as it was back at the ranch. He was the first man up in the morning and usually the busiest during the day. He packed and drove the wagon, prepared three hot meals a day, doctored cuts (one favored coagulant was kerosene oil), sewed buttons and settled bets.

The cook wielded subtle but enormous power, and trail hands were at pains to stay in his favor. For example, all the coffee had to be hand ground. One favorite brand was Arbuckle's, which came with a stick of peppermint packed in each one-pound bag. When the cook hollered "Who wants the candy tonight?" some of the toughest men in the West would fight for the privilege of cranking the grinder. At night the cook would often stay up until the last man save the night guard was bedded down. Then he would carry out the final chore in his long day: pointing the chuck wagon's tongue toward the North Star to give the trail boss a sure compass heading in the morning.

Under the paternal eye of a pipe-smoking cook, the boys of the Bar CC Ranch take a dinner break on Cherokee land in what later became Oklahoma. Sleeping tents like the canvas tipis behind the men were rare luxuries on the plains.

Taking leave of his pots and pans, a cook gets a shave. On the range cowboys rarely cared what they looked like, but an invitation to dinner at a nearby ranch would send the dandies among the crew scurrying for a shave or a haircut.

Bending to the stewpot, a cook for the huge 861,000-acre Matador Ranch in west Texas stirs up supper, usually a mess of sowbelly and beans. The tentlike tarpaulin on poles over the wagon indicates that this is a roundup and the outfit will stay put for a day or two. On the trail the cook had to move twice a day and rarely had time to rig a shelter.

Gathering in front of the chuck wagon at a water hole in the Oklahoma Panhandle, a roundup crew holds still for an itinerant photographer who came by while five of the men—and one horse—were having a soak. During the late 1800s gypsy photographers rode the range, taking pictures like this and selling prints to the cowboys for 50 cents apiece.

As evening falls six range hands settle down to listen to a tale told by a gesticulating comrade. Actually, cowboys rarely stayed up long after they had finished supper, since each hand had to take his regular two-hour stint on night guard.

A crap game gets underway on a blanket close by the chuck wagon. To avoid trouble, most cattle barons prohibited gambling around the home ranch; but rules relaxed on the range at roundup when the men of several outfits got together.

Propped against a pile of bedrolls, a herd boss grabs a moment to write a letter home, while the cook helps himself to a piece of soap. Literate men who could keep ranch records as well as handle men and cows were hard to find and commanded up to four times the pay of ordinary hands.

6 | Towns that boomed on beef

After the Civil War a number of raucous boomtowns sprang from the flat prairie at the junctions of Texas longhorn trails and freshly built railroad tracks. Most of these burst forth in Kansas, and no one had ever seen their like. They were all dust and raw weatherboard, hard-handed cowpunchers and longhorns—sometimes 30,000 animals inundating a village of 500 souls.

To the beef broker, a cattle town was the place where he could close $20,000 deals on a handshake. To railroad men, whose freight trains had been rolling west fully loaded and going back empty, beef partly offset a five million dollar a year imbalance of trade. To the cowboy coming up the trail, the cattle town was a glorious oasis—a place to get a bath and haircut, a woman and a bottle of "Kansas sheep dip," as he called his whiskey. The town also afforded him a chance to gamble his meager wages on anything from a nickel game of horseshoes to a poker hand that swallowed his whole wad.

The first of the cattle towns, Abilene, started up in 1867 and boomed for four years. Then, as the railroads moved west, the cows and cowboys went with them. The last and busiest, Dodge City, shown here in its embryonic stage, thrived 10 seasons, filling pockets with dollars, its Boot Hill cemetery with dead gunslingers and the Santa Fe Railroad's cars with steers.

The outskirts of Dodge City, Kansas, in 1872 presented a dreary façade of mud-chinked log cabins and tents. A dozen years later Dodge was the busiest trailhead town, with 19 saloons, a lush casino and a seasonal population of 2,000.

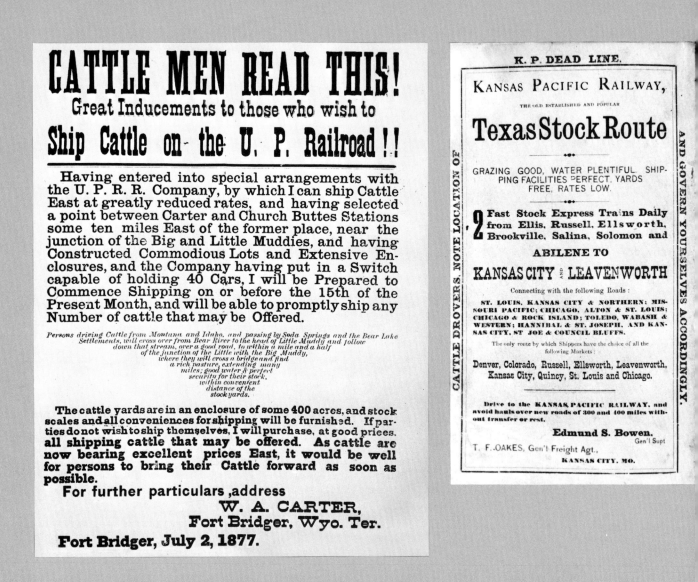

CATTLE MEN READ THIS!

Great Inducements to those who wish to

Ship Cattle on the U. P. Railroad !!

Having entered into special arrangements with the U. P. R. R. Company, by which I can ship Cattle East at greatly reduced rates, and having selected a point between Carter and Church Buttes Stations some ten miles East of the former place, near the junction of the Big and Little Muddies, and having Constructed Commodious Lots and Extensive Enclosures, and the Company having put in a Switch capable of holding 40 Cars, I will be Prepared to Commence Shipping on or before the 15th of the Present Month, and will be able to promptly ship any Number of cattle that may be Offered.

Persons driving Cattle from Montana and Idaho, and passing by Soda Springs and the Bear Lake Settlements, will cross over from Bear River to the head of Little Muddy and follow down that stream, over a good road, to within a mile and a half of the junction of the Little with the Big Muddy, where they will cross a bridge and find a rich pasture, extending many miles; good water & perfect security for their stock, within convenient distance of the stock yards.

The cattle yards are in an enclosure of some 400 acres, and stock scales and all conveniences for shipping will be furnished. If parties do not wish to ship themselves, I will purchase, at good prices, all shipping cattle that may be offered. As cattle are now bearing excellent prices East, it would be well for persons to bring their Cattle forward as soon as possible.

For further particulars, address

W. A. CARTER,
Fort Bridger, Wyo. Ter.

Fort Bridger, July 2, 1877.

K. P. DEAD LINE.

KANSAS PACIFIC RAILWAY,

THE OLD ESTABLISHED AND POPULAR

Texas Stock Route

GRAZING GOOD, WATER PLENTIFUL. SHIPPING FACILITIES PERFECT, YARDS FREE, RATES LOW.

2 Fast Stock Express Trains Daily from Ellis, Russell, Ellsworth, Brookville, Salina, Solomon and

ABILENE TO

KANSAS CITY and LEAVENWORTH

Connecting with the following Roads :

ST. LOUIS, KANSAS CITY & NORTHERN; MISSOURI PACIFIC; CHICAGO, ALTON & ST. LOUIS; CHICAGO & ROCK ISLAND; TOLEDO, WABASH & WESTERN; HANNIBAL & ST. JOSEPH, AND KANSAS CITY, ST JOE & COUNCIL BLUFFS.

The only route by which Shippers have the choice of all the following Markets :

Denver, Colorado, Russell, Ellsworth, Leavenworth, Kansas City, Quincy, St. Louis and Chicago.

Drive to the KANSAS PACIFIC RAILWAY, and avoid hauls over new roads of 300 and 400 miles without transfer or rest.

Edmund S. Bowen,
Gen'l Supt

T. F. OAKES, Gen'l Freight Agt.,
KANSAS CITY, MO.

CATTLE DROVERS, NOTE LOCATION OF

AND GOVERN YOURSELVES ACCORDINGLY.

CIRCULAR.

TO DROVERS AND DEALERS IN SOUTHERN CATTLE.

Messrs. _____

The following facts are respectfully offered for your consideration: The Town of

WICHITA,

Located at the mouth of the Little Arkansas River, offers the following facilities for the transaction of your business: Straight, short and safe route is opened to the southern herding grounds, by which you can make TWO trips each season instead of one. It is the center of a splendid stock country, where stock will thrive six weeks earlier and later, than on the line of the Pacific Railroad. It is the natural point where buyer and seller should meet, to their mutual advantage. Here the drover can close out his entire drove without sacrificing a portion of it, and the buyer can take only such as are fit for shipment, leaving the balance in a rich pasture to recruit, or sell to settlers at good rates. Here the drover can procure all needed supplies for his return trip at as low rates as at any western point on the Railroad. A permanent

MILITARY POST

Has been established at Wichita, thus affording perfect protection for the herds, and at the same time by constant communication with the other Southern and Southwestern Posts, will keep the shortest and most practicable route entirely free from all obstructions. An excellent Ferry will soon be in operation at this point, furnishing safe transit for teams and cattle at all stages of water.

Yours, Respectfully,

E. H. DURFEE & CO.

Atchison, Topeka & Santa Fe
RAILRORD
FROM
ATCHISON, KAS. TO GRANADA, COL.
SHORT LINE Between MISSOURI RIVER
AND
Colorado, New Mexico and Arizona.

THE ROAD BEING NEW—WITH GOOD LINE—EASY GRADES, AND EQUIPPED WITH FIRST CLASS ROLLING STOCK AND POWER, OFFERS SUPERIOR ADVANTAGES TO SHIPPERS AND TRAVELERS.

The Live Stock Business
IS MADE A SPECIALTY. ROOMY AND SUBSTANTIAL YARDS ARE LOCATED AT CONVENIENT DISTANCES, AND EXPERIENCED STOCKMEN ON HAND TO LOAD STOCK.

AT GRANADA, GREAT BEND, NEWTON AND WICHITA
GOOD STOCK SCALES ARE PROVIDED.

Large Resting and Feeding Yards
AT
HUTCHINSON,
WITH GOOD ARRANGEMENTS FOR FEEDING, AND CLEAR WATER RUNNING THROUGH THEM, ARE PROVIDED FOR

COLORADO CATTLE.

Large Sale Yards at Atchison.

THE RATES TO
Atchison, Leavenworth and Kansas City
ALWAYS THE SAME.

And are guaranteed to be as low as by any other Line from corresponding points. Stock in Train Loads will be run extra, and will receive special attention.

For Particulars, Address

G. H. NETTLETON, Supt.,   M. L. SARGENT, Gen. Frt. Agt.,
            Topeka, Kas.   Topeka, Kas.
STOCKWELL & HAMILTON, Stock Agts., Atchison, Kas.

Handbills from hard-selling livestock brokers and from railroad men competing for beef deluged cattlemen before the start of the spring cattle drive. Such flyers also appeared as newspaper ads and even adorned the trunks of cottonwood trees along the trails to Kansas and the northern range.

Range hands use long prods *(above)* to force steers up a chute into rail cars—18 to a carload. This was a tedious chore that followed the long drive. The men hated the work, but it gave them a lasting nickname: "cowpoke."

The focus of business at all cattle towns was the shipping-yard area, like this one in Magdalena, New Mexico. The pens built in 1867 at Abilene, first of the boomtowns, could handle up to 120,000 head of cattle per season.

Cattle-town businessmen, like the barkeeper standing in the "office" doorway of a New Mexico saloon, gouged most of a cowboy's trail wage. Cowboys also splurged in general stores like Dodge City's Wright, Beverley and Company, which did a daily business of $1,000 in the boom season.

Bartender George Masterson, brother of Sheriff Bat, presides over the gleaming interior of Dodge City's premier dance hall and gambling palace, Varieties, in 1878. Though cattle-town saloons served mostly beer, at Varieties a trail hand or drover with fancy tastes could try French brandy.

181

THE ABILENE CHRONICLE.

VOL. I. ABILENE, KANSAS, THURSDAY MORNING, MAY 12, 1870. NO. 9.

AN ORDINANCE

To Prevent Gambling.

Be it ordained by the Trustees of the town of Abilene,

SEC. 1. Every person who shall set up or keep any table or gambling device of any kind, adapted, devised, and designed for the purpose of playing any game of chance for money or property, and shall induce, entice, or permit any person to bet or play at or upon any such gaming table or gambling device, or on the side or against the keeper thereof, shall on conviction be fined in a sum not exceeding three hundred dollars nor less than twenty dollars, and imprisoned in the common jail of the town not exceeding thirty days.

SEC. 2. Every person who shall bet any money or property upon any gaming table, bank, or device prohibited by the foregoing section, or upon any game with cards, shall on conviction be fined in a sum not exceeding one hundred dollars nor less than ten dollars.

SEC. 3. Every person who shall permit any gaming table, bank, or device prohibited by section one of this ordinance, to be set up or used for the purpose of gaming in any house, building, shed, tent, booth, shelter, lot or premises to him belonging, or by him occupied, or of which he hath at the time possession or control, shall on conviction be fined not exceedidg five hundred dollars nor less than fifty dollars, or imprisoned in the common jail of the town not exceeding thirty days, or by both such fine and imprisonment.

SEC. 4. This ordinance shall take effect and be in force from and after the 20th of May 1870.

T. C. HENRY, Chairman.

Attest: G. L. BRINKMAN, Clerk,

AN ORDINANCE

Respecting Vagrancy

Be it ordained by the Trustees of the town of Abilene,

SEC. 1. Any person who may be found loitering around houses of ill-fame, gambling houses, or places where liquors are sold or drank, without any legitimate means of support, or shall be the keeper or inmate of any house of ill-fame or gambling house, or engaged in any unlawful calling whatsoever, shall be deemed a vagrant, and upon conviction thereof may be fined in any sum not exceeding five hundred dollars, and unless such fine shall be paid the person so offending shall be committed to the common jail of the town, and shall work the same out on any public work of the town at the rate of two dollars per day for each day so committed.

SEC. 2. This ordinance shall take effect and be in force from and after May 20th 1870.

T. C. HENRY, Chairman.

Attest: G. L. BRINKMAN, Clerk.

AN ORDINANCE

To Regulate the sale of Spirituous Intoxicating Liquors.

Be it ordained by the Trustees of the town of Abilene,

SEC. 1. That before a libense shall be granted to any person or persons applying for the same, to sell spirituous and intoxicating liquors within the incorporate limits of the town of Abilene, Kansas, or after the 20th day of May, 1870, any person so applying shall present to the Town Trustees a petition signed by a majority of the residents of the town of Abilene, of twenty-one years and over, both male and female, recommending said applicant as a suitable and safe person to vend the same, and requesting that a license be granted to him for such purpose.

SEC. 2. That upon every license granted as aforesaid, there shall be levied and collected a tax of one hundred dollars for the year, for the use and benefit of the town of Abilene, for every period of twelve months from and after the 20th day of May 1870.

SEC. 3. That all licenses granted under this ordinance shall terminate on the 20th of May 1871.

SEC. 4. That any person or persons, who, without procuring a license as herein aforesaid, shall sell or cause to be sold, any intoxicating liquors, shall, upon conviction, be fined any sum not less than five dollars nor more than forty dollars for each offense, and shall be imprisoned in the town jail until said fines and costs are paid.

SEC. 5. That before any person or persons be licensed to sell spirituous or intoxicating liquors under the provisions of this ordinance, they shall in their application state the name or names of the person or firm applying for the same, and shall state therein the house in which said liquors are to be sold. No transfer of said license from one party to another party, or from the place licensed to a different place shall be valid, unless application be first made to the Trustees of the town, and authority granted therefor.

SEC. 6. This ordinance to take effect from and after May 20, 1870.

T. C. HENRY, Chairman.

Attest: G. L. BRINKMAN, Clerk.

AN ORDINANCE

To Prohibit Drunkeness and Disorderly Conduct.

Be it ordained by the Trustees of the town of Abilene,

That any person found in a state of intoxication within the corporate limits of the town of Abilene, or any person guilty of noisy, riotous conduct, or threatening violence against any person or persons, or against the town of Abilene, or running horses on the public streets or alleys, or of lassoing any animal, or leading any wild animal with lasso, or lassoing any person or persons, or of discharging fire-arms within the town limits, shall on conviction thereof before the Court, be fined in any sum not less than five dollars nor more than twenty-five dollars for the first offense, and for the second offense not less than ten dollars nor more than fifty dollars, with costs of prosecution added in both first and second offense, and may be committed to the town jail for any length of time not exceeding five days, provided at the end of that time all costs and fines are paid.

This ordinance shall be in full effect and force from and after the 20th of May, 1870.

T. C. HENRY, Chairman.

Attest: G. L. BRINKMAN, Clerk.

AN ORDINANCE

Relating to the Carrying of Fire Arms and other Deadly Weapons.

Be it ordained by the Trustees of the town of Abilene,

SEC. 1. That any person who shall carry, within the limits of the town of Abilene, or commons, a pistol, revolver, gun, musket, dirk, bowie-knife, or other dangerous weapon upon his or their person or persons, either openly or concealed, except to bring the same and forthwith deposit it or them at their house, boarding house, store room or residence, shall be fined in a sum not less than ten dollars nor more than fifty dollars; and it shall be the duty of any town constable, or policeman of this town, to arrest and disarm any person violating this ordinance, and to deposit the arms so taken with the captain of the town police, to be by him kept until he is, by the magistrate taking cognizance of the offense of carrying arms as aforesaid, authorized to deliver the same to the person or persons from whom the same shall have been taken.

SEC. 2. Any and every person who shall be in violation of this ordinance, within the town of Abilene, or commons, and who shall refuse to deposit his or their arms with the constable or policeman as aforesaid, or shall resist any officer who may attempt to disarm him or them according to the provisions of section one of this ordinance, shall be imprisoned in the common gaol of the town not less than twenty-four hours nor more than ten days, and fined not less than $10 nor more than one hundred dollars: Provided, that the provisions of this ordinance shall not apply to the constable or any officer of the town of Abilene, while in the discharge of their duties as such constable or policeman.

SEC. 3. That any person who shall intentionally discharge any pistol, revolver or gun, within the town of Abilene, in any street, alley, highway, lot, house or other place where the life or limb of any person could be endangered, shall be punished by a fine not less than ten dollars nor more than one hundred dollars.

SEC. 4. This ordinance shall take effect and be in force from the 20th of May 1870.

T. C. HENRY, Chairman.

Attest: G. L. BRINKMAN, Clerk.

AN ORDINANCE

Relating to Houses of Ill-Fame.

Be it ordained by the Trustees of the town of Abilene.

SEC. 1. That any and every person or persons who shall keep or maintain, in this town, a house of ill-fame or prostitution, or a house in which disorderly, licentious, obscene, lewd, profane or indecent conduct or language is permitted or allowed, shall be fined not less than twenty-five dollars nor more than two hundred dollars, and the fact that such language occurring in said house shall be prima facie evidence that the same is permitted or allowed by the person who maintains or keeps such house.

SEC. 2. That any and every person who shall be an inmate or resident of a house of ill-fame or prostitution in this town, or who shall visit or frequent any such house for lewd, licentious, obscene or indecent purposes, shall, on conviction, be fined not less than ten dollars nor more than one hundred dollars, and the fact of any person being found in any such house in the night time, between the hours of eight o'clock, P. M., and five o'clock, a. m., shall be prima facie evidence of his or her frequenting the same for such purpose.

SEC. 3. That any and every person who shall attend, visit or frequent any place in the last preceding section mentioned, and engage or take part in any of the acts, conduct or language therein specified, shall be fined not less than ten dollars nor more than one hundred dollars for each and every offense.

SEC. 4. That any person or persons who shall hereafter knowingly let, lease or rent any house, hall, tenement or other place in this town to any person or persons, for the purpose of keeping or maintaining therein any place as described in the preceeding sections of this ordinance, shall, on conviction, be punished by a fine not exceeding one hundred dollars, and not less than ten dollars for each day that he, she or they allow the same to be tenanted for such purpose or purposes, or who shall suffer the same to be used after any of the Constables of this town have given notice that the same has been declared a house of ill-fame.

SEC. 5. Be it ordained, that any person convicted for keeping a house of ill-fame, or being an inmate thereof, as provided in the foregoing sections, shall be removed by any of the town Constables without the corporate limits of this town, upon the order of the Court.

SEC. 6. This ordinance shall be in force from and after the 20th of May 1870.

T. C. HENRY, Chairman.

Attest: G. L. BRINKMAN, Clerk.

AN ORDINANCE

Relating to Sundry Offences.

Be it ordained by the Trustees of the town of Abilene:

SECTION 1. That any person found guilty of committing any of the several acts and offenses prohibited in this town, shall be subjected to the penalty herein provided for them respectively.

SEC. 2. That for disturbing the peace of the town, or any lawful assembly of persons, or of any neighborhood, family, person or persons, or for indecent, obscene, improper or abusive language or conduct, or for any assault or affray, a fine of a sum not less than one nor more than one hundred dollars.

SEC. 3. For throwing stone or brick or pieces of wood or other hard substances in or across any building, street or alley of this town, or at or against any house, building, vehicle, person or animal, a fine shall be imposed of not less than one nor more than fifty dollars, at the discretion of the Court.

SEC. 4. For discharging any fire-arms, setting off fire crackers or squibs, throwing any fire balls or combustible substance, or making bonfires, within the limits of the town, a fine shall be imposed of not less than one nor more than twenty-five dollars: Provided, that this section shall not apply or be enforced on the first day of January, nor on the fourth day of July of each year: And provided further, that this provision may be applied to other days by the Trustees: Neither shall this section apply to the person authorized to keep a pistol gallery, nor to any gunsmith who may carefully discharge any fire-arms in the prosecution of his business, nor shall it apply to the person duly authorized to shoot dogs running at large in the town.

An abundance of laws, a minimum of order

When the riders on a long drive crested the last rise and in the distance saw the wisps of smoke or the flickering lamps that signaled trail's end, each cowhand felt a surge of almost irrepressible desire. Typically the men had been one to four months in the saddle, usually in the same clothes every day, with boots worn out, hats caked by dust and grime, and no companionship save one another and the cows. They seldom had shaved and had been bathed only by the muddy waters of river fords. Now, with the cattle town finally in sight, each man knew what he needed most of all, and it was neither a drink nor a woman. He needed to be clean again. "'Twas first to the cardhouse and then down to Maisie's," intoned that mournful ballad "The Cowboy's Lament." But most real-life trail riders went first to the bathtub and then to the haberdasher, if only because neither Maisie nor the cardhouse would truly welcome a man so long as he had the look and smell of a summer in the saddle.

Yet even the simple pleasure of cleanliness was not available for everyone right away. Somebody had to watch over all those cows, and if the trail herd arrived behind a lot of other outfits, the cattle might have to be held half a dozen miles from the settlement, with regular guards set and only a few cowhands at a time from any one outfit free to go in. (A few trail bosses, like the one cowboy Baylis John Fletcher remembered, were such stern bluenoses that they restricted all their men to brief daytime visits.)

It was sheer agony for the men on watch to sit in the saddle, grimy as ever, staring at the lights of the distant pleasure palaces and dreaming of what they might be doing if only they were loose in that "Sodom of the plains," as one contemporary newsman described a cattle town. It was even worse, sometimes, to start in for a long-awaited spree and then suddenly find oneself called back to duty. "It was my night off," wrote one frustrated cowboy, "and I went in to whoop 'em up; but a big cloud came up after I had paid $1.25 for a haircut and a shave, and I had to go back to the herd and stand guard all night during a severe storm."

But sooner or later every trail hand managed to break free, however briefly. When his chance came he grabbed at it with a whooping, pistol-firing vengeance. "Well-mounted, and full of their favorite beverage," noted the *Annals of Kansas* in an 1886 survey, "the cowboys will dash through the principal streets of a town, yelling like Comanches. This they call 'cleaning out a town.'" Their visit was often their only opportunity of the year to whoop it up. On the trail or back at the ranch, cowhands had to behave, but at trail's end the rules—and even local ordinances like those at left—often went by the board. Here the cowboy repeatedly acted out his classic role as a free-spending, hard-drinking roisterer, sometimes by accident and at other times with a certain self-conscious purpose. "We ordered toddies, like we had seen the older men do, and drank them down," wrote one strutting youngster in 1867.

In the town a small regiment of profiteers was ready to embrace him and to relieve him of his hard-earned trail money at almost any time of the day or night. Starting in early spring, the townsfolk would place bets as to when the first herds would arrive. Along the streets the jerry-built false-front buildings of unpainted pine were crammed with marked-up merchandise, human and otherwise. In 1877 one local newspaper reported with somewhat chauvinistic license that the town was "bracing herself for the cattle trade. Places of refreshment are being gorgeously arrayed to beguile the festive cow-

Grumpy ordinances like these issued in Abilene did less to quench crime than to make money. In Caldwell, court fines contributed the bulk of the city's income.

boy." The same paper also noted that "accommodations for a large influx of people are being made by the hotels and restaurants, and with a view to the adage of 'live and let live.'"

Into this receptive atmosphere the cowboy rode, pausing briefly to scrape off the grime in a rooming-house tub or a bathroom attached to a saloon. Then, clean-shaven and refurbished, he stepped forth to pleasure himself in a bustling world whose sights and sounds seemed altogether marvelous after the lonely vastness of the range. Down by the stock pens, filled with cattle due to be shipped that day or the next, trains hooted and clanked, and wooden chutes drummed with the hoofs of reluctant cows being poked and shoved aboard. On the main streets horses raised clouds of dust from the unpaved thoroughfares, while human footsteps echoed on the wooden sidewalks—an amenity that the frontier provided to spare pedestrian boots from the mud that followed an occasional rainfall.

Knots of cowboys swaggered along these sidewalks, joking boisterously among themselves and shouting profane greetings to old friends not seen since a year or two ago back in Texas. At intervals a stray longhorn might charge down the street, with a cowboy, his lariat circling, galloping close behind. On one corner a black minstrel might be strumming his ballads, luring a small crowd toward a crony who was bellowing out the bids at an impromptu horse auction. (In one cattle town livestock auctions were held at a spot called Horse Thief Corner, a nickname reflecting local suspicion regarding the source of the animals being sold.) On a bare spot of ground, two snarling dogs might be locked in mortal combat, surrounded by cowhands betting on the outcome. From across the way might come the hard laughter of a group of prostitutes, lusty women with names like Hambone Jane, Big Nose Kate, the Galloping Cow and Squirrel Tooth Alice. Occasionally at the peak of the season the sidewalk babble would be heightened by a barker for a street show, inviting the cowhands to come see the freak pig or watch the performance of The Armless Wonder.

Through the open doorways of saloons, which in some cattle towns for a while outnumbered other establishments by as much as 2 to 1, could be heard the rumble of other voices amplified by infusions of the local liquor. In the background poker chips rattled, and gamblers called the cards while presiding over games of poker, faro and monte. Above the din a cowboy would suddenly raise a boozy shout of "Keno!" signaling a winner's bonanza in a game of progressive numbers played across a grid. "Occasionally," observed one priggish reporter in 1877, "some dark-eyed virago or some brazen-faced blonde will saunter in among the roughs of the gambling houses and saloons, entering with inexplicable zest into the disgusting sport, breathing the immoral atmosphere with gusto."

When evening came on, the strains of fiddles sang through the night air as the cowhands paired up with bar girls for a wild, foot-stomping night of frontier dancing. Or if the town was really up to date a brass band on a saloon balcony might begin blatting out a favorite melody such as "The Lakes of Killarney" or "The Girl I Left behind Me," while next door a piano player might be tinkling the popular tune "Pop Goes the Weasel." "Even the Mayor of the city indulges in the giddy dance with the girls," recounted a cattle-town newspaper in 1877. "And with his cigar in one corner of his mouth and his hat tilted to one side he makes a charming looking officer."

In the midst of this boomtown cacophony there were contrasting islands of tranquillity. Ponies waited patiently in front of the shops and saloons, sometimes tethered to hitching posts but more often restrained only by the fact that the reins were hanging to the ground. On the veranda of the best hotel elegantly dressed Northern meat packers and Midwestern feeders made deals with Texas drovers, sealing the exchange of thousands of head of cattle and many thousands of dollars with a few

Brass checks, stamped with names of soiled doves, were legal tender in up-and-coming Western towns. The usual price was a dollar.

quiet words, a handshake and a drink. The sidewalks were strewn with silent knots of cowhands who because of bad luck or lack of money or their own abstemious ways — or perhaps sheer exhaustion — were bypassing the seamier action of the town. A Wichita resident described them as "loitering principally on the benches erected for their accommodation in front of the different dry goods and grocery stores, whittling thoughtfully with their jackknives."

Over the entire scene hovered the stern silence of disapproval that emanated from the cattle town's handful of respectable citizens, for all of these settlements had in their structure a basic schizophrenia that, in time, would undo them — or at least alter them beyond recognition. The towns grew at first as combination cattle markets and roughhewn frontier watering spots, opening for business when the weather became good enough for trail driving and shutting down with the November snows. Most of the regulars who served this trade were profiteering seasonal operators — notably the saloonkeepers whose premises would close with the year's last drive, the dapper gamblers in from the riverboats and the East, and the prostitutes who wintered in the bagnios of Memphis, St. Louis and New Orleans when the cowboys were back in Texas.

But early on, the cattle towns also attracted homesteaders and farmers in search of new lives and new opportunities. The grangers gravitated toward the towns because there they found at least a few of the amenities of civilization, however rude, and as time passed, these settled citizens infused the cattle markets with steady Bible-thumping ways. Moreover, the orderly grangers drew in a supporting cast of equally sober-minded doctors, lawyers, ministers and teachers who, in the dark cold months of winter, became the town's permanent population. Often they numbered only in the hundreds. Then, beginning in the spring, they would be inundated by perhaps 1,500 cowhands, drovers and buyers, plus hundreds of hangers-on.

To these settled residents the hordes of cowboys and the other transients who preyed on them seemed bizarre and alien creatures, no more welcome than a summer hailstorm. A staid Kansan said edgily of the cowboy: "His large spurs jingled loudly, suggesting fatality like a rattlesnake's rattling." No matter that the economic base of the town was the cattle trade; the respectable farmers and their respectable wives despised the summer people. An occasional cowboy, too, was repelled by the atmosphere the fast-buck merchants had created. One wrote, following a liberty visit to a cattle-shipping center: "Attended the Sabbath school this A.M. and was delighted as it was the most pleasant hour I have spent since leaving home."

Many of the cattle-business promoters were themselves of two minds about all the hoopla and shooting. On the one hand they wanted to create the kind of wide-open spot that cowboys would want to visit. "If we make a devil of a place," advised a promoter, "we shall have a devil of a cattle trade." On the other hand,

Nailed to a well on Front Street, this 1878 Dodge City sign — besides pushing a local tonic — informed arriving cowboys that toting guns was prohibited. Despite the ordinance, Dodge had five killings that year.

while it was very profitable to have the ordinary cowhand's dollars circulating through the stores and saloons, a good hunk of the real money was in steady trade, and in the land speculation and construction that came along with permanent settlement or followed close on its heels. In the light of this wisdom a straight-eyed cattle-town editor sagely observed that "people who have money to invest go where they are protected by law." Sooner or later, in almost every town, enough of his peers came to agree, and they would band together to create a town government, complete with elected mayor and a squad of marshals and deputies, who were counted on to be faster with their fists and their guns than were the trail hands and the bullyboys.

As time passed, the cattle towns became increasingly strict, at least in their public posture toward the cowboys. "We expect them to have all the fun they can get," announced one local editor, "but they must ac-

knowledge that the citizens of our town have a right to insist upon a strict compliance with the city's laws. Visitors had better bear that in mind," he added, "and also the fact that we have a police force determined to do their duty." Signs of warning went up at the entrances to the main thoroughfares. One, which was posted on two pine boards, bore this legend: "All persons are hereby forbidden the carrying of firearms or other dangerous weapons within the city limits under penalty of fine and imprisonment. By Order of the Mayor." Another (above) opened with a stern warning and ended with an advertisement for a patent medicine.

As an extra show of purpose, a number of stiff laws were passed, backed by a system of fines. And yet there lingered a continuing and reasonable doubt about the seriousness of some of these early attempts at law and order. For one thing, most of the fines were well within the limits of what a boisterous cowhand or en-

186

terprising prostitute could afford to pay for a misdemeanor. Many residents seemed both to understand and to benefit from this subtle fact of city life: one town totted up $5,600 from fines in a single cattle season so that the levies actually became not punishment but in effect licensing fees and a steady source of municipal income. "The revenue derived from fines on gambling and prostitution," noted one newspaper in 1879, "will pay the police force."

Thus the tide of reform often found itself frustrated by a pragmatic and highly mercantile boys-will-be-boys attitude toward the cowhands, even when they were very bad boys indeed, and occasionally they were. "A humorous cowpuncher named Todd lassoed Mr. Bowring, a prominent citizen," ran a report, "and dragged him several hundred yards as rapidly as his horse could run." The police never bothered about the matter. In another town a puncher rode his pony into the anteroom of a favored amusement center, the roller-skating rink — one of several similar places that sprang up in the unlikely surroundings of the frontier. (Bowling alleys provided another popular diversion.) Giddy with booze, he tried to spur the horse onto the rink itself before two attendants persuaded him that the healthiest thing all round would be his departure, which he effected with no threat of arrest. A local newspaper of August 20, 1878, told this story: "One of the cow boys, becoming intoxicated and quarrelsome, undertook to take possession of the bar. A row ensued. Several cattle men engaged in the broil and some of them were bruised on the head with six shooters. Several shots were accidentally fired. We are glad to chronicle that none were seriously hurt and nobody shot."

Unfortunately the outcome was not always so happy. "A cowboy named Taylor rode into a saloon and announced that he intended cleaning out the house," said another story of the era. "He was heavily armed, but before he carried his threat into execution he was shot by an unknown man, his head nearly severed from his body. There is much excitement among the cowboys over Taylor's death, and fears are entertained that trouble will ensue."

Thus the cattle towns rolled on in an atmosphere of live and — with exceptions — let live, with some cowboys themselves stoutly maintaining that despite all the stories about them, they were indeed basically fun-loving fellows. "There is a good deal of exaggeration about us cowboys," complained one puncher. "We're not near so bad as we're painted. We like to get up a little racket now and then, but it's all in play."

The places that gave rise to this roistering, and evoked such conflicting emotions, were unique in American history. They were a special sort of boomtown — as wide open as the wildest of the mining camps — that sprouted where Texas cattle trails intersected westward-reaching railroads. For two decades following the Civil War, thousands of Texas drovers and Texas cowboys rode into these cattle towns and were joined by Northerners and Easterners who came to buy the cows and to do a little reveling themselves in the curious confusion of the cowboy Shangri-las. The first such town to spring from the prairie was called Abilene, but it might just as well have been called Newton, Ellsworth, Wichita, Caldwell, Ogallala or Dodge City. For these were the names of the most notorious of the towns, whose high-living ways were copied by other cattle markets across the West. However, the pacesetters were all in Kansas or just over the border. At the outset, virtually everything about them was designed, first, to handle longhorns and, second, to assuage the frustrations of the Texas cowboy.

In Abilene or Ellsworth or one of their lesser competitors along the Texas trails — Hays City, Hunnewell, Ellis or any of a dozen others — the trail hand could drink at an Alamo saloon or buy new clothes at the Long Horn store. He could take a bath or find a girl at the Cowboy's Rest. Or his boss could make a deal at the Drovers' Cottage. And if one cattle boomtown swiftly died of farmers' piety backed by toughening law enforcement, no matter. For the promoters could make a fortune in a single good year and then could easily shift the action a few miles down the railroad track to another wild new marketplace.

Each of these cattle towns had a different life span, though all boasted very similar boom-and-bust life cycles. Newton, for instance, lasted just one season — 1871, when the Atchison, Topeka and Santa Fe Railroad reached town. The speed with which Newton grew and died was astonishing, even for a cattle town. A cowboy who passed through in May 1871 recalled: "A blacksmith shop, a store and about a dozen

Like most cattle towns, Newton, Kansas, grew up and out-
ward from the railroad tracks. Unlike some cattle-town
residents, however, the people of Newton did not have to
put up with cows tramping through town. Joe McCoy, fresh
from his Abilene venture, built the Newton stockyards a dis-
creet distance from town — a mile and a half to the west.

A. F. HORNER. STORE

dwellings made up this town at the time, but when we came back through the place on our return home 30 days later, it had grown to be quite a large town." Of all its new-sprung buildings only one had plastered walls, and that was the railroad station. The rest were Cattle Town Classic—bare weatherboard with false fronts mixed in with a motley assortment of shacks and tents. Grass still grew in the streets when the first cows arrived; prairie dogs poked their heads up through the grass, and water came from two wells on the main street. Stronger drink, costing 25 cents a glass, flowed at 27 establishments. The seamiest saloons were in the red-light district, which Newtonites called Hide Park. A writer for *The Wichita Tribune* exclaimed that "you may see young girls not over 16 drinking whisky, smoking cigars, cursing and swearing until one almost loses the respect they should have for the weaker sex. I heard one of their townsmen say that he didn't believe there were a dozen virtuous women in town."

Wichita should not have talked, especially not in such pompous phrases. For Wichita, according to one estimate, was on its way toward establishing some sort of cattle-town record for total soiled doves: 300. Among the most thoroughly soiled were the doves who labored in a dance hall appropriately named Rowdy Joe's, a family enterprise whose management was shared by Joe's wife, Rowdy Kate. Texans acclaimed it "the swiftest joint in Kansas," and in cattle season it cleared more than $100 a night on drinks alone.

During its brief life as a cattle town Newton never managed to put together a municipal police force, for the lack of which the local gamblers—who seemed to feel they needed more protection than anybody—pooled

some money to pay the salaries of a couple of private enforcers. The enforcers did little, according to contemporary accounts, to keep the peace. "The firing of guns in and around town was so continuous," said one resident, "that it reminded me of a Fourth of July celebration. There was shooting when I got up and when I went to bed." Such tales earned the town the sobriquet of Bloody Newton. No accurate statistics were kept, but the more conservative estimates say that in Newton's one year of glory nine people were shot to death. Some put the casualties as high as 50.

These stories of lethal violence, however, particularly those having to do with total casualties, do not always stand up to careful historical research. No question that there was action galore—and too much killing. But here, as elsewhere, the stories that people seized on and remembered were the rowdy and the gory ones. A good many of the accounts came from nearby and out-of-state newspapers whose horror tales about cattle towns tended to be artfully emphasized or purposefully exaggerated. The cattle markets, being close together in both time and place, became bitter rivals for the beef-and-cowboy trade that flocked to good shipping points with plenty of rough entertainment. Aware of this, the news editors, in cahoots with local business leaders, lost no chance to make a rival market's two pistol shots fired skyward in celebration sound like two dozen Winchesters exchanging volleys across the public square.

The towns also did a fair amount of sniping at each other on matters other than plain violence. Wichita and Ellsworth engaged in a running editorial battle of belittlement. "If the lack of water and short grass are required to the well-being of Texas cattle," sneered *The Wichita City Eagle,* "then Ellsworth is the point." To which the *Ellsworth Reporter* riposted that everyone knew cattle tended to be "wild and unruly, and easily stampeded by any degree of annoyance from flies and mosquitoes which prevail to an alarming extent this year in and around Wichita, and which owe their increased number to the humid and sultry weather experienced there during the spring and summer."

Along with slinging mud at rivals, the local boosters promoted their own town's virtues with typical frontier gusto. Ellsworth advertised the hometown stockyards as "the biggest in the state" and trumpeted a local hotel as the finest in any state (and indeed the new Grand

These Mexican *toreros* starred in a Fourth of July fete in Dodge *(opposite)*. "They are a fierce lot," said a reporter, but "their all-redeeming trait is that they cannot be forced to drink a drop of strong liquor."

Central Hotel had been put up at a startling cost of $27,000, a mighty fat sum in those days). Ellsworth businessmen collected a subscription of $1,000 to pay off the influential Texas cattle baron Shanghai Pierce (who had been on the payroll at Wichita only the year before) for the six weeks he spent drumming up beef business for the town among his cronies.

Wichita countered by appropriating $2,500, some of which went for kickbacks to drovers to bring in their herds, some for laying out a new trail, some for circulars extolling the excellence of the Wichita stockyards. One year a delegation of cattle-hungry businessmen offered to pay $50 in damages to a farmer whose crops on the outskirts of Wichita had been trampled by cows, and another year the city council passed a resolution guaranteeing unimpeded passage for cattle right down the main street of town if the drovers so desired. During

the summer of the kickbacks, Wichita—which had already killed off Newton's business—shipped 30,000 head more than Ellsworth.

Early in the Wichita bonanza one enterprising citizen, a land developer named William (Dutch Bill) Greiffenstein, figured out an ingenious way to help promote the town further while at the same time putting some money into his own pockets. He built a bridge over the shallow Arkansas River, placing it so that incoming traffic would pass his various business enterprises. The drovers, having already pushed their herds through the Red River and lesser streams, paid to get their cows safe and dry into Wichita. Local farmers also paid—50 cents to cross the bridge with a wagonload of produce and 25 cents to go out empty. In five months Dutch Bill racked up $10,000 in tolls.

The railroads, too, sometimes pitched into the scramble for cattle business. During 1880 the Atchison, Topeka and Santa Fe slashed its carload rate out of Caldwell from $40 to $10. Whereupon the Kansas City, Lawrence and Southern at neighboring Hunnewell dropped its own rate to match. And while the businessmen engaged in such sophisticated techniques to entice the big drovers, the boosters did not forget that what the cowboy himself came to town for was fun. Wichita's *Eagle* proudly reported the goings-on at the town's pony track, where a cowboy could get rich quick by betting on the right nag and have a whooping good time, win or lose. On one Saturday afternoon "more than one thousand men were present," said the *Eagle,* and added slyly, "besides five carriages of soiled doves." Another time the paper noted: "Pistols are as thick as blackberries." But it insisted: "Notwithstanding this a man is as safe in Wichita as anywhere else if he keeps out of bad company."

This note was struck with increasing frequency as time passed. Ellsworth was claiming to be "the most orderly city; here is order and law." And Caldwell, among other towns, really undertook to do something about it. In 1879 the town elected as mayor a sober dry-goods-and-grocery merchant and set up a police force. In Wichita a vigilante group, headed by a shotgun-toting lawyer named S. M. Tucker, faced down and marched off to jail a trigger-happy Texan named Hurricane Bill, who had been rustling local cattle and shooting up the town. From then on Wichita was considerably quieter, though it was by no means prim.

No matter how orderly they tried to become, however, or how much zest they put into puffery, none of the other towns managed to last as long as Dodge City or to surpass its enduring reputation as a place where drovers could profitably bring their cows and where trail hands could have a blowout. Dodge had been in existence for some years before the first big shipment of cows went out in 1876. It was adjacent to Fort Dodge, and thoughtful saloonkeepers, with thirsty soldiers in mind, opened establishments just at the edge of the military reservation. Dodge boomed as a shipping center for buffalo hides, and during this period it established its reputation for rowdiness: 24 men were said to have been killed in a single year.

The proprietors of the Dodge City dives recognized very early the merit of low-cost volume business. When the cattle came, with the Texans as escort, the saloonkeepers did not raise their prices, and the Long Branch Saloon even dispensed free eggnog on Thanksgiving Day. It also dispensed the favors of three ladies ostensibly hired as singers. The singers drew so much business that A. B. Webster, who ran the rival Old House, persuaded his friend Mayor Lawrence Deger to throw them in jail, which left Webster's own stable of girls free to profit from the dip in competition.

As the cattle trade increased, Dodge City promoters spared no effort to make cowboys and drovers feel welcome there. The town proclaimed itself the "cowboy capital of the world," and advertised that "the grass is remarkably fine, the water plenty, drinks two for a quarter and no grangers. These facts make Dodge City the cattle point."

That it was until the mid-1880s, boasting the gaudiest dance halls, the prettiest girls, the most unruly cowboys and, on the whole, the least effective law enforcement—despite the presence of Sheriff Bat Masterson and Deputy Marshal Wyatt Earp. Dodge City lost no opportunity to show where its true heart lay —with the Texas cowboy. When a Texan, already under indictment for rustling, died a slow death of a gun

wound, the local *Ford County Globe* eulogized him as "a good young man, having those chivalrous qualities so common to frontiersmen. He had many friends and no enemies among the Texas men who knew him. His brother cowboys permitted him to want for nothing during his illness, and buried him in grand style when dead."

Perhaps Dodge City's finest hour came in 1884, by which time the cattle trade was foundering badly and Caldwell had produced a dying gasp of competition. Looking toward the Fourth of July holidays, the inventive saloonkeeper A. B. Webster conceived a celebration certain to lure cattle shippers back to Dodge and to stun any lingering rivals. It would be a Spanish bullfight. Webster raised $10,000 from fellow businessmen, built a crude ring, rounded up 12 fierce-looking longhorns, hired five formidable Mexican *toreros* and lured 4,000 spectators. Some of them came from so far away they traveled to Dodge by train; others arrived on horseback and found the hitching posts all taken and cow ponies picketed in the vacant fields. When it was over, a neighboring newspaper observed: "Quite a number of our boys visited Dodge last week to see the bullfight. Some of them returned looking as though they had had a personal encounter with the animals." One did not return at all, having been killed just after the bullfight in a shoot-out with a gambler named Dave St. Clair at A. B. Webster's saloon.

Despite the killing, Dodge was delighted with the promotion. "Caldwell is way behind the times as a cattle town," crowed the hometown newspaper. "They didn't have any bullfight on the Fourth."

The great bullfight, however, was by no means a universal success. Editorial writers as far away as New York described the undertaking as inhumane and un-American. And worse yet, the promotion itself did not help to stave off the ultimate fate that swallowed up all the cattle towns. In 1885 the state legislature passed a new quarantine law that closed all of Kansas to the tick-infested cattle that were being driven up from Texas. By the end of that year the trails were blocked by lines of barbed-wire fence. Finally — and ironically — the very railroads that had provided the original impetus for the cattle towns also helped to make them anachronisms. They did this by the simple expedient of extending their lines into Texas.

In the 20-year sweep of the towns' existence as cattle markets, Dodge City had perhaps been, as it claimed, the grandest. Newton, in its brief existence, was probably the most violent. Yet none of these later cattle centers ever truly surpassed the very first of the trail's-end boomtowns, Abilene.

The cattle-town mold was set in Abilene. Virtually everything that ever was to happen later in Newton or Ellsworth or Wichita or Caldwell or Dodge had already happened first in Abilene between 1867 and 1872.

During these five years more than a million cows went through Abilene. In this brief time, too, Abilene took on a special significance beyond the singular role of the pioneer Kansas cattle town. For it was here that respectable citizens had their first confrontation with the cowboy as a major American figure — and won their first victory over him, an omen that almost nobody noticed at the time.

As the prototype among the cattle towns, Abilene emerged full-blown from the head of the most ingenious cattle-town promoter of them all, an ascetic-looking but tough, rich but ambitious young Illinoisan named Joseph Geiting McCoy. In fact, it was McCoy who, in a sense, invented both the concept and the reality of the cattle town. One of 11 children born to a Springfield family that grew rich from dealing in local beef, Joe McCoy got the first gleam in his eye when two friends, one just having returned from the Civil War, described the millions of longhorn cattle grazing over the Texas plains — all of them begging for sale. "It was not long," wrote McCoy, who always referred to himself in the third person, as befitted a man of his importance, "before he was casting his eye over the map of the western states" in search of a suitable market site. He hit upon Kansas as a place "whereat the southern drover and northern buyer could meet upon an equal footing, and both be undisturbed by mobs or swindling thieves."

In the spring of 1867 McCoy boarded a train for Salina, Kansas, the western tip of the Union Pacific Railroad. En route the train halted for an hour while workmen repaired a bridge, and McCoy alighted to find himself in the prairie village called Abilene. The name, which early settlers had chosen from the Bible, meant "city of the plains."

It was as unprepossessing a city as ever McCoy had seen. He found it "a small, dead place, consisting of about one dozen log huts." A single post bearing a number and a peg for a mail pouch indicated to the brakeman where to stop the train. A mere handful of people actually lived in Abilene. Tim Hersey, who claimed to have been the first arrival, served food to stagecoach passengers in a log cabin. According to one local historian, *New York Tribune* editor Horace Greeley during his famous Western rovings described it as the last place to get a square meal. Josiah Jones, a rotund and amiable sort, ran a saloon and fed the native prairie dogs, trapping a few that he tried to sell to travelers at five dollars a pair. Business was not very good.

The train went on to Salina, which apparently showed no interest in McCoy, and returned by way of Junction City, where land prices were too high. McCoy began, somewhat reluctantly, to consider Abilene. The village had certain fairly obvious advantages: it lay west of Kansas lands that had been settled by farmers but was squarely on the Kansas route of the Union Pacific Railroad Eastern Division (later renamed the Kansas Pacific). On the other hand, it had no station, cattle pens or ramps, and it was well within the quarantine line. None of these drawbacks fazed McCoy. He had made up his mind. This would be the place.

He called on the Governor of Kansas and soon had the latter's assurance that the quarantine would not be enforced. McCoy, the irresistible promoter, also visited the Union Pacific and extracted its promise to install switches and sidings, and a commitment to carry cattle at five dollars a carload — with not a cow in sight and none promised, except by McCoy. Meanwhile, McCoy grabbed up 250 key acres of land.

Back home in Illinois, McCoy had enlisted his brothers and some friends in the scheme and had also dipped into the family money. One brother worked on getting backing from Eastern retailers in New York. Another Illinoisan named T. C. Henry, who proved to be as shrewd as McCoy, came to help promote the venture — as well as a few real-estate schemes of his own.

A cowboy band assembles for its portrait in 1886. Started as a promotional gimmick by local Dodge City boosters, it had starred at the Cattlemen's Convention in St. Louis two years earlier. Though the band's leader told reporters he conducted with a loaded six-shooter in case anyone blew off-key, the "cowboys" were mostly professional musicians.

Drover J. D. Reed

Drover Seth Mabry

W. W. Sugg, another Illinois acquaintance and himself a dealer in cattle, mounted a horse and, upon McCoy's bidding, gamely rode 200 miles into the Indian Territory, where he collared Texas drovers and pointed the way to Abilene.

In less than two months the transformation of the prairie village was underway. McCoy ordered fancy lumber from Missouri to build a set of stock pens sturdy enough to contain 3,000 stamping and bawling longhorns; nearby he had workmen set up a 10-ton scale that would weigh 20 cows at a time. He also erected a livery stable, a barn, an office and an 80-room hotel. McCoy called the hotel the Drovers' Cottage.

And one day in August, before the construction in Abilene was even finished, the cattle began to come. On September 5, twenty carfuls rolled away to Chicago. By the time the season ended in November another 1,000 carloads had pulled out of Abilene.

The venture made news as far away as New York, where the *Tribune* reported that McCoy's stockyards could "load a train of 40 cars in two hours." Visitors by the hundreds were flocking to Abilene to cash in on the boom, said the *Tribune,* adding, with the unabashed bigotry characteristic of the era, "Some of them are paying 'lightning prices' for ready-made clothing to two Jews, who have extemporized a store out of an empty corn-bin, and are selling the goods they receive from Fort Leavenworth, at from 150 to 200 per cent profit, almost as fast as they can take them from the boxes."

In a single hot summer McCoy's vision had been realized; yet his work was far from finished. The following season, when double the number of cattle started north, rumors began to spread that they were bringing with them an epidemic of the dreaded Texas fever. That news scared off buyers from Abilene, threatening McCoy's infant market with extinction.

McCoy's solution to this problem was as ingenious —and unlikely—as his original creation. By his own modest account he seized everyone's attention with another piece of spectacular promotion and then followed it up with some mesmerizing salesmanship, the total effect of which was to bury the fever scare under a blanket of hoopla. He began by staging one of the precursors of the Wild West shows. On McCoy's instructions a band of cowboys went out on the prairies west of Abilene in search of buffalo. They captured several, including a mammoth bull weighing 2,200 pounds, and hoisted them aboard a waiting train by block and tackle. He later added some elk and wild horses, and set off for St. Louis and Chicago in a stock car draped with a brilliant banner touting Abilene and the fat beeves to be had there. With them went the cowboys—Texans in neckerchiefs and spurs, and Mexicans in black velvet trousers and red sashes. These colorful plainsmen displayed their prowess in riding, roping and throwing the obstreperous animals.

The extravaganza, the sort of show Buffalo Bill Cody would later make famous, delighted the buyers, and ac-

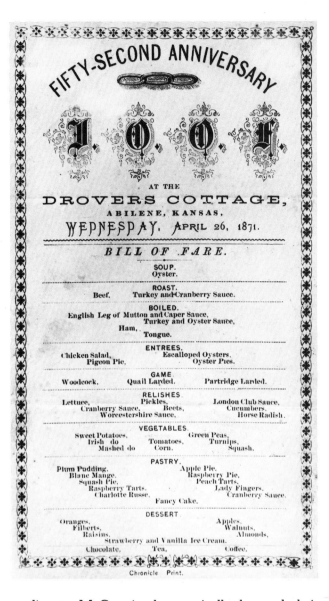

FIFTY-SECOND ANNIVERSARY

I.O.O.F.

AT THE

DROVERS COTTAGE,
ABILENE, KANSAS,
WEDNESDAY, APRIL 26, 1871.

BILL OF FARE.

SOUP.
Oyster.

ROAST.
Beef.   Turkey and Cranberry Sauce.

BOILED.
English Leg of Mutton and Caper Sauce,
Turkey and Oyster Sauce,
Ham,
Tongue.

ENTREES.
Chicken Salad,   Escalloped Oysters,
Pigeon Pie,   Oyster Pies.

GAME.
Woodcock.   Quail Larded.   Partridge Larded.

RELISHES.
Lettuce,   Pickles,   London Club Sauce,
Cranberry Sauce,   Beets,   Cucumbers,
Worcestershire Sauce,   Horse Radish.

VEGETABLES.
Sweet Potatoes,   Green Peas,
Irish do   Tomatoes,   Turnips,
Mashed do   Corn,   Squash.

PASTRY.
Plum Pudding,   Apple Pie,
Blanc Mange,   Raspberry Pie,
Squash Pie,   Peach Tarts,
Raspberry Tarts,   Lady Fingers,
Charlotte Russe,   Cranberry Sauce.
Fancy Cake.

DESSERT.
Oranges,   Apples,
Filberts,   Walnuts,
Raisins,   Almonds,
Strawberry and Vanilla Ice Cream.
Chocolate,   Tea,   Coffee.

Chronicle Print.

name." In just two years the mud-hut settlement of 1867 had become a national marketplace.

Even in its own time Abilene was famous the country over. One early resident, who as a boy delivered ice from the hardware store (where it was kept frozen) to the saloons where it chilled the Texans' drinks, later asserted that "every schoolboy in the far eastern states, when seeing the long trains of long horned cattle going through the country on the railroads, knew that they were from Abilene." Pride and nostalgia may have led the old man to exaggerate — but he was not far wrong.

By 1870 to 1871 Abilene was reaching bustling maturity as the pacesetting cattle town. And with maturity came change and conflict. Along with its burgeoning cattle trade, Abilene now boasted a furniture store, a jewelry store, two churches and a newspaper, *The Abilene Chronicle*. It had a prospering new population of blacksmiths, tinsmiths, saddlers, grocers, dry-goods and clothing merchants, doctors, lawyers, dentists, ministers, teachers and bankers, all of whom were learning to depend on one another and on the growing farm population for their livelihood. Settlers intending to farm were arriving by the hundreds; T. C. Henry's real-estate office, around the corner from the railroad depot, sold from 10 to 15 farms a day.

A three-block walk would take the visiting cowboy or prospective settler through the heart of town. Henry H. Hazlett's Farmer's and Drover's Supply Store stood at the western end of Texas Street, named for the cattle trade that kept it busy for six months of the year. It was not, strictly speaking, a street, but a kind of grubby esplanade. Hazlett's store was the first of a number of establishments inviting the cowboy to spend his money before he proceeded any farther. "I had to sow my wild oats," one cowboy remembered in later years, "and I regret to say that I also sowed all of the money I made right along with the oats." He was not the only one. "It has cost us much since we have been here," wrote another cowboy to his parents from Abilene, "and Charlie made $4.50 plastering a house."

A block beyond Hazlett's was another money trap, the Great Western Store, where Jake Karatofsky, a more recent arrival than Hazlett, had come with the boomtown trade. He sold "boots, hats and gents' furnishing goods" at handsome markups. Thomas C. McInerney, also on Texas Street, employed from 10 to

cording to McCoy it also magically lowered their resistance to his drumfire of persuasion about the basic virtues of his Texas cattle. (The fact is that their own meat was untainted by disease even though longhorns could fatally infect other cows.) As his final coup, McCoy invited everyone in sight to come to Abilene for a real, live buffalo hunt. They went, killed their share of the shaggy beasts and then, thoroughly under the spell of Joe McCoy, allowed themselves to be herded down to Abilene's stockyard. By then the fever had conveniently waned, and McCoy showed and lavishly praised the thousands of fine longhorns waiting for someone to bid on them. Someone did. Before the end of the summer of 1868 Abilene was back on top of the cattle business again. The following year 150,000 head of cattle were received in Abilene. The town won such a reputation that one visiting Texan remarked that he had never seen "such a little town have such a mighty big

DOCKET, POLICE JUDGE, CITY OF CALDWELL, KANSAS

THE CITY OF CALDWELL, Plaintiff.	IN THE POLICE COURT.
vs.	
No	BEFORE James D' Kelly POLICE JUDGE.
One Mollie Last name unknown	In and for the City of Caldwell, Sumner County, State of Kansas.
May Bates Defendant	

One Mollie Last name unknown Defendant arrested on the complaint
of Wm Horseman charging that on the 17 day of
May A.D. 188 1, at the said City of Caldwell, the said Defendant

Index,	10
Docket,	10
Number,	10
Title,	10
Complaint,	30
Warrant,	50
Subpœna,	
Swearing Wit's,	
Trial,	50
Judgment,	25
Solis	25
Entering Judgm't,	25
oh	10
at	10
Commitment,	25
Attorney	2.50
Entries,	
Filing Papers,	
Mav	2 00
Arrest	25
WITNESSES.	

Wm Horseman being duly sworn
on oath says says that on the 17th day
of May A D 1880 in the City of Caldwell
County of Sumner and state of Kansas
One Mollie Last name unknown did then
and there unlawfully Violate the City
Ordinance by being an inmate of a
House of Ill fame in the City of Caldwell
The charge being distinctly read to her and
she required to plead and she plead guilty
And was fine in the sum of Five
dollars and cost of suit and stand com
mitted until fine and cost is paid
Sent to prison

Fine and cost paid
Paid to treasure

FINE,	5 00
COSTS,	
TOTAL,	13 10

Witness my Hand: James D' Kelly Probate Jud

20 men in cattle season to fashion cowboy boots with high heels, red tops and Lone Star designs.

Just to the east of Hazlett's, conveniently facing the jail, was the Bull's Head Saloon, marked by a signboard painted with an enormous red bull. It was one of seven or more bars where the cowboy could drink, gamble and get a girl — the kind of place where, according to a reporter on the *Kansas State Record,* "dealers in card board, bone and ivory most do congregate."

However, the Bull's Head and its brother saloons were crude compared to the original Alamo in the next block. This handsome oasis had glass doors instead of wooden ones and paintings of Renaissance-like nudes on the walls. Mirrors doubled the apparent size of the main barroom, reflecting the rows of whiskey, brandy and rum bottles, the glass tumblers arranged in pyramids, the polished brass fixtures and the gold that lay loose on the green baize of the gaming tables. At such tables in Abilene and the other cattle towns across the Kansas plains drovers and cowboys played for stakes in the thousands. One cowboy remembered seeing a Texan gamble away a whole herd of cows.

Past the Alamo and the railroad depot stood the splendid frame house of T. C. Henry, who continued to flourish on the Abilene boom — and who transferred his loyalty from the cattlemen to the farmers. He was the principal author of the town's first ordinances for law and order.

Dominating the next corner, the last one before the stockyards, stood McCoy's elegant Drovers' Cottage, the grandest place in town. It towered three stories high, standing out from the other buildings in yellow paint, with green trim and venetian blinds. Behind the Cottage was a stable with room for 100 horses and 50 carriages. The food in the dining room was reputed to be as good as that of the poshest Eastern restaurant (*menu, page 197*), and its lounges were praised as places where businessmen could think and talk in genteel quiet. On its broad veranda, too, drovers could relax, make deals or just sit and watch the trains.

Around the corner from the Drovers' Cottage squatted the stockyards, where every day of the summer the cattle pawed the ground and cracked their horns together as they waited their turn to be weighed, sent up the ramp and loaded onto the trains. Within sight of the stockyards but on the other side of the tracks rose the substantial home that McCoy had built for his family.

Scattered among the rest of the landmarks was an assortment of hardware stores; blacksmith shops; boarding houses, where the cowboy might get a bath and sleep on clean sheets for the first time in months; a photography studio, where many a cowboy posed in his new-bought duds to show the folks back home; and several grocery stores. Notwithstanding the saloons and the gambling houses, groceries were often the biggest selling items in town, for they fed the trail outfits as well as local residents (a Wichita grocer was to run up sales of $12,000 a month in 1873).

And of course there was the bank, which helped initiate the practice of bestowing outrageous favors on cattlemen, sometimes at the expense of other borrowers. (A bank in Wichita granted loans to Texas drovers at 3 or 4 per cent, while an outraged farmer had to cough up a usurious 36 to 60 per cent.) For a long time the small tradesmen also favored the cattlemen, whom they found to be splendidly openhanded. "If a stockman wants a jug of vinegar," said one man, "he pays for both. If a granger wants the same, he wants to pay for the vinegar and have the 25-cent jug thrown in."

A little distance away from the center of Abilene — about half a mile, more or less, the location shifting according to public tolerance — was another major business center: the red-light district. It was nicknamed the Devil's Addition, and an Abilene lumber dealer was sure he knew why: "Money and whiskey flowed like water down hill, and youth and beauty and womanhood and manhood were wrecked and damned in that valley of perdition." Another name for it was McCoy's Addition, possibly because Joe, in his role as town leader, responded to citizens' demands to get rid of the girls by moving them just outside of town.

Many of the subsequent Kansas shipping sites followed this practice. But the soiled doves (they also were known as nymphs du prairie, calico queens and painted cats) were as hard to contain in their quarter as longhorns in a loose cowpen. In Abilene itself the girls sometimes went skinny-dipping in the Smoky Hill River in the company of their customers. And in Ellsworth a legend stubbornly persists — though no contemporary account can be found to support it — that a belle named Prairie Rose strode down the main street one day covered with nothing but a pair of six-shooters.

on the Early 70's and 68 & 9 the long
buried here so called, "Boot Hill"
element - killed in brawls & dru
boots on, Wild Bill marshall-
started Boot Hill first some 70'
70's This photo shows where ii
on unexpectedly on 5 or six
found with the bullet in he
milk-made stones and wode

Road workers outside Hays City, Kansas, display a corpse and coffins turned up during a grading operation. Boot Hill was a cattle-town institution, where gamblers and other frontier toughs were interred with their boots on, or tucked like a rough pillow underneath their heads. The inscription is by an anonymous contemporary, possibly the photographer.

Wild Bill Hickok, dandied up with a pair of pearl-handled pistols, was marshal at Abilene for eight months in 1871. In that time he shot two people, one a policeman.

For the first three seasons in Abilene, despite rising pressure from the farmers and a few businessmen, no one seriously tried to keep law and order; there were not even any town officials to do so. The citizens in neighboring towns said of Abilene during the cattle season that "hell is now in session." And one newspaper, in the extravagant language of the era, intoned: "Murder, lust, highway robbery and whores run the city day and night. Seventeen souls snatched from this earth, seventeen souls taken in their sins, ushered before their God without a moment's warning, all of this done at our county seat."

However, as time passed, the farm element grew increasingly powerful—but also impatient at the rank favoritism shown the cowboys and with the lawlessness that grew out of it. The farmers had come to stay and to raise their children, one result of which was that a stone schoolhouse was going up at the edge of town. It would not do to have liquored-up cowhands galloping around the school grounds. Nor anywhere else, if Abilene was ever going to be known as something better than "the meanest hole in the state."

Finally the townfolk decided they had been pushed beyond the point of tolerance. They petitioned successfully to the probate court for the right to incorporate and to elect city officials (rather than having to rely on the lax administration of a county government). T. C. Henry became chairman of the new entity, a role that allowed him to act as a sort of provisional mayor until the town should hold an election. One of his major acts was to sign his name to the ordinances prohibiting firearms, fining prostitution and requiring licenses for saloonkeeping and gambling. These ordinances, effective May 20, 1870, appeared on the front page of the *Chronicle (page 182)* and on billboards along the roads, where they were shot full of holes by cowboys.

Henry set about to hire a marshal, but the first two candidates took one look at the rip-roaring main street and hopped the midnight train out again. Undaunted, the provisional mayor redoubled his efforts and finally came up with a willing recruit. The new man was one Thomas James (Bear River Tom) Smith, a redhead with gray-blue eyes, a low voice and a straight and nimble body. He had been a New York policeman and a worker on the Union Pacific Railroad. At a bloody frontier riot in Bear River, Wyoming, he had performed yeoman service while bleeding from a severe gun wound. The site of that exploit gave him his nickname, and his performance won him the post of marshal at the next town the railroad reached.

In Abilene, Bear River Tom addressed himself first to enforcement of the antigun law. Smith kept his own gun, but it showed only as a bulge under his coat, and he was seldom seen to draw it. He got the chance to show his mettle on a Saturday night soon after he took office, when a desperado known as Big Hank strode into town flaunting a six-shooter on his belt. Smith demanded the weapon, and Big Hank refused to give it up. Smith struck him "a terrible blow" on the jaw, relieved him of the gun and ordered him out of town. To the astonishment of all those who witnessed the scene, Big Hank went.

With him went news of the incident. In one of the cowboy camps that circled the town a tough hand named Wyoming Frank bet his fellows that he could overcome the marshal. He installed himself on the main street of Abilene the first thing Sunday morning and when Bear River Tom made his appearance greeted him with abuse.

Smith walked up to the offender and quietly asked for the gun. Wyoming Frank backed away toward a saloon; Bear River Tom kept walking and drove him right inside it. There Bear River Tom punched the cowboy, threw him onto the floor, took away the gun and told him to get out. Like Big Hank the day before, Wyoming Frank meekly did as he was told.

As T. C. Henry described the episode some 30 years afterward, Frank's capitulation produced stunned silence in the crowded saloon. Then the saloonkeeper spoke up. "That was the nerviest act I ever saw," Henry remembered hearing him say. "You did your duty, and that coward got what he deserved. Here is my gun. I reckon I'll not need it so long as you are marshal of this town."

One by one the others in the crowd stepped forward to surrender their weapons, and the gun-toting issue was settled. From then on all visitors to Abilene left their weapons at a saloon, a hotel or a store and picked them up again only when they were ready to leave. Abilene had peace at last, and so grateful were the town officials that they raised Smith's pay from $150 to $225 a month, an astonishing sum for a peace officer in a place where trail bosses might make only half as much.

Ironically, Bear River Tom himself died in line of duty, at the hands not of a cowboy or transient gunslinger, but of a settler. In November 1870, after five months of awesomely effective peace-keeping, he went out into the country one night in pursuit of a farmer who was wanted for murder. He got the man at his dugout, but a friend of the farmer's lurking nearby—himself implicated in the farmer's crime—seized an ax and chopped off Smith's head.

In the wake of this incident it appeared that no normal man would so much as consider the job as Abilene's next marshal. But the following April, with another cattle season looming, the energetic Mr. McCoy, who by now was mayor, found a candidate utterly unfazed by the fate of his predecessor. And why not? For what farmer with an ax was going to frighten James Butler (Wild Bill) Hickok? Without a qualm Wild Bill signed on for Bear River's starting salary of $150 a month.

Wild Bill Hickok was a former Union Army scout and a devout gambler. He was known throughout the frontier as a fast draw—perhaps the fastest—and was thought by Abileners to have killed more white men than any other frontiersman. He reigned in Abilene from a table at the Alamo, where he drank whiskey and played cards. Whereas his predecessor, Bear River Tom, had relied for authority on a steady gaze and calm voice, Hickok relied on his guns, which he wore with the butts turned forward, an arrangement he believed favored a sure aim on a quick draw.

Unfortunately it turned out that Hickok was all too quick on the draw. For a time he was successful in keeping order, and the cattle season of 1871 passed without serious incident until early fall. Then one evening in October, while Hickok was having a drink, he heard a shot on the street. He rushed outside and there found a crowd of 50 carousers led by a man who brandished a gun and claimed to have picked off a dog, though none was in sight. Both men fired; Wild Bill shot the other man dead. A fellow policeman, Mike Williams, then dashed up in the darkness, startling Wild Bill, who fired again and instantly killed his friend.

Even for Abilene that was too much. Once and for all the town resolved to be rid of ruffians, rid of shooting, rid of gunslinging lawmen. "He acted only too ready to shoot down, to kill outright, instead of avoid-

203

ing assassination when possible, as the higher duty of a marshal," one early citizen remembered. "Such a policy of taking over justice into his own hands exemplified, of course, but a form of lawlessness." In December the city officials discharged Hickok and hired a successor for $50 a month, one third of Wild Bill's salary and only a fifth of the popular Bear River Tom Smith's.

They also resolved—in an agonizing but firm decision—to be rid of the fundamental cause of all the ruckus. Both the cows and the cowboys would have to go. That winter T. C. Henry drew up a manifesto:

We the undersigned members of the Farmers' Protective Association and Officers and Citizens of Dickinson County, Kansas, most respectfully request all who have contemplated driving Texas Cattle to Abilene the coming season to seek some other point for shipment, as the inhabitants of Dickinson will no longer submit to the evils of the trade.

The manifesto appeared in the *Chronicle* over 52 signatures on February 8, 1872. It was republished there three times and later printed in Texas newspapers, the list of signatories growing with each reprinting until 366 names eventually appeared. Texas drovers got the message. In 1872 they headed for Ellsworth and Wichita, and Abilene's days as a cattle town ended as abruptly as they had begun.

As Abilene's cattle boom folded, the fly-by-nights who had exploited the cowboys boarded the trains and moved down the line to the next cattle town. So, for that matter, did many who ran legitimate businesses. Jake Karatofsky opened a new store in Ellsworth and later two more in Wichita. A Texas promoter, Moses B. George, had the Drovers' Cottage disassembled, loaded onto a flatcar and shipped to Ellsworth, where he reopened it under the same name. Even Joe McCoy moved on; he designed the stock pens for the town of Newton, later promoted Wichita to prospective beef buyers and still later in his many-faceted career counted cows for the U.S. Census Bureau.

Abilene settled into permanent respectability, and the *Chronicle* was quick to echo the townfolk's sigh of relief. "Business is not as brisk as it used to be during the cattle season," it editorialized when the summer of 1872 came, "but the citizens have the satisfaction of knowing that 'hell is more than 60 miles away.'"

Heading for home, cowboys clamber onto a caboose for a final snort after delivering their herds. Some trail hands returned all the way to Texas by rail, but others rode east to the Mississippi, then caught steamboats to the Gulf ports.

7 | The code of the West

Kansas farmers Daniel, Alpheus and Burch Berry lie dead
and Roy Berry *(left, rear)* wounded after a shoot-out over
water rights with a prominent ranching family, the Deweys.
The only casualty in the Dewey ranks was the horse.

Although ranchers and cowboys made something of a fetish of individualism, they nevertheless behaved, or pretended to behave, by an unwritten set of rules that came to be known collectively as the code of the West. It was a most peculiar code—in part a canon of ethics, in part a rationalization for rapacity and sometimes an excuse for murder.

In its more benign application the code was a sort of frontier version of the Golden Rule. A cattleman fed a visitor because he might himself be far from home next month. He asked no questions of strangers because in leaner days he might himself have preferred not to have his affairs pried into. He returned stray cattle because his own livestock might wander.

Nevertheless, the rancher was not bothered by inconsistencies in his use of the code. Protection of property was an integral part of the canon, so he erected fences; meanwhile he cut his neighbor's fences (freedom of the plains was also enshrined in the code).

The Sunday-school aspect of this unwritten book of laws disappeared entirely when the cattleman felt himself threatened. The code gave him the right to set up vigilance committees whose members acted as sheriffs, prosecutors, judges and executioners, dispensing justice on the spot. If no vigilantes were available for the job, he took matters into his own hands; the grim results of one such episode are pictured below. In the final analysis the code was whatever a man said it was—and if some of the noblest deeds of the Old West were performed in its name, it also accounted for some of the most sordid.

A roughhewn credo for the frontier

Since there was little or no law in the Old West, the cowboy made his own rules from the outset. In his unwritten code there were certain principles understood by nearly everyone, and stories of the range are filled with examples of their observance.

A man's word. In Lavaca County, Texas, one February day in 1874, cattleman Willis McCutcheon sized up a spunky young lad named West and decided that despite his youth he'd do to drive the McCutcheon firm's first herd of the year to Ellsworth, Kansas. "You'll get half of whatever these cows bring over the price per head after expenses," McCutcheon promised. The boy said that would do.

The drive was halfway to Ellsworth when a five-hour blizzard killed the trail crew's remuda of 78 horses. Having promised to get the cattle through, West traded some cows—and with them part of his profits—for six horses and a mule. A month later he managed to get the cattle to the Kansas market. He sold them off a few at a time during the summer and fall.

When West finally returned to Lavaca County in December, McCutcheon's bookkeeper figured the profits, deducting the value of the lost horses (West made no objection). "Are you going to buy a herd of your own, or start a bank?" the bookkeeper joked as he handed over the young man's profit—75 cents. West smiled and pocketed the coins without a complaint at the outcome of a deal that he had sealed with his word.

Rough justice. In 1876 cattlemen near Fort Griffin, Texas, formed a vigilance committee to put down an epidemic of horse thieving. On April 9 the vigilantes, patrolling at night, caught a man in the act and immediately hanged him from the nearest pecan tree. Beneath the dangling body they left a pick and shovel in case someone cared enough to dig a grave. Of such activities a local newspaper commented: "As long as the committee strings up the right parties, it has the well wishes of every lover of tranquillity."

The code violated. Two cowpunchers out looking for work rode up to a Texas ranch in time for dinner, expecting the customary offer of a free meal. The boss fed them, but afterward demanded 50 cents in payment. Outraged at this violation of Western hospitality, the men roped a three-year-old steer belonging to their host and used a saddle ring to brand on its flanks the message: "Meals—50 cts." The steer was left to roam the range and proclaim the owner's ignominy.

The contractual bond of a man's word, the noose for all horse thieves, the obligation of hospitality to a visiting cowboy—these were among the cardinal principles of the code, but there were a great many more. Certainly rules were required, because the conditions of life in the West cried out for some regulation of man's activities. Opportunities for dubious deeds were almost unlimited. On the open range wandering cattle were virtually unprotected from rustlers. With boundary lines in constant dispute fences were sometimes uprooted as fast as they could be strung across the land. The consequent confrontations frequently led to gunplay—and when this happened the code itself often broke down. But in such an atmosphere of violence it is surprising that any rules prevailed at all.

Indeed, the code of the West and the violence that helped create it not only existed side by side in an inextricable symbiosis, but together formed the principal breeding ground for the legend that Westerners themselves soon began to export to the credulous East, initially in the form of dime novels and Wild West shows that glorified both the code and the violence.

May Lillie aims a six-gun that won her reputation as The Girl Dead Shot. She married impresario Pawnee Bill and starred in his Wild West extravaganza *(page 221).*

One aspect of the Western code was the practice of reporting lost and found livestock. Finders sometimes sold strays and sent the money to the owners. This ad is from *Field and Farm,* January 13, 1894.

In its simplest form the code was merely a common ethic of fair play, and it worked reasonably well. At the N Bar Ranch in Montana, for example, the foreman fired a hand because he failed to pay a prostitute her promised fee. On the bank of the Colorado River in Texas a young puncher, asked to take the lead in swimming the herd across, said that while he was not a good swimmer and was afraid of the water "I am a hired hand and will not shirk my duty." He made it.

Some of the fine points of the code dictated horsemen's etiquette. No one borrowed a horse from another man's string without his permission (which was rarely given). One did not whip or kick a borrowed horse. When two mounted cowboys approached each other on the trail both were supposed to keep course and perhaps pass a friendly word; to veer off was to suggest furtiveness—or even danger. But a wave of greeting was considered bad form—it might scare a horse. If one man dismounted, the other did too, so they would meet on equal terms. A man on foot did not grab the bridle of a mounted man's horse, for that could be taken as an intrusion on the rider's control.

Other rules of the code governed the practicalities of rangeland housekeeping. Cowboys were expected to close pasture and corral gates behind them, and to remove their sharp-roweled spurs when they entered another man's house. On roundup a cowboy did not wait for his fellow hands to arrive before beginning his meal; he helped himself and began eating at once so he would be out of the way when other punchers came to dip food from the common pots and pans.

In matters of money, most cowboys bound themselves to be trusting and trustworthy. One North

Dakota hand gave back part of his wages for digging postholes because he realized later he had dug one of them too shallow. At payoff time on the range bosses might dump sacks of money on the ground and leave them there, unmolested, for days at a time until the boys came by to pick up their wages. On a handshake cattle buyers would take whole herds sight unseen. G. W. Rourke, a railroad agent at Dodge City, recalled, "I've seen many a transaction in steers, running as high as 5,000 head and involving more than $100,000, closed and carried out to the letter, with no semblance of a written contract." In the market crash of 1873 Texas cattlemen, stuck with notes totaling $1.5 million to Kansas banks, paid off the debts almost to the penny—at the price of personal ruin for a number of the ranchers.

In such straightforward activities and transactions the code worked well for both sides. When differences of opinion or disputes arose, however, the cowman tended to change his definition of the code. Taking matters into his own hands, he rationalized his behavior as following a code, but this time the code was distinctly one-sided. Now the emphasis was on might rather than right. Property—legitimately owned or not—took precedence over people. It was true, as upholders of this unilateral ethic sometimes argued, that on the frontier vigilance committees helped to bring order where none existed. And in the name of swift justice a number of deserving stage robbers, horse thieves, fence cutters and even a few cattle rustlers got strung up. But too often these demimobs killed on mere suspicion. Some of the vigilance committees did double duty as musclemen for the cattle barons who sometimes acted more like robber barons. And too often these

Four men re-enact a wire cutting on a Nebraska ranch. Fencing became a critical issue after 1874, when Joseph F. Glidden patented a practical barbed wire, allowing settlers to bar cattle herds from farmland.

armed groups were able to subvert what justice there was on the range. One night in 1879 night riders hanged a prostitute and a saloonkeeper whose principal crime had been to set up small homesteads on land coveted by the powerful cattlemen. The vigilantes were arrested. But their members included some ranchers, and they persuaded the local press, and ultimately the jury, that the victims were blackhearted cattle thieves. The vigilantes were acquitted.

The cowmen's attitude toward rustling illustrates how their code of ethics could be strained. The penalty for stealing cattle seemed to depend, in large part, on who you were or how you did it. When Texas teemed with wild longhorns right after the Civil War cowmen routinely branded unmarked animals as their own, considering them a natural resource — which in most cases they were — comparable to the nuggets of gold that miners found in creek beds. Cowman John James Haynes told how he built a pen to trap strays and confined them there without water or grass until they were tame enough to drive to other pens. "We kept this up until we had about a thousand head of maverick yearlings," he said. Years later, long after the last wild longhorn had been corralled, some cowmen still would pick up any unbranded cow on sight and claim it, even if the rightful owner was just over the next divide. One rancher wrote, tongue in cheek, that since many ranchers neglected to brand their cattle by the time they were a year old, "I adopted some of those neglected yearlings and put my brand on them."

In time an understanding grew that a maverick belonged to the owner of the range where the animal was found and could be branded accordingly (page 133). But the fact was that range ownership itself was a crazy quilt of overlapping claims, and the finder might be genuinely uncertain about which rancher really owned any part of a given pasture. So enterprising individuals naturally interpreted the rule in their own favor.

Rustling, in short, was not generally regarded as a grave breach of ethics when it was done among friends and with decent restraint. Between neighboring barons a little maverick snitching met with smiling tolerance. One cattleman announced that he was serving a friend at dinner with "something you've never eaten before —your own beef."

Key employees of the big outfits also qualified under this loose set of rules and were permitted by their bosses to do a bit of freelance rustling. A ranch foreman might register a brand of his own, hoping some day to start a herd. Riding his boss's range 20 miles from any other human being, he finds a maverick. He builds a fire and heats his running iron. Somehow the design comes out as his own brand, not the boss's. Pretty soon the foreman has a little herd of cattle all his own, grazing right on the boss's grass in a coulee where no one would bother to look.

Some big ranchers, having started this way themselves, maintained a certain respect for such initiative. When a veteran cowpuncher named George Clutts arrived at Charlie Goodnight's ranch in Texas and asked for a job, Goodnight greeted him with the challenge: "George, they say you're a cow thief." The cowboy replied, "They say the same thing about you, Mr. Goodnight." Impressed by this brash logic, the cattle baron instructed his foreman to find Clutts a job.

It was the stranger—the lone cowboy with little means or the farmer — who found that this capricious set of rules did not apply to him. For the solitary rustler there was a simpler code, which dictated summary punishment. In Texas a lone rustler named John Leaverton was caught slapping his brand on the favorite calf of a rich rancher in Adobe Walls; when he imprudently showed fight he was killed on the spot. In 1875 cowmen in Mason County, Texas, broke into jail to grab five rustlers and swiftly executed three of them (the sheriff appeared in time to save the other two). Elsewhere around the West, ranch managers like John Clay of the VVV in South Dakota openly sanctioned lynching of cattle thieves. The crime in such instances appeared to be lack of social or business connections as much as actual rustling.

Most rustlers, not surprisingly, dropped any pretense of ethical behavior. Not only did they simply appropriate mavericks they found, but they also manufactured artificial mavericks, usually by nullifying the instinct that keeps cow and calf together for nearly a year. The simplest method was to pen a bunch of calves and drive their mothers away. Other cattle thieves slit the calves' tongues so they could not suckle, or cut their eyelid muscles so they could not see to return to their mothers, or burned them between the toes to keep them from walking to the cows. Once the calves got used to grazing instead of suckling, they would drift off from their mothers, and the rustlers could brand these new mavericks as their own.

Equally ingenious and iniquitous was the practice of brand changing, a dark science by which a skilled man could, with a couple of quick strokes, transform a V into a diamond and wind up with a cow of his own. The mere possession of a running iron—a metal rod with a curved end that could be used to alter a brand —came in time to qualify a man for the noose. Rustlers then learned to burn brands with cinch rings or telegraph wires. Sometimes they created a temporary brand by cutting away a cow's hair with a jackknife. Another even more subtle rustling technique was to put a wet sack between the hot branding iron and the hide of the cow. This so-called cold-branding method served to delude the true owner into believing that his calves were branded. But after hair grew over the temporary marks the rustlers could burn in their own brands —deep, permanent and unblurred by the earlier marking.

The problems of law enforcement and codes of behavior became really chaotic when, as sometimes happened, the rustlers banded together with farmers and townsmen in open defiance of the cattlemen. In certain areas they actually controlled enough votes to elect sheriffs, judges and county commissioners. Frequently the confrontations that followed developed into range warfare. In 1892 the established cattlemen of Johnson County, Wyoming, reacted to the threat of organized rustling by importing 20 gunslingers from Texas. The mercenaries arrived on a special train, laid siege to the first band of rustlers they found, killed one and suddenly found themselves in trouble. Rustlers came all the way from the Platte to the Powder River to join their comrades. Reinforced by nesters, disaffected cowhands and assorted other enemies of the cattle barons, the outlaws closed in with a countersiege so devastating that the ranchers sent a cry for help to the Governor's mansion. Law—or at best the power of local authority—finally prevailed. The Governor called in the militia, which rescued the hired gunfighters and their leaders.

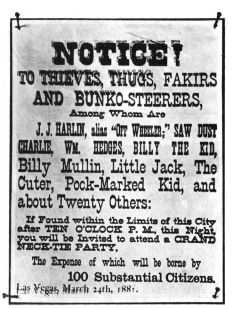

NOTICE!
TO THIEVES, THUGS, FAKIRS AND BUNKO-STEERERS,
Among Whom Are
J. J. HARLIN, alias "OFF WHEELER," SAW DUST CHARLIE, WM. HEDGES, BILLY THE KID, Billy Mullin, Little Jack, The Cuter, Pock-Marked Kid, and about Twenty Others:

If Found within the Limits of this City after TEN O'CLOCK P. M., this Night you will be Invited to attend a GRAND NECK-TIE PARTY.

The Expense of which will be borne by
100 Substantial Citizens.
Las Vegas, March 24th, 1881.

Although cattle rustling might be winked at under some circumstances, there were hard and fast rules for dealing with the horse thief. Unlike official laws written long before in the East—where horse stealing was a misdemeanor because the animal was worth only about $25—the unwritten law of the Western plains measured horse theft severely because it could leave a man afoot in hostile country. Thus the code's penalty for horse stealing was instant execution. Granville Stuart, who had been known to give fair warning to cattle rustlers before lynching them, felt no such compunctions when he and his vigilantes went after some horse thieves in 1884. Trapping part of the gang in a cabin, Stuart's men set the house afire and killed three of the thieves. Four of the horse stealers escaped to the banks of the Missouri, tied some logs into a raft and floated away, only to be arrested downstream by a group of soldiers and turned over to a U.S. marshal. But neither the marshal nor the law could protect the horse thieves from the vigilantes. "At the mouth of the Musselshell," Stuart reported, "a posse met the marshal and took the prisoners from him. Nearby stood two log cabins close together. A log was placed between the cabins, the

ends resting on the roofs, and the four men were hanged from the log."

The cattleman's code was almost equally severe on the sheepherder. Sheep grazed grass down to the roots, then cut the roots with their sharp hoofs, ruining the pasturage for cattle. Furthermore, the ranchers believed—wrongly—that sheep could spoil lush pasture simply by walking across the range; all sheep secrete a sticky fluid from a gland between their toes, and ranchers accepted the myth that cattle were repelled by the smell. The coming of sheep thus seemed to represent a theft of the grassland that cattlemen regarded as their rightful property. Vigilance groups rode out at night to get it back. One August evening in the Big Horn Basin of Wyoming, masked cowmen, using guns, dynamite and clubs, killed 4,000 sheep, burned wagons and ran the remaining sheep out of the country. In Colorado 1,000 sheep were driven over a cliff—a method of mass slaughter quaintly known as rimrocking. In South Dakota 32 cattlemen killed a sheepherder, and then, in an afterthought remarkably generous in the history of the cattle-vs.-sheep vendetta, gave his widow $1,000 in gold to square things. Many Texans put a much lower value—something around zero—on the lives of sheepherders since so many of them were foreigners. Grazing sheep was a job that attracted Basques, Frenchmen, Mexicans, Scots and Englishmen.

The arrival of barbed wire on the range triggered a crisis for the code and revealed how Janus-faced it could be. By his use of the fence, or his efforts to destroy it, the cowboy simply changed the rules to serve his own situation: if the cattleman jealously protected his land (plus perhaps a little more that didn't actually belong to him) he built a fence; but if he preferred open land (or had little he could claim) he cut others' fences down.

The first Westerners to see barbed wire were so mystified by it that they guessed it might be intended for horses' bits. But the remarkable utility of barbed wire as a cheap, strong fence soon became obvious, and many cowmen began to enclose the land. In Archer County, Texas, the fence mania was so great that at

Superdudes abroad in the wilderness

The excitement of the Old West drew thousands of overcivilized types to play at being frontiersmen. A fair number of these adventurers, called dudes after the colloquialism for a dandy or a fop, pitched in and did real cowboys' work. But a notable minority never shed their tailored clothes, their prim manners or their grandiose style.

Perhaps the prissiest of the early dudes was Richard Trimble, a well-to-do New Yorker who went strolling among the cows with his poodle Mifouche. And the most spectacular was certainly the Grand Duke Alexis, third son of the Czar of Russia, who swept into Nebraska in 1872 with two sleeping cars, a diner and a refrigerator car stocked with grouse, quail and caviar. The Grand Duke set off on a buffalo hunt guided by none other than Civil War hero General Philip Sheridan and staffed by General George Armstrong Custer, Buffalo Bill Cody and 1,000 Sioux. The Grand Duke's first volley of gunfire did the buffalo no damage. When he finally killed one with a gun borrowed from Buffalo Bill he treated the whole party to magnums of champagne, and on departing he gave Cody a purse of gold and General Custer an embrace, with kisses on both cheeks.

The most memorable of all dudes, however, was 25-year-old Theodore Roosevelt, who came West in 1883. When he first arrived at Little Missouri, a bleak sagebrush outpost in the Dakota Badlands, Teddy looked like an Eastern city boy if ever there was one. He was bookish, pale and thin. His face was full of teeth, he wore

T. R. strikes his fiercest hunting stance.

big round eyeglasses and he bounded about crying things like "Bully!" and "Deelighted to meet you."

His guide, Joe Ferris, expected the worst—and he got it, but not as anticipated. On the first day, after a 45-mile ride through running streams, timbered hills and even quicksand, the horses limped into camp and the guide fell into bed—but not T.R. He sat up well past midnight, talking politics with his host, a transplanted Scot named Gregor Lang. Next morning at 6 a drizzle was falling. Ferris was sure he would have a day of rest. But T.R. bounded up ready for action.

This lasted for a week, with T.R. riding and talking tirelessly, and blazing away futilely at game that his weak eyes really could not discern in the rifle sights. But nothing dampened his pleasure or his persistence. When Ferris brought down a bounding deer that Teddy had missed, Roosevelt happily exclaimed: "By Godfrey! I'd give anything in the world if I could shoot like that." Attempting to defend himself against a charging bull, he accidentally struck his forehead with the butt of his gun and blood poured into his eyes, but he raised his gun and fired again. His host found T.R.'s grin "apparently built in and irradicable." By week's end T.R. had decided to stay indefinitely. He invested the sum of $14,000 and went into ranching for himself.

He throve on the vigorous new life. His chest filled out, his neck thickened and, even dearer to this cheerful egoist, he won the respect of the cowmen. He learned to stay in his saddle even when his horse bucked so hard he lost his hat, his gun and his glasses. One night in a saloon a rowdy announced, "Four Eyes is going to treat." Roosevelt put up with this for a while, and then said philosophically, "Well, if I've got to, I've got to." Whereupon he stood up and knocked the man flat in best frontier style.

At this the veteran cowboys paid him the supreme accolade: they altered his nickname from Four Eyes to Old Four Eyes, Old denoting approval and affection.

For his own part Roosevelt was to cherish his memories of the cowboy's world for the rest of his adventure-filled life. Nearly 20 years later he was to say that it was in the West that the "romance of my life began."

216

one time the county seat could be reached only by snipping someone's barbed wire. Such overzealous wiring outraged the open-range ranchers, who felt that the whole outdoors should be free to everyone. Fencing also antagonized small stockmen, who began to find the choice water holes fenced off; nesters, whose small farms were completely enclosed; and even the cowboys, who felt that cheap fencing material would reduce the need for range riders.

In an unlikely alliance farmers, rustlers and some small ranchers banded together to destroy all fences. When Texas cowman R. A. Davis built a four-strand fence around a 1,000-acre pasture, he discovered two days later that it had been cut in 3,500 places. The Galveston *News* reported in 1883 that 20 miles of fence on the property of the Hickey Pasture Company had been hacked to bits because the neighbors needed the enclosed water.

It was inevitable that the confrontation between the fencers and the fence cutters, like that of the rustlers and the ranchers, would erupt into shooting. Whether it flared over fences, water rights, sheep or cattle, gunplay somehow came to be the gaudiest and most popular symbol of the cowboy.

The gunfight, according to the popular mythology of the West, was the ultimate expression of the cowboy's code. A man was not a man unless he could coolly face death and fight for his good name. This was the American equivalent of the European duel, with similarly punctilious rules of conduct and the same emphasis on honor above all else. In historical fact, however, the classic gunfight was virtually the invention of the pulp novelists and the 19th Century journalists. Only a few such shoot-outs ever occurred. In an 1893 duel on the Kansas plains two cowboys faced each other with Winchesters at 50 paces, advanced with each shot, fired seven times apiece and simultaneously fell dead at 10 paces. In a less dignified but similarly lethal variation of this confrontation, George Littlefield, later to be a cattle baron and a leading banker of Austin, got into a dispute with a neighbor just after the Civil War. The two adversaries came within pistol range at camp on a roundup. Each pulled a gun, each squeezed the trigger — and both guns misfired. Littlefield's adversary fled behind a tree, then peeped cautiously around it. At that instant Littlefield got his gun working; he scored a clean kill.

However unclassical, these were undeniably real face-offs. But they took place nearly 25 years apart. Most other gunfights occurred not between cowboys but in the Western underworld, among the gamblers, toughs and professional criminals who walk the dark corridors of any society. There was, for example, nothing particularly honorable about William (Billy the Kid) Bonney and Jesse James, both of whom were pathological killers. Wyatt Earp was primarily a barroom bouncer, bush-league gambler and petty politician, who may also have dabbled in a little rustling. The code of these gunslingers was what Westerners called a rattlesnake's code. The fact is, it lacked even the rattlesnake's fair warning.

In the rare cases when real cowboys did exchange gunfire honor and rules were conspicuously missing. There were Wyoming range wars, Texas fencing battles and family feuds involving gunplay. In most such instances the intent was simply to shoot a man in the front, back, side or wherever the shot would take effect. Most commonly, however, bullet wounds among cowboys occurred in the course of drunken cattle-town sprees. A Wyoming newspaper recounted a typical episode: "A large number of cowboys, who had been working the beef roundup, came into town yesterday and started to paint the community a crimson color. A large number of them became fighting full of whiskey and several scrimmages occurred. In the evening Leon Williams endeavored to take Harry Mason, who had got very quarrelsome, to bed. Mason started off quietly but soon turned and shot Williams through the right breast and shoulder, the ball passing out near the collarbone. Sheriff M. Doze was at once called, and when he attempted to arrest Mason the drunken cowboy emptied all the chambers of his six-shooter at him. Fortunately they failed to take effect. Doze, nothing daunted, immediately knocked Mason down and placed him under arrest."

Most cowboys, though they may have heard tales of such incidents, or perhaps even witnessed one, assiduously avoided taking part. Looking back on his own broad experience on the range, cowpuncher Jo Mora wondered why some cowboys packed pistols during the safest roundups and the most mundane ranching chores. He commented, "Why we packed guns on jobs of that kind and in that way is a mystery to me now."

A feast of pulp for a hungry audience

When Teddy Roosevelt was ranching in the Dakotas, he once helped capture a trio of bandits whose saddlebags turned out to contain a stack of dime novels with such titles as *A History of the James Boys*. These real-life desperadoes were among the millions of Americans who, beginning in the 1870s, began to revel in—and sometimes even try to imitate—the bold adventure of the range as depicted in pulp fiction about the West.

Among the leading purveyors to this market was the firm of Beadle and Adams, from whose offices came some 2,200 titles like those shown here. In them, killers like Jesse James and Wild Bill Hickok appeared as swashbuckling gallants. Occasionally a genuine frontier hero would remind the public that most of the stories were balderdash: the famed scout Kit Carson, seeing a dime-novel cover of himself slaying seven Indians with one hand while clutching a grateful maiden with the other, laconically observed, "I ain't got no recollection of it." But nobody cared. Western buffs gobbled up the action—and such manly dialogue as that shown at right.

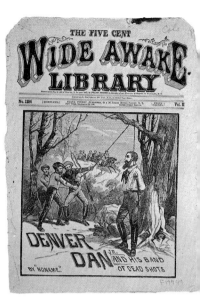

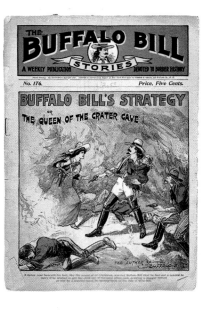

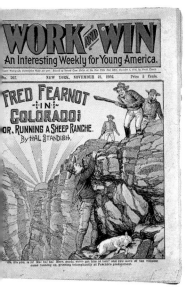

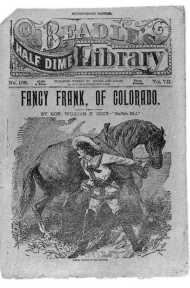

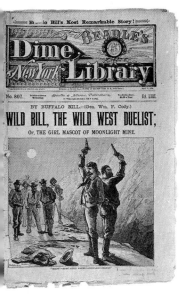

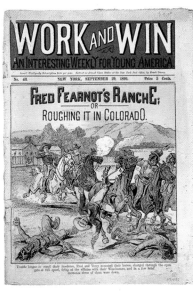

THE JAMES BOYS AND THE 49ERS.

CHAPTER II.

JESSE JAMES WORKS A COFFIN FOR A BIG HAUL.

Crack!

Crack!

Crack!

Unluckily for old Jack Farley, his aim was not equal to his courage.

His shots were both bad misses.

A shower of cold lead came in answer.

With a deep groan, the brave old engineer tumbled back, seriously wounded.

"Kill him, Ned—kill him, boy!" he cried, thrusting the smoking pistol into Ned Jackson's hand.

What Ned might have done if he had been given a chance it is hard to say.

As it was he had no opportunity to do anything.

Two big, burly fellows sprang into the cab.

He was seized and pinioned in an instant.

The revolver was wrenched from him.

Roughly the young fireman was ordered to descend into the snow.

Of course he had to do it.

The brakeman and conductor were in the same fix.

The masked outlaws had spread themselves along the line of the train.

Some were armed with rifles, others with revolvers.

The latter now scrambled upon the platforms.

There were men to stand guard at either end of the cars, and men to go inside and relieve the frightened passengers of their money, watches, jewelry and diamonds, if they had any.

If any one had thought of fight they speedily abandoned the idea.

The hold-up had been too cleverly planned, too skillfully executed.

There was positively no other way but for everyone to give up, and be thankful if they came out of the scrape with their lives.

Meanwhile, Jesse James was walking up and down through the snow, watching the movements of his men, giving directions where needed, making sure that everything was going to his mind.

Presently he encountered a tall, thin, cadaverous-looking man, and stopped to talk.

It was Frank James, the famous outlaw, fully as notorious as his brother, and credited by many with a longer head.

"Well, Frank, everything seems to be working all right," Jesse remarked.

"Right as the mail, far as I can see," replied Frank.

"I was sorry we had to shoot Jack Farley."

"So was I."

"Still it could not be helped."

"Certainly not. If these engineers will be fools and fire at us, they must take the consequences."

"Right you are; but I feel a sort of affection for the old man; you see this makes the third time we held him up."

"And the unlucky one for him. Is he badly hurt?"

"Bill Chadwell says no;—the wound is in his left shoulder. Bill thinks he'll get over it all right."

"Glad to hear that. Are you still determined to carry out your plan, Jess?"

"I am."

The solution to Mora's mystery was that cowboys, like other 19th Century Americans, reveled in the glamorized image of the Old West. But unlike their less lucky Eastern admirers, the cowhands had a chance to act the role. The Mayor of Dodge City, Robert Wright, observed that cowboys "delight in appearing rougher than they are." They swaggered down cattle-town streets, pistols waggling dangerously on their hips as though ready for a face-off with any man—until a reminder from the sheriff about gun ordinances caused them to meekly surrender their weapons. Some cowboys came to enjoy their swashbuckling image so much that they went to elaborate ends to construct incidents of phony violence for the benefit of gullible visitors from the East.

One favorite gambit in railroad towns was the fake shoot-out. A bunch of the boys would wait inside a hotel or saloon until a train pulled in. While the passengers gawked, the cowhands would fire off a volley of shots, then pick up the limp form of a volunteer "corpse" and carry him out the door and around a corner. Cowpuncher Teddy Blue Abbott recalled an impromptu performance that he and some fellow hands put on near the Fort Kearny station of the Union Pacific Railroad. They made a dummy, placed a noose around his neck and, just as a train pulled in, threw the rope over the crossbar of a telegraph pole and jerked the dummy into the air. As the appalled passengers gaped at the phony lynching, the "vigilantes" fired away at the swaying dummy, shot the rope in two, and proceeded to drag their straw victim across the plain at a full gallop, continuing to riddle him with bullets. Aboard the train women fainted, children screamed and a public-spirited passenger raced into the station to telegraph news of the mayhem to the Nebraska territorial capital.

At this stage the code of the West had become part of the larger legend. And some canny businessmen realized that the legend was a marketable commodity. The first to profit were the publishers of dime novels, treating their readers to a barrage of paperbound books about Western derring-do. Though real-life action could hardly come up to the level of the pulp fantasies, nonetheless a few promoters tried to entertain Eastern audiences with cowboys in the flesh. In a venture billed as the "Grand Buffalo Hunt," held at Niagara Falls in 1872, Wild Bill Hickok, together with a few Indians

and Mexicans, roped three buffalo, while some local Indians put on a lacrosse-playing exhibition nearby.

The premier merchandiser of the live Western show was William F. (Buffalo Bill) Cody. Born in Iowa in 1846, he had done a bit of Pony Express riding, a lot of buffalo shooting, some gallant scouting, a little Indian fighting, a smidgen of cowpunching and a great deal of boasting. (In this latter capacity he was encouraged by the prodigious literary output of one Colonel Prentiss Ingraham, who wrote 121 wildly exaggerated dime novels supposedly based on Cody's life.)

Beginning in the 1870s, Cody embarked on a career as producer and star of a series of Western melodramas that toured the small-town stages and even hit Broadway on March 31, 1873. But he finally found his true calling in the town of North Platte, Nebraska, in 1882. Idling away an afternoon in a saloon, he heard that the town had no festivities planned for the Fourth of July, and, irrepressible showman that he was, he resolved to provide one. He quickly worked up a program designed to display cowboy skills, offering prizes for shooting, riding and bronco busting. Although he expected only about 100 cowboys to enter the contests, 1,000 applied. Cody perceived that with some added frills he had a magnificent theatrical property on his hands. By the following year he had organized his show. He called it "The Wild West," and it was a flamboyant outdoor exhibition of Western prowess.

This and other spectacular live-action shows, along with the dream stuff of dime novels and the romanticized reports of Western travelers, forever fixed the popular image of the cowboy's glamorous life. The cowboys, of course, continued to cooperate in the making of their own myth (partly through antics like those of a puncher in Cody's troupe who shot at a steak served to him in a London restaurant, claiming that it was still alive and "jerking around on the plate"). Even among themselves, and in the privacy of their own range, they tended to move through their sweaty, dusty lives with a certain posturing pride that is still discernible in photographs 100 years old (*pages 224-233*). Self-abnegation was not a part of the cowboy character, for meek men did not last long on the Great Plains. And if in trying to live up to the legend cowboys reached a little high for a share of immortality, it was only because they thought that they deserved one. Perhaps they did.

PAWNEE BILL'S HISTORIC WILD WEST

AMERICA'S NATIONAL ENTERTAINMENT

BEAUTIFUL DARING WESTERN GIRLS AND MEXICAN SEÑORITAS IN A CONTEST OF EQUINE SKILL.

NO DISAPPOINTMENT   POSITIVELY GIVING TWO GRAND AND COMPLETE PERFORMANCES EACH DAY   RAIN OR SHINE

AMERICA'S NATIONAL ENTERTAINMENT

A FEATURE OF THE WORLD'S FAIR. GENUINE GAUCHOS FROM THE PAMPAS OF SOUTH AMERICA.

Top dog of Wild West showmen, Buffalo Bill *(with beard)* appears with some of his troupers on a London stage against a backdrop of the Western plains. A former Army scout, Cody first appeared on stage in Chicago in 1872 and later traveled with an exposition that featured the sharpshooting of Ohio cowgirl Annie Oakley, mock attacks by real Indian braves — and Bill's own fancy riding and roping. He advertised his European tour with a map *(inset)* picturing the cities he had played.

In the Old West's heyday the cowboy sits for his portrait

Huffman, NEW STUDIO, Miles City, Montana. Graham Block,

Like any other man with a tough job that calls for special accouterments, the cowboy liked nothing better than to get in front of the camera all decked out with the tools of his trade. Fresh in from the range, he would scrape off the trail dust, pull on some clean duds and then head for the pineboard photographic studio that seemed to spring up in virtually every major cow town. There he posed—with his friends, alone, or sometimes even with his horse *(page 233)*.

The resulting compositions, framed in cheap cardboard and often stamped with the photographer's name, provide a surprising and sometimes poignant look at the real cowboy of the Old West. Though he clearly thought of himself as a fearsome swashbuckler, in reality he often looked painfully young and vulnerable, the more so for the prominently displayed six-guns, which usually were studio props. Or he might poke a hole in the cowboy image by sitting with a pair of high-laced Sunday-go-to-meeting shoes *(right)* peeking out from beneath his trail-worn britches.

Other times, unshaven and lined up beside his rangewise buddies, he looked every bit as rough as his romanticized reputation. In each pose, however, there emerged one special characteristic: unmistakable pride in being a cowboy.

226

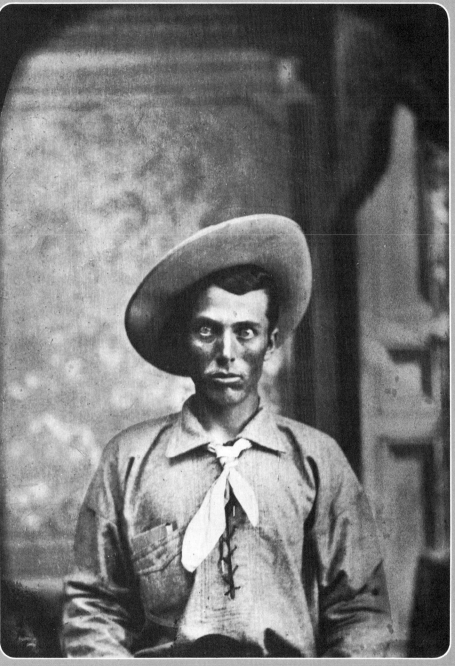

TEXT CREDITS

Chapter I: 17—excerpts from "The Cowboy at Home" by John Baumann from *The Cornhill Magazine,* vol. II, 1886, pp. 294 ff; excerpts from "Driving Cattle from Texas to Iowa" by George C. Duffield, from *Annals of Iowa,* third series, vol. 14 (April 1924), courtesy of Iowa State Department of History and Archives, Des Moines, Iowa, pp. 243-262; 18—excerpts from "My First Five-Dollar Bill" by J. L. McCaleb, from *The Trail Drivers of Texas,* vol. I, J. Marvin Hunter, ed., Argosy-Antiquarian Ltd., New York, 1963, pp. 126-132. Chapter II: portions based on excerpts from *Charles Goodnight: Cowman and Plainsman* by J. Evetts Haley, new edition copyright 1949 by the University of Oklahoma Press. Chapter III: 86—letter from S. P. Conrad to James Haft, courtesy Fred A. Rosenstock, Denver, Colorado, reproduced in *When Grass Was King* by Maurice Frink, W. Turrentine Jackson and Agnes Wright Spring, copyright 1956 University of Colorado Press, pp. 81-82; 87—recipes adapted from *Cowpokes Cookbook and Cartoons,* by

Ace Reid, copyright 1969 by Ace Reid, c/o Draggin' S Ranch, Kerrville, Texas; 82—X I T Ranch rules from *The X I T Ranch of Texas,* by J. Evetts Haley, copyright 1967 University of Oklahoma Press, pp. 241-245; 92—excerpts from *The Camp Life of a Cowpuncher,* by Carroll Doshier, courtesy Panhandle Plains Historical Society, Canyon, Texas. Chapter IV: based on Chapters 1 to 5 of *Back Trailing on Open Range,* by Luke D. Sweetman, copyright 1951, The Caxton Printers, Ltd.; 133—list of brands partly compiled from *The Manual of Brands and Marks,* by Manfred R. Wolfenstine, copyright 1970 by the University of Oklahoma Press. Chapter V: based on excerpts from *Up the Trail in '79,* by Baylis John Fletcher, new edition copyright 1968 by the University of Oklahoma Press. Chapter VII: 209—excerpts from "Courage and Hardihood on the Old Texas Cattle Trail," from *The Trail Drivers of Texas,* vol. I, J. Marvin Hunter, ed., Argosy-Antiquarian Ltd., New York, 1963, pp. 126-132.

PICTURE CREDITS

The sources for the illustrations in this book are shown below. Credits from left to right are separated by semicolons and from top to bottom by dashes.

Cover: *The Cowboy* by Frederic Remington, courtesy Amon Carter Museum, Fort Worth, Texas. The paintings and sculpture reproduced on pages 2 through 15 courtesy Amon Carter Museum, Fort Worth, Texas, except 10-11 courtesy Montana Historical Society, Helena. 2—*The Outlaw,* Frederic Remington. 6,7—*A Dash for Timber,* Frederic Remington. 8,9—*Wild Horse Hunters,* Charles M. Russell. 10,11—*The Toll Collectors,* Charles M. Russell. 12,13—*Loops and Swift Horses Are Surer Than Lead,* Charles M. Russell. 14,15—*In Without Knocking,* Charles M. Russell. 16—Courtesy Montana Historical Society, Helena. 18—Courtesy Library of Congress. 19—Map by Jean Held. 22—J.C.H. Grabill, Courtesy Bettmann Archive. 23,24,25—Drawings by Nicholas Fasciano. 27—Courtesy Denver Public Library, Western History Department. 28—Lady Evelyn Jephson Cameron, courtesy Montana Historical Society, Helena—Courtesy Montana Historical Society, Helena. 31—Courtesy the Library, University of Texas Archives, Austin. 32—F. M. Sherman, courtesy Denver Public Library, Western History Department. 34,35—Dan Coolidge, reproduced through the courtesy of the Bancroft Library, University of California, Berkeley. 36,37—W. H. Jackson, courtesy The National Archives. 38,39—W. H. Jackson, courtesy Denver Public Library, Western History Department. 40,41—Courtesy State Historical Society of Colorado Library. 42,43—© Charles J. Belden, courtesy Denver Public Library, Western History Department. 44,45—Courtesy National Oceanic and Atmospheric Administration. 46,47—Courtesy Denver Public Library, Western History Department. 48—Courtesy State Historical Society of Colorado Library. 49—Milligan, courtesy Denver Public Library, Western History Department. 52—Dean Austin, *Charros at the Roundup,* James Walker, courtesy Carl Dentzel Collection. 55—Courtesy California State Library, California Section Picture Collection. 57—Courtesy William Wittliff, The Encino Press. 58—Courtesy State Historical Society of Colorado Library; Courtesy Western History Research Center, University of Wyoming; Courtesy Western History Collections, University of Oklahoma Library—Courtesy Southwest Collection, Texas Tech University (3). 59—Courtesy Montana Historical Society, Helena, except top center and bottom left, courtesy Western History Research Center, University of Wyoming. 60—Courtesy Montana Historical Society, Helena; Courtesy Western History Research Center, University of Wyoming; Courtesy

State Historical Society of Colorado Library—Courtesy Montana Historical Society, Helena (2); Courtesy Denver Public Library, Western History Department. 63—Courtesy Denver Public Library, Western History Department. 64—Courtesy Kansas State Historical Society, Topeka. 66—Courtesy Wyoming State Archives and Historical Department. 68,69—Brown Brothers. 70,71—J.C.H. Grabill, courtesy Library of Congress. 72,73—Courtesy Montana Historical Society, Helena. 74,75—Courtesy David R. Phillips Collection; Courtesy Arizona Historical Society—Courtesy State Historical Society of Colorado. 76,77—Courtesy the Library, University of Texas, Austin. 78,79—Brown Brothers. 80—Joseph E. Smith, courtesy David R. Phillips Collection. 83—W. G. Walker, courtesy Western History Research Center, University of Wyoming. 84,85—Culver Pictures. 87—Courtesy Montana Historical Society, Helena. 90,91—© Charles J. Belden, courtesy Denver Public Library, Western History Department. 93—Lady Evelyn Jephson Cameron, courtesy Montana Historical Society, Helena—Erwin Smith, courtesy Texas State Archives, Austin. 94,95—Courtesy Southwest Collection, Texas Tech University. 96,97—Courtesy State Historical Society of Colorado Library. 98 through 103—L. A. Huffman, courtesy Coffrin's Old West Gallery, Miles City, Montana. 104—Benschneider, courtesy Colorado State Museum. 105—Robert Royal, courtesy Royal Armour Museum, Madrid, photograph authorized by the Patrimonio Nacional—Drawing by Nicholas Fasciano. 106,107—Robert Markow, courtesy Arizona Historical Society; Shelly Katz from Black Star, courtesy Joe Ruiz Grandee Gallery; Benschneider, courtesy Colorado State Museum; Robert Markow, courtesy Arizona Historical Society—Drawing by Nicholas Fasciano. 108—Benschneider, courtesy Arizona Historical Society; Shelly Katz from Black Star, courtesy Joe Ruiz Grandee Gallery; Benschneider, courtesy Arizona Historical Society; Benschneider, courtesy Joe Ruiz Grandee Gallery—Drawings by Nicholas Fasciano. 109—Benschneider, courtesy Arizona Historical Society; Shelly Katz from Black Star, courtesy Joe Ruiz Grandee Gallery; Benschneider, courtesy Joe Ruiz Grandee Gallery. 110,111—Courtesy Montana Historical Society, Helena. 112, 113—Reproduced through the courtesy of the Bancroft Library, University of California, Berkeley. 114, 115—Erwin Smith, courtesy Library of Congress. 116,117—W. G. Walker, courtesy Collection of Fred and Jo Mazzulla. 118—© Charles

J. Belden, courtesy Whitney Gallery of Western Art, Cody, Wyoming. 120—Map by Rafael D. Palacios. 122—Drawings by Nicholas Fasciano. 124—F. J. Haynes, courtesy The Haynes Foundation. 125,126, 127—Drawings by Nicholas Fasciano. 128—No Credit. 130—Courtesy Denver Public Library, Western History Department—Courtesy State Historical Society of Colorado Library; Courtesy Montana Historical Society, Helena. 131—Drawing by Nicholas Fasciano. 133—Courtesy Montana Historical Society, Helena. 134—Copied from *We Pointed Them North: Recollections of a Cowpuncher* by E. C. (Teddy Blue) Abbott and Helena Huntington Smith, copyright 1954 by the University of Oklahoma Press. 136,137— © Charles J. Belden, courtesy Whitney Gallery of Western Art, Cody, Wyoming. 138, 139—Erwin Smith, courtesy Library of Congress. 140—*Through the Alkali,* Charles M. Russell, courtesy Thomas Gilcrease Institute, Tulsa, Oklahoma. 142—Drawing by Nicholas Fasciano. 143—From copy in Philip Ashton Rollins Collection of Western Americana, Princeton University Library. 145—Maps by Nicholas Fasciano. 146,147—*Stampeded by Lightning,* Frederic Remington, courtesy Thomas Gilcrease Institute, Tulsa, Oklahoma. 148,149—*Trail Herd to Montana,* W.H.D. Koerner, courtesy Whitney Gallery of Western Art, Cody, Wyoming. 150,151—Drawings by Nicholas Fasciano. 152,153—*The Longhorn Cattle Sign,* Frederic Remington, courtesy Amon Carter Museum, Fort Worth, Texas. 154—No Credit. 156—Courtesy Rare Book Division, The New York Public Library, Astor, Lenox and Tilden Foundations. 158,159—*Hard Winter,* W.H.D. Koerner, © Ruth Koerner Oliver. 161—Drawing by Walter Johnson. 164, 165—Courtesy Western History Collections, University of Oklahoma Library. 166, 167—Erwin Smith, courtesy Library of Congress. 168, 169—Courtesy Kansas State Historical Society. 170—Erwin Smith, courtesy Library of Congress—F. M. Sherman, courtesy Denver Public Library, Western History Department. 171,172,173—Courtesy Denver Public Library, Western History Department. 174—Courtesy Nebraska State Historical Society; Courtesy Kansas State Historical Society, Topeka. 175—Courtesy Kansas State Historical Society, Topeka; Courtesy Rare Book Division, The New York Public Library, Astor, Lenox and Tilden Foundations. 176,177—Joseph E. Smith, courtesy David R. Phillips Collection; Courtesy Montana Historical Society, Helena. 178,179—Joseph E. Smith, courtesy David R. Phillips Collection. 180,181,182—Courtesy Kansas State Historical Society, Topeka. 184—Collection Fred and Jo Mazzulla. 185 through 191—Courtesy Kansas State Historical Society, Topeka. 192—Courtesy Dickinson County Historical Society, Abilene, Kansas. 194,195—Courtesy Kansas State Historical Society, Topeka. 196—Courtesy Rare Book Division, The New York Public Library, Astor, Lenox and Tilden Foundations. 197—Courtesy Dickinson County Historical Society, Abilene, Kansas. 198—Verne F. Ryland, courtesy City Clerk's Office, Caldwell, Kansas. 200, 201—Courtesy Denver Public Library, Western History Department. 202—Courtesy Kansas State Historical Society, Topeka. 204, 205—Erwin Smith, courtesy Library of Congress. 206, 207—Courtesy Kansas State Historical Society, Topeka. 208—Courtesy Henry Hornblower II. 210—Courtesy Denver Public Library, Western History Department. 211—Courtesy E. A. Wright. 212—Solomon D. Butcher Collection, courtesy Nebraska State Historical Society. 214—Courtesy Western History Collections, University of Oklahoma Library. 215—Courtesy Kansas State Historical Society, Topeka. 216—Brown Brothers. 218,219—Courtesy Denver Public Library, Western History Department; Courtesy Sy Seidman. 221—Courtesy Denver Public Library, Western History Department. 222, 223—James E. Hunt, courtesy State Historical Society of Colorado Library; Courtesy Buffalo Bill Museum, Cody, Wyoming. 224—L. A. Huffman, courtesy Montana Historical Society, Helena. 225—Courtesy Wyoming State Archives and Historical Department. 226—Courtesy Henry Hornblower II. 227—Courtesy Kansas State Historical Society, Topeka. 228,229—Courtesy Montana Historical Society, Helena; from *We Pointed Them North: Recollections of a Cowpuncher,* by E. C. (Teddy Blue) Abbott and Helena Huntington Smith, copyright 1954 by the University of Oklahoma Press. 230—Courtesy Montana Historical Society, Helena (2); Joseph E. Smith, courtesy David R. Phillips Collection—Joseph E. Smith, courtesy David R. Phillips Collection (2); Frank Dean, courtesy State Historical Society of Colorado Library. 231—Joseph E. Smith, courtesy David R. Phillips Collection; Courtesy Wyoming State Archives and Historical Department; Courtesy Western History Research Center, University of Wyoming—Courtesy *The Cattleman;* Courtesy Denver Public Library, Western History Department (2). 232,233—Courtesy Denver Public Library, Western History Department; Courtesy Texas State Archives, Austin.

BIBLIOGRAPHY

Abbott, E. C. (Teddy Blue) and Helena Huntington Smith, *We Pointed Them North: Recollections of a Cowpuncher.* University of Oklahoma Press, 1966.

Adams, Andy, *The Log of a Cowboy: A Narrative of the Old Trail Days.* University of Nebraska Press, 1964.

Adams, Ramon F., *Come an' Get It: Story of the Old Cowboy Cook.* University of Oklahoma Press, 1953.

The Old-Time Cowhand. The Macmillan Company, 1961.

Arnold, Oren, and John P. Hale, *Hot Irons: Heraldry of the Range.* The Macmillan Company, 1940.

Atherton, Lewis, *The Cattle Kings.* Indiana University Press, 1961.

Brisbin, James S., *The Beef Bonanza; or How to Get Rich on the Plains.* University of Oklahoma Press, 1959.

Brown, Mark, and W. R. Felton, *Before Barbed Wire.* Bramhall House, 1956.

Burroughs, John Rolfe, *Guardian of the Grasslands.* Pioneer Printing & Stationery Co., 1971.

Clay, John, *My Life on the Range.* University of Oklahoma Press, 1962.

Cleland, Robert Glass, *The Cattle on a Thousand Hills: Southern California, 1850-1880.* Huntington Library, 1951.

Cox, James, *The Cattle Industry of Texas and Adjacent Territory.* Antiquarian Press, Ltd., 1959.

Dale, Edward E., *The Range Cattle Industry: Ranching on the Great Plains from 1865 to 1925.* University of Oklahoma Press, 1969.

Dobie, J. Frank, *A Vaquero of the Brush Country.* Little, Brown and Company, 1960.

The Longhorns. Grosset & Dunlap, Inc., 1957.

Drago, Harry Sinclair, *Great American Cattle Trails.* Bramhall House, 1965.

Duke, Cordia Sloan, and Joe B. Frantz, *6,000 Miles of Fence: Life on the XIT Ranch of Texas.* University of Texas Press, 1961.

Dykstra, Robert R., *The Cattle Towns.* Alfred A. Knopf, 1968.

Edwards, J. B., "Early Days in Abilene." *The Abilene Daily Chronicle,* 1938.

Emmett, Chris, *Shanghai Pierce: A Fair Likeness.* University of Oklahoma Press, 1953.

Fletcher, Baylis John, *Up the Trail in '79.* University of Oklahoma Press, 1968.

Fletcher, Robert H., *Free Grass to Fences, The Montana Cattle Range Story.* University Publishers Inc., 1960.

Frantz, Joe B., and Julian E. Choate Jr., *The American Cowboy: The Myth and the Reality.* University of Oklahoma Press, 1968.

Frink, Maurice, *Cow Country Cavalcade: Eighty Years of the Wyoming Stock Growers Association.* Old West Publishing Co., 1954.

Frink, Maurice, W. Turrentine Jackson and Agnes Wright Spring, *When Grass Was King.* University of Colorado Press, 1956.

Gard, Wayne, *The Chisholm Trail.* University of Oklahoma Press, 1969.

Frontier Justice. University of Oklahoma Press, 1968.

Gressley, Gene M., *Bankers and Cattlemen.* University of Nebraska Press, 1971.

Haley, J. Evetts, *Charles Goodnight: Cowman and Plainsman.* University of Oklahoma Press, 1970.

The XIT Ranch of Texas and the Early Days of the Llano Estacado. University of Oklahoma Press, 1967.

Henry, Stuart, *Conquering Our Great American Plains.* E. P. Dutton & Co., 1930.

Hough, Emerson, *The Story of the Cowboy.* Gregg Press, 1970.

Hunter, J. Marvin, ed., *The Trail Drivers of Texas,* vols. I and II. Argosy-Antiquarian, Ltd., 1963.

Jones, Mat Ennis, *Fiddlefooted.* Sage Books, 1966.

McCoy, Joseph G., *Historic Sketches of the Cattle Trade of the West and Southwest.* Ralph P. Bieber, ed., Southwest Historical Series. The Arthur H. Clark Co., 1940.

Mercer, A. S., *The Banditti of the Plains.* University of Oklahoma Press, 1968.

Miller, Nyle H., and Joseph W. Snell, *Great Gunfighters of the Kansas Cowtowns, 1867-1886.* University of Nebraska Press, 1967.

Mothershead, Harmon Ross, *The Swan Land and Cattle Company, Ltd.* University of Oklahoma Press, 1971.

National Live Stock Association, *Prose and Poetry of the Live Stock Industry.* Antiquarian Press, Ltd., 1959.

Osgood, Ernest S., *The Day of the Cattleman.* University of Chicago Press, 1929.

Pelzer, Louis, *The Cattleman's Frontier: A Record of the Trans-Mississippi Cattle Industry 1850-1890.* Russell and Russell, 1969.

Sandoz, Mari, *The Cattlemen.* Hastings House, 1958.

Siringo, Charles A., *A Texas Cowboy or Fifteen Years on the Hurricane Deck of A Spanish Pony.* University of Nebraska Press, 1966.

Smith, John D., *The Wild West.* Doubleday & Co., Inc., 1894.

Snyder, A. B., *Pinnacle Jake.* Peter Smith, 1971.

Streeter, Floyd Benjamin, *Prairie Trails and Cow Towns.* The Devin Adair Co., 1963.

Stuart, Granville, *Forty Years on the Frontier.* A. H. Clark and Co., 1967.

Sweetman, Luke D., *Backtrailing on Open Range.* The Caxton Printers, Ltd., 1951.

Vestal, Stanley, *Queen of Cowtowns: Dodge City.* Harper and Bros., 1952.

Von Richthofen, Walter Baron, *Cattle-Raising on the Plains of North America.* University of Oklahoma Press, 1969.

Ward, Fay E., *The Cowboy At Work.* Hastings House, 1958.

Webb, Walter Prescott, *The Great Plains.* Grosset & Dunlap, Inc., 1957.

Wolfenstine, Manfred R., *The Manual of Brands and Marks.* University of Oklahoma Press, 1970.

ACKNOWLEDGMENTS

The editors of this book wish to thank the following persons and institutions for their assistance: Dan Farris, Mammoth Lakes, Calif.; Wayne Gard, Dallas, Texas; Dr. Gene M. Gressley, Director of Rare Books and Special Collections, University of Wyoming, Laramie; Joseph W. Snell, Assistant State Archivist, Kansas State Historical Society, Topeka, and Clifford P. Westermeier, Professor of History, University of Colorado, Boulder, who read and commented on portions of the text.

Paul Rossi, Tucson, Ariz., and Joe Ruiz Grandee, Joe Grandee Gallery and Museum of the Old West, Arlington, Texas, who assisted in the preparation of picture essays.

Also, Garnet Brooks, Membership Chairman, National Cowboy Hall of Fame, Oklahoma City, Okla.; Alfred L. Bush, Curator, Princeton Collections of Western Americana, Princeton University, N.J.; Roland Christiansen, Bishop, Calif.; Mr. and Mrs. William Claflin Jr., Belmont, Mass.; Jim Davis, Picture Librarian, Western History Department, Denver Public Library, Colo.; Eugene D. Decker, Archivist, Kansas State Historical Society, Topeka; Carl S. Dentzel, Director, Southwest Museum, Los Angeles, Calif.; Robert R. Dykstra, Associate Professor of History, University of Iowa, Iowa City; Dr. Joe B. Frantz, Professor of History, University of Texas at Austin; Richard I. Frost, Curator, Buffalo Bill Museum, Cody, Wyo.; Sam Gilluly, Director, Montana Historical Society, Helena; Mary Elizabeth Good, Public Information Specialist, Thomas Gilcrease Institute of American History and Art, Tulsa, Okla.; Mildred Goosman, Curator, Western Collections, Joslyn Art Museum, Omaha, Neb.; Frances M. Gupton, Registrar, Amon Carter Museum of Western Art, Fort Worth, Texas; Jack D. Haley, Assistant Curator, Western History Collections, University of Oklahoma Library, Norman; Archibald Hanna, Curator, Yale University Western Americana Collection, New Haven, Conn.; Paul W. Horn, Editor, *The Cattleman,* Fort Worth, Texas; Henry Hornblower II, Boston, Mass.; Daniel W. Jones, Director of Research, Special Projects, NBC, New York City; Jerry L. Kearns, Head of Reference, Prints and Photographs Division, Library of Congress, Washington, D.C.; Marie E. Keene, Assistant Librarian, Thomas Gilcrease Institute of American History and Art, Tulsa, Okla.; Bill Kelsey, Kelsey's Sierra Studios, Bishop, Calif.; Joan Paterson Kerr, New Haven, Conn.; Dr. Chester Kielman, Director, Texas Collection, Barker Texas History Center, University of Texas at Austin; Dean Krakel, Managing Director, National Cowboy Hall of Fame, Oklahoma City; Mary Abbott Matejcek, Lewistown, Mont.; C. Boone McClure, Director, Panhandle-Plains Historical Museum, Canyon, Texas; Dr. Harold McCracken, Director, Whitney Gallery of Western Art and Buffalo Bill Historical Center, Cody, Wyo.; Harriett C. Meloy, Librarian, Montana Historical Society Library, Helena; Mrs. Marjorie Morey, Photo Archivist, Amon Carter Museum, Fort Worth, Texas; David J. Murrah, Assistant Archivist, Southwest Collection, Texas Tech University, Lubbock; Ruth Koerner Oliver, Santa Barbara, Calif.; Robert W. Richmond, State Archivist, Kansas State Historical Society, Topeka, Kans.; Jerry L. Rogers, Associate Director for Ranch Headquarters, Museum of Texas Tech University, Lubbock; Charles G. Roundy, Research Historian, Western History Research Center, University of Wyoming, Laramie; Alice L. Sharp, Librarian, State Historical Society of Colorado, Denver; Mrs. Eric Steinfeldt, Curator of History, Witte Memorial Museum, San Antonio, Texas; John Barr Tompkins, Head, Public Services, Bancroft Library, University of California, Berkeley; Stewart P. Verckler, Historian, Dickinson County Historical Society, Abilene, Kans.; Fredric R. Young, Dodge City, Kans.

Printed in U.S.A.